The Naked Path of Prophet series

volume 1

The Naked Path of Prophet

A new translation of 1 Samuel 1 - 17,
a warning about kings, christs, & organized religion

translation & commentaries by

Brian J. Shircliff

VITALITY
buzz, bliss + books

The Naked Path of Prophet:
a new translation of 1 Samuel 1 - 17,
a warning about kings, christs, & organized religion
vol 1 of The Naked Path of Prophet *series*
Copyright © 2021, 2024 by Brian J. Shircliff (updated edition - 2024)

Published by VITALITY buzz, bliss + books LLC
vitalitybuzz.org

VITALITY buzz, bliss + books LLC publishes original creations to grow the mission of VITALITY Cincinnati Inc, a 501(c)3 education-based nonprofit: sharing holistic self-care from neighborhood to neighborhood, person to person, and breath by breath since 2010.

The opinions and ideas expressed herein are those of the author and do not necessarily represent the opinions of the VATRONS of VITALITY buzz, bliss + books LLC or the Board of Trustees of VITALITY Cincinnati. Any errors, of course, are solely the author's.

Every effort has been made to give credit to other people's original ideas through the text itself and the recommended resources that follow this text. If you feel something should be credited to someone and is not, please get in touch through our website and every effort will be made to correct this text for future printings. Thank you!

We invite you to honor your mind, your body, your whole self. Do only what you know to be right for you. While the invitations offered here in this book, on our websites and social media, and in our classes are geared to be gentle and easily modified by the participant to fit the participants' needs, please consult your medical doctor or health professional before undertaking any practices.

Artists Sean Long and Julie Lucas contributed their work to this edition. Thank you!

ISBN: 978-1-954688-01-8
Library of Congress Control Number: applied for

to do the great is always an excavation —

and then a climbing up and out

in gratitude

to the VATRONS for the first edition of this volume
& our book *Inspiring Stories of Hands-On Healing*

Cynthia Allen & Larry Wells, Mary & Tim Cronin,
Bob Donovan, Ed & Carol Ewbank, James Gaunt,
Jeffrey Chad Hartman, Judith Johnson,
Maggie & Russ King, Margaret Kupferle,
Sarah Elizabeth, Bob Reineke, Laurie & Dan Roche,
Tonia Smith, Scott Stiens, Howard Thoresen,
Annie Weisbrod, Amy & Steve Whitlatch

with these VATRONS for this volume

Harry Cullen Blanton, Mary Ann Blome,
Angie Grimsley, Melissa McNeill, Mary Ann Meyer,
Mary Muntel, Stephanie & Eric Nichols,
Michael Preston, Cynthia Reese, Pam Schreiner,
Lucille Schultz, Alli Shircliff & Rafael Gallardo,
Karehma Simon, Jennifer Lynne, Debbie VanKuiken,
Lada Tyro, Carol T. Yeazell, anonymous friends

I am extremely grateful to Helen Buswinka and Amy
Fogelson for reading and improving immensely a draft
of this new edition.

This revised and updated volume in *The Naked Path of Prophet* series was translated and written over a span of many years and many voyages, including one long stay in Paris to hear Thomas Römer's Genesis 1 - 11 lectures at Collège de France in March 2024. Much of this translation was polished in Paris, that 2000-year-old, multi-layered city that often reminds me of the many layers of the Bible.

Professor Römer has offered me and many wise counsel over the years through his lectures, his writings, his conversation. I've always appreciated his fresh approaches to all things...something that comes, I think, with knowing a subject deeply over decades, from many angles and even linguistic perspectives.

May all who seek to grow human wisdom on Earth, especially through biblical scholarship, dare to ask YAHWEH for a double-helping of Professor Römer's spirit, charisma, humor, and vast knowledge of the biblical tradition(s).

CONTENTS

Inner-Styles & After-Styles

Resources for Further Discovery

CHOOSE WELL!

x

An Intention
for *The Naked Path of Prophet* Series
(included in every volume)

This series has interest in the questions of the various scholarly theories about the origins and redactions (assembling + editing) of the Bible...

but this series will not try to solve those riddles.

Biblical scholar Thomas Römer's books offer excellent summaries of many of the most current theories about the origins of the Hebrew scriptures, especially *The Invention of God* and the *L'Ancien Testament*; biblical scholars of the Westar Institute/Jesus Seminar have done much to help unravel the Christian traditions' layers to reveal the ecstatic roots of Jesus and the world-resounding message of Paul about this peasant Jesus and what God did for him. Maybe you've checked out *The Gospel of Jesus* by Robert W. Funk, Arthur J. Dewey & the Jesus Seminar or *The Authentic Letters of Paul* by Arthur J. Dewey, Roy W. Hoover, Lane C. McGaughy, & Daryl Schmidt.

Inspired by these and other scholars' excavations of the Bible, this *Naked Path of Prophet* series aims:

first, to reveal more of the cleverness of the Hebrew puns in the biblical texts and then bring forward this cleverly-styled wordplay/poetry into a clearer English translation

...so that more people can identify such style running through much of the Bible and, if they find such style helpful for our 21st century world, then bring it forward in new ways;

and second, to reveal a significant idea for our time and all time, which continually gets passed over by scholars and by religious leaders and the faithful of any and all traditions, namely, that the Bible being a collection of many differing imaginations and writers could be divided into two competing camps: **the hierarchically-minded** and **the circularly-inspired**

...so that more people can identify which imagination is used within their own family, classroom, workplace, religion, and governments and that, by knowing the differences between circular-imagination and hierarchical-imagination, have the ability to choose which is most life-giving and helpful in any moment.

Hierarchical Imagination

A hierarchy has a human-leader over various strata of minor leaders over various sub-classes of humans. A hierarchy is a system where some humans have more value and more power than others. Often there is even a non-class of humans... untouchables who have no value or enslaved-people of all sorts, sex-slaves of all genders or eunuchs or maid-slaves or wet-nurses, each of whom might be valued/valuable but having very few if any rights to their own human personhood. This is what hierarchies do — they sort and place people based on their value to the system that those with power create and those without power accept until revolution boils over and there is a paradigm shift with some people losing and/ or gaining power and privilege within the new hierarchical system...unless an entirely different and more circularly-minded system is chosen.

The hierarchical imagination often uses a podium from which one person addresses the masses who follow. There is little conversation in such a system, even when the group is small. The speaker stands over and above the followers who hear and obey. Perhaps the followers take issue with some of the speaker's announcements so the followers find ways to safely communicate their disagreements through channels long after the speech. Often such 'communication' is made passive-aggressively because it's the only safe way to 'communicate' in such a system. The speaker/leader then either takes those communications into account or delivers another speech that clamps down even more on the communicators or changes the system entirely so that the system becomes more circular than before and people have more influence in decision-making. In a hierarchical system, it is impossible to commune with the leader who ranks above all unless there is revolution or unless the top-dog leader changes the rules of the system to make the system more circular. But even then, the people that top-dog leader rules might not want or might not accept a more circularly-inspired system.

The hierarchical imagination plays out in royal-slave systems, in despot-follower systems, in guru-follower systems, in organized religion's leader-follower systems, in celebrity-follower systems...each and all of any era.

With the hierarchical imagination, people can and often do awful things to each other. The hierarchical system depends on it. And when people know no other option besides the hierarchical system, desperation can settle in quickly...tragic motivation to want to climb a rung higher and then another rung higher...moves that see people in the way or people down below as enemies or problems to solve. With a hierarchical-mindset, it's easy to point out that a person is evil or bad or wrong.

Someone with a circularly-inspired imagination realizes instead that people are not bad or wrong but instead are stuck inside hierarchical-systems, ways of imagining that have limited who they are and all that is.

All too often, hierarchical-imagination limits one's map of the Infinite, what we're all too often tempted to call 'reality.' As we keep growing and have more experiences in life, 'reality' keeps changing doesn't it?

Circularly-Inspired Imagination

A circularly-inspired imagination is much different, of course. With this imagination, each human recognizes the equal-value of all humans and sometimes even of all life, of every living thing. Such a circular imagination perfects itself as an entirely holistic imagination...where participants recognize on their own — often through very different experiences — that there is no separation between creatures...where it is readily recognized that we all exist within a larger and highly interdependent whole, as a Universe, the One-Verse, the Infinite, THE ALL. That is to say, we all exist in 'God.' When we recognize we participate in such a Whole, it's a lot easier to live more harmoniously with every creature, with all inside that ever-expanding circle.

The circular imagination often invites everyone to sit in a circle, with no one person any higher or more valued than another. A circle invites speakers and hearers and co-hearers alike to use all senses in communicating...even a deep look into someone's eyes or listening carefully to the subtle sounds someone makes or getting a wisp of the feeling in the air communicates a great deal. A circle breeds a sense of equality, a sense that we're all in this together and that we all will be needed in some diverse and equally-valued way to move forward in our shared life together on the planet. Could there be a leader or moderator or convener of the circle? Of course. But such leaders of a circle try to be very mindful not to interject their opinions or will upon the circle; instead, circularly-inspired leaders ensure that all ideas are heard, that everyone who desires to speak gets to speak, that those with information share what they know and invite ideas and people to evaluate information openly and wisely and to grow information's usefulness through deliberation and discernment. There is equal access to knowledge and opportunity in a circular system, even if knowledge and opportunity are not 'free,' even if they must be merited through effort and growth.

Circularly-inspired imaginers know well that some experience inspired them to a larger vision of THE ALL. Someone with a circularly-inspired imagination knows that an experience can free anyone stuck in a hierarchical-imagination — an experience as simple as a breath or a gasp from an ecstatic's clever rap or wild story or a deep look into someone's eyes. A circular-imaginer knows too that the awakening that comes from an experience must happen within each person and unfold within each person in that person's own time and in its own original way. It's not possible to make someone know THE ALL. Such an awakening erupts out of nowhere — is ecstatic in that way. Mentoring relationships can help, of course, especially when a mentor invites the mentee to spend some time in some activity, some study, so that some awakening might happen in the mentee's own time. Sensible mentors know too that what awakened themselves might not be the same thing that will awaken their mentees. Indeed, no two experiences are ever the same, right?

Beyond these mentor-mentee relationships, there have been glimpses of the circular imagination being lived out today or in times past, though they all too often either get snuffed out by hierarchs or the hierarchically-minded or devolve to a hierarchical-system because some who once perceived something of THE ALL can no longer stay with that vision and imagination, for whatever reason.

Sometimes, too, we live and act more circularly in one arena of our lives but think and act more hierarchically in others. For example, what a gift it is to be pro-LGBTQ+ and you and I invite to the round-table all people who feel different in terms of their sexual identity and their gender identity...but what good is that if we still think that people of our own ethnicity or skin-tone are better (or worse) than others? What a gift it is to be antiracist...but what good is it if you and I hate women or nonbinary humans? Or what good is it to greet everyone we meet as an equal but then buy our t-shirts or shoes made in sweatshops owned by millionaire CEO's or buy coffee or chocolate grown and picked by slaves?

We need to get to the root issue — and it's not racism, it's not homophobia or the patriarchy or transphobia or anything like that. Those are all nasty symptoms of the hierarchical imagination killing us all.

Democracy...
circularly-inspired or hierarchically-motivated?

Perhaps you're wondering where democracy rests between these camps?

Democracy — or rule by the people — attempts to break free from the hierarchical imagination with democracy's more circular attempts to allow all voices — at least those of a certain age — to be heard and with every person of age getting an equal vote. But all too often democracy devolves into hierarchy when celebrity-presidents of every party — and even the parties themselves — are followed at every word by their followers, all too often with little discernment as to the value or wisdom of what the leader or party offer. In smaller groups in a more local place, of course, circular-democracies can thrive. In larger groups, it can be quite difficult...unless there is a common appreciation for what ultimately gives life.

Some roots of circularly-inspired imaginations

So...hopefully you're becoming curious about how a circular imagination actually works or could be helpful in the 21st century, and how it has been lived out in past eras. Well, my friends, that's the very heart-intention of *The Naked Path of Prophet* series with its devoted interest in YAHWEH's wild and sexy wind. All are called by the wind/breath, we've been reminded by the wise ones through the centuries, few choose themselves or allow themselves to notice the sensations of the wind.

Jesus was interested in the circular imagination...his authentic parables and wisdom sayings and table-fellowship reveal that...but he lost first to the hierarchs of the religion of his region's day and then after his death to those wanting a more hierarchically-minded church.

Paul was interested in the circular imagination...the very rhetoric of his authentic letters to early Jesus-interested communities call for a more circular approach to governance where God rules and all people are valued equally below <u>and</u> because of God who raised up even a peasant (Jesus)...but Paul lost first to Rome and then to Peter's hierarchically-minded camp which projected Rome's sense of order and destruction onto Jesus-interested communities, and still does.

And where and how did Jesus and Paul get interested in a more circular imagination?

Perhaps they were inspired by the wandering ecstatics and their little quips of wordplay and poetry, clever parables or episodes of story, and exceedingly bizarre actions for, perhaps, nearly 1000 years before Jesus and Paul ever set foot on Earth. Those little ecstatic bits were becoming the Bible, at least the first half of it. It's a circular-style and circularly-minded imagination that seeps out in the poems of the likes of Amos and the Isaiahs and Jeremiah and more, in the stories of 1 & 2 Samuel and much of 1 & 2 Kings, in large portions of Genesis once called "J/Yahwist" because of these storytellers' penchant for calling the divine "YAHWEH." Likely a band of multiple storycrafters through the generations, I've chosen to call this group 'the band of YAH.' Much later after their first tellings of these stories, the ancient Levitical priests (possibly with some later help from the Deuteronomic scribes) assembled these stories into what today we call Genesis, the first book of the Bible. The band of YAH is expert at flattening triangles/hierarchies into circles, often with humor.

Rather interestingly, this circular-style and imagination seems to seep out during the most difficult and oppressive times in history both before Jesus' time, during Jesus' lifetime, and long after.

Perhaps you've caught a wisp of It?

Perhaps you've had an experience of YAHWEH brought on by Its life-giving, inspiring, encircling wind? Such an experience is starkly different from the institutions we humans have built century after century to try to honor such wind....

Do we take the time to discern the differences?

As collision after collision happens in our world — as hierarchs assert power over hierarchically-minded and circularly-minded — it concerns me how challenging it seems to be for us humans to distinguish a hierarchically-minded imagination from a circularly-minded imagination. It's not easy. Everything gets so murky swimming in the midst of the shipwreck — not to mention the traumatic experiences that led to the collisions that got us swimming in those dangerous waters in the first place.

How often we try to swim away to safety...but....

I've watched friends leave church-communities — led by pastors who openly proclaimed their status as hierarchs — immediately jump right into the next church-community or even an entirely different religious tradition, both being led by friendlier hierarchs of the same hierarchical system/imagination that still aggravates my friends, though they're not entirely clear why. The very person upon whom their original church was founded — Jesus — was up-ending the hierarchical imagination of his day with his clever parables and wisdom sayings, and with being present and loving with those he is said to share meals/time...women, tax collectors, children, the ill...people who were not regarded as people in Jesus' time. Sadly, so few of my own Christian tradition cannot discern the differences between what Jesus was saying and doing and what Peter or Pilate or the Sanhedrin-leaders were said to be saying and doing in the gospel stories we've inherited. This inability to discern hierarchical-mindedness from circular-mindedness happens in every religious tradition, not just my own Christianity. It's even present in yoga...tragically, it's nearly everywhere and we are the ones who pass on this hierarchical-imagination unwittingly.

I too went right along with and even invested in the hierarchical system within my own religious tradition...for far, far too long...hoping it would change and thinking my queer outside-on-the-edges life/teaching would change things someday and somehow...until I realized my staying within my low place in the massive hierarchy as a lay religious educator was still giving power and credence to the hierarchical system. Finally I realized I had to swim away from my position and even my local parish to preserve my own life. I too often found the same hierarchical imagination in so much of yoga and have sought out other styles of movement as well.

And so I hope that my church-going and religious friends of all traditions and yoga-friends swim away from the shipwrecks of all hierarchical imaginations before it's too late to even notice what's in the breeze and always has been — life! Such a realization of the wind of life is precisely what welcomed every awakening and 'miracle' that gave birth to a religion in the first place...and all too often just a short time later the circular, spiral-rich experience concretized in messy hierarchies that stifle the original experience that was so rich and life-giving and able to be accessed by anyone living on the planet. Such access to that circular, spiral-rich experience is always available...for anyone who breathes and can sense such breath.

Organized religion of any sort cannot bear the circular imagination that must wait on YAHWEH alone — the very breeze of life — and not anyone directing or liturgizing, not anyone creating formulas or potions or laws or concert-sets to cull their divinities to act.

As we'll soon discover, the ecstatic/prophetic imagination of the Bible's prophets does indeed call on YAHWEH to act...but it's the very experience of sitting, breathing, contemplating, perhaps even spitting just-created-in-the-moment stylish rhymes and rhythms and stories or gasping or laughing with them that stirs the breeze to act. Could it perhaps even be as simple as uttering 'YAHWEH'? When you open your mouth or nostrils, in pours that wildness of YAHWEH. Dare you let YAHWEH have Its sexy, ecstasy-inducing way with you?

In a world undergoing such vast changes from day to day, in a world where the old orders no longer satisfy, might we have the courage today to play with such an open, circular style? Might we do so because we've had an ecstatic experience that makes us suspicious of the dangerous hierarchical systems of today and yesteryear? Might we do so because we'd like to let such an ecstatic-style expand and discover if it has something new to offer human life on the planet? Or just because it's fun and feels good, in YAHWEH's surprising ways?

No matter —

   play.

Play is the very style of YAHWEH as these circular-styled biblical texts mentioned above point out again and again...after all, within a circle, we can be pleasantly surprised together, we can see deeply into each other's eyes, hear more clearly each other's sounds and make meaning from them, taste the possibilities of life's abundance together, smell each other's scents that drift to us in the breeze, touch gently and lovingly the open hands of one another...

circle around!

let the breeze blow!

play!

open yourself to a refreshing surprise!

How did 1 & 2 Samuel
come to be in the Bible?

As I reminded in *A Wildly Sensual YAHWEH*, many people will be shocked to discover that God did not write the Bible.

Neither did Moses.

Neither did Jesus.

And neither did David for that matter.

The Saul and David and Solomon stories are almost certainly a fiction told with a clear purpose. There's a chance that the character David of 1 & 2 Samuel was a real human being, the one-time leader of the House of David, of the line of kings hailing from Judah/Israel, but even the archaeological evidence to support that is scant at best. What we know for sure is that the 'King David' that modern religious-believers and scholars proposed to have lived around 1000 BCE and to have kickstarted Israel after Saul's disastrous reign did not exist. It's likely Saul didn't either.

And read it carefully in 1 & 2 Samuel and 1 Kings — David and Saul and Solomon come off as complete fools. The priests caring for the ark do too.

But not the prophets — the ecstatics.

And that's the entire point of 1 & 2 Samuel and much of 1 & 2 Kings. Note well that Chronicles was written centuries after these books to try to boost the narrative of 'David as founder of Jerusalem' and the power that the priests could claim with that narrative — all of them with hardly any interest in the ecstatics/prophets. Indeed, Chronicles was written by priests to try once and for all to hide the ecstatics/prophets and their wildly clever style(s) and their significant sway that not only stole attention from the royals and the priests but especially called out both palace and temple.

Why isn't that all obvious to the casual Bible reader? Exceedingly complex layering of biblical texts through multiple generations of editing, subtracting, adding, wondering on paper/animal-skin sometimes makes it challenging to notice what's been done to hide the ecstatic/prophetic imagination — whether it's 1 Samuel into which this book zooms or Genesis as *A Wildly Sensual YAHWEH* explored or the wordplay/poems of prophets like Amos and the Isaiahs and Jeremiah and Jesus as future volumes in *The Naked Path of Prophet* series will delve deeply. Even the Bible's four gospels try to obscure Jesus' real vision for life; any careful reader can know a very different Jesus in Jesus' sayings and parables when the narrative is removed from around those sayings and parables that most likely go back to him. Jesus' imagination is wild — maybe too wild for the gospel writers so they added things around his sayings/parables and often even changed his sayings/parables to dim Jesus down and promote their own agendas. Keep in mind that Jesus' sayings/parables were spoken out loud and orally shared for at least one generation and possibly two generations before they were written down by gospel writers.

The differences between an oral-culture and a writing/reading-culture are stark.

Sometimes people write to hide, to bulldoze over an idea, to control the idea, especially in an oral culture like the ancient Mediterranean eastern seaboard where it's likely that 95% of the population could not read. Writing seems like magic to a non-reader. And a tale that was popular orally becomes suspect when someone who writes and reads points to a scroll and says, "No, you have it all wrong — the story goes this way."

I suspect much of the Bible was written to command such sway, to determine the path of the story at the hands of the power-brokers — royal court and government administrators and priests — to swell their power over the people and over the misfits, the ecstatics/prophets who cared nothing for palaces or temples or even reading/writing.

The books of 1 & 2 Samuel challenge those power-brokers.

You see, the original kernel of 1 & 2 Samuel is a collection of stories about the foolishness of those who aspire to royal and priestly power and about the clever wisdom of the ecstatics/prophets on the mountaintops with their more circular, usually all-accepting vision of life. I suspect roving bands of ecstatics told these 1 & 2 Samuel stories through Ancient Israel/Judah for generations, perhaps as Homer's stories were told through Greek villages for generations to help people understand love and honor played out on the battlefield and within a nation, to stir one's responsibilities to both.

In *A Wildly Sensual YAHWEH*, I named the band who crafted the ecstatic stories of Genesis 'the band of YAH' after YAHWEH because this band's stories do not shy away from calling 'God' YAHWEH while the priests did and often still do. The Levitical priests actually make it a commandment to not say the Divine's name — including 'YAHWEH' — out loud, perhaps a move to dampen the power of the band of YAH's stories and to keep common people from having an ecstatic experience. Say 'YAHWEH' out loud a few times — what happens for you?

The band of YAH was likely many generations of crafters; biblical scholars today note that those who told the Jacob stories were probably not the exact same people who told the Abraham/Sarah or Isaac/Rebekah or Joseph stories. But these different generations of storycrafters do seem unified in the ways they use verbs and especially in using "YAHWEH" as the name for the divine instead of the more generic "ELOHIM" which is a plural word that can be understood as "the one

God" but can also mean "gods and goddesses" and sometimes makes it difficult to understand which ELOHIM is which ELOHIM in the Bible. The ecstatic-prophets and other Bible-crafters using "YAHWEH" instead of "ELOHIM" make it very clear, and YAHWEH in 1 & 2 Samuel and Genesis often has a lively personality...much like the wind. After all, YAHWEH was originally a storm-divinity.

First and Second Samuel — if indeed they were ever really separated — was probably also conceived through the generations. Like the band of YAH, the crafters of 1 & 2 Samuel usually refer to the "One God" as YAHWEH. I call the band who crafted 1 & 2 Samuel 'the band of X' after the word 'ecstasy' — the original word for 'prophet' in Ancient Hebrew.

Imagine these roving bands of Hebrew-speaking bordercrossers arriving in Israelite villages to share a tale about the dangers of priests/organized-religion and the dangers of monarchy/ royal-courts — all with a good laugh that has the hearer thinking deeply about the story the next day. Today, we call these people comedians, people who get us laughing across the borders of how we once conceived the world. The word 'Hebrew'/AYBR actually means 'bordercrosser.' And the ways we guess the Ancient Hebrew language was spoken makes these stories wildly punny, as we'll soon encounter. Most translations of 1 & 2 Samuel do not draw the readers' attention to these puns and plays with Hebrew sound to boost meaning... but *The Naked Path of Prophet* series sure aims to do just that.

Reading Ancient Hebrew to oneself from a text is far different from hearing it out loud. I suspect this is why biblical scholars have difficulty understanding what I've been noticing in the texts by reading them out loud to myself. I asked a scholar-friend I met at the Society of Biblical Literature if he read the biblical texts of his expertise out loud and he told me that he hadn't in decades. He went off and tried it and came back to tell me that the meanings he discovered when he heard the sounds of the text were far richer. Precisely.

If we are to understand these bands of Hebrew-bordercrossers who became the Israelites — for many of us our actual ancestors or spiritual ancestors, for all of us our linguistic ancestors — we'd be wise to step into their sound chamber as best we can by reading the texts out loud, especially the texts of the prophets/ecstatics. This translation offers a way to do that for both lay readers who know no Ancient Hebrew and scholars who sometimes miss the sound-meaning potential with the transliteration systems they've created. The range of meanings offered by 1 & 2 Samuel change drastically when we catch the sounds that play with each other in Ancient Hebrew — and even wonder why the band of X would phrase things the way they carefully did and not another way.

The sounds within the stories might even enchant you, dear reader, into an ecstatic experience. The band of X, as I call these storycrafters, was very much after ecstasy through a style all their own...and yet a style they heard within them and around them...a style as close as breathing the life-giving atmosphere into and out of themselves.

Most scholars argue that 1 & 2 Samuel are the work of some generation(s) of the Deuteronomistic School/Party — the ring that empowered the monarchy of Israel/Judah, the hierarchical system that benefits the top rungs at the expense of the bottom rungs, the subjects of the king. The Deuteronomists — the top rung of bureaucrats who seated the king — most certainly had a hand in editing and cataloguing 1 & 2 Samuel as they did with most of the Hebrew Bible. Chapter 12 alone in 1 Samuel reveals the heavy hand of the Deuteronomists' influence on the text. But I argue that the original composers of 1 & 2 Samuel — the band of X — have entirely different language, linguistic style, vision, values, and motivations than the later Deuteronomists who brought 1 & 2 Samuel into their opus, the Hebrew Bible. And the band of X's differing values and styles hearkened back to a bordercrossing/Hebrew past... who the Israelites were before Israel/Judah had big cities....

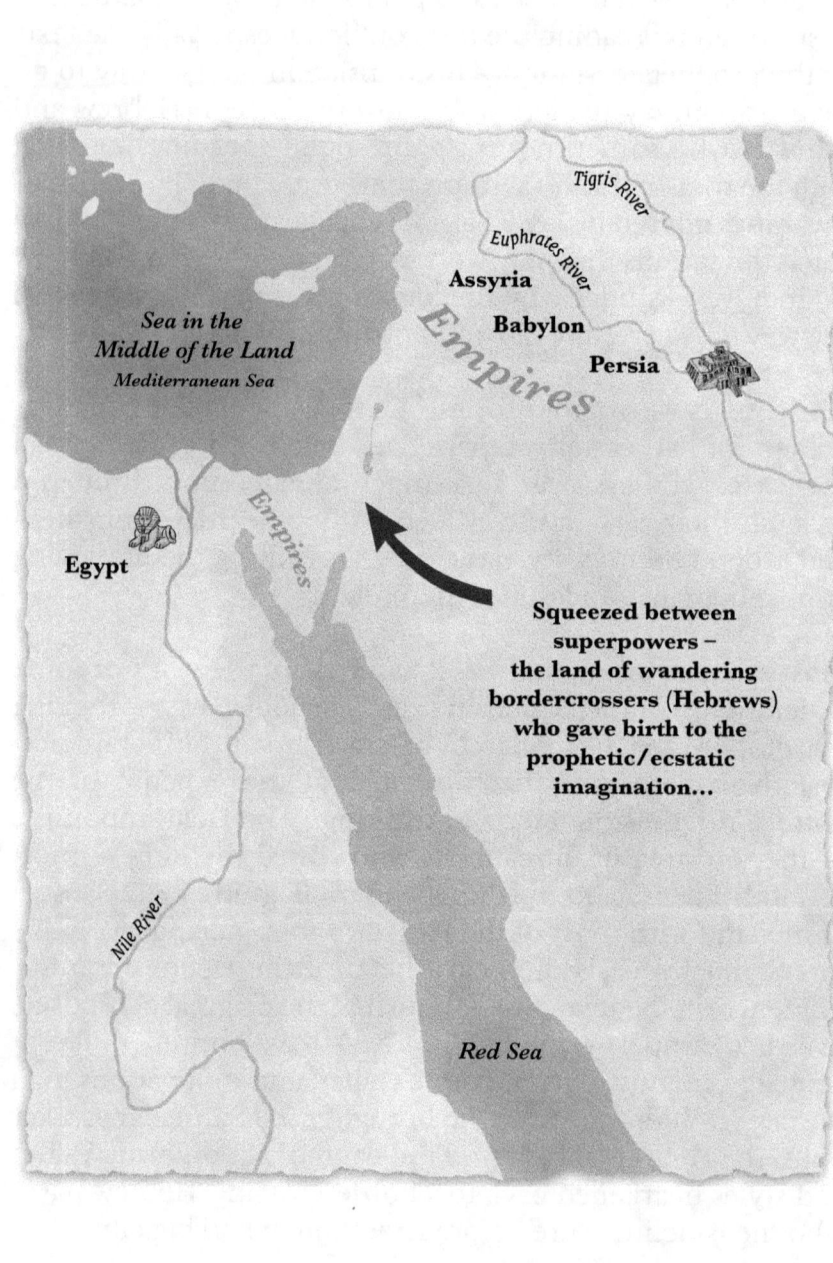

Who were the Israelites?

Originally, the group that became the Israelites was a band of disparate peoples trying to avoid the grips of empire. Long before the pivotal 12th century BCE when the beginnings of 'Israelites' emerged, Egypt and Assyria were the powerful empires in control of much of the Levant, the region of the eastern Mediterranean seaboard. But a perfect storm of factors ruined these empires — famine, wild storms, and invasions by the so-called Sea Peoples and potentially others. As archaeologist Eric H. Cline notes in *1177 B.C.: The Year Civilization Collapsed*, new possibilities for human life in the region emerged once those controlling empires of Ancient Egypt and Assyria were weakened.

Empires demand that people pay with taxes or with sweat/slavery, that people worship in their way(s) of theological understanding, that people speak in their way. Sometimes such demands are meted out with punishment/death; sometimes by more of a 'social contract' type of understanding. If you want to participate in the life offered by the empire, you'd better pay and worship and speak as the empire demands — or be a misfit by stepping out of the hierarchy completely, a move which could cost you your life if you chose to stay within the empire's reach.

People under the grips of Egyptian and Assyrian control and taxation and forced-religion and forced-labor before 1200 BCE might escape and choose to be nomadic, to be away from cities under direct control by the empire. Being nomadic meant people could take their wealth — animals/livestock — into the wildernesses where empires usually don't invest in the authorities/troops/organization needed to maintain control.

The Abraham-Isaac-Jacob tales of the band of YAH in Genesis celebrate that freedom, tales perhaps told to look back to how good their Hebrew-bordercrossing ancestors had it before the forces of empire encroached on their freedom. The name 'Abraham' actually has AYBR/'bordercrosser, Hebrew' in it (especially if you transliterate the first letter slightly differently) with Abraham and Sarah being the ones called out of empire's grasp into a wilderness where YAHWEH does wonders with them and multiplies them greater than the greatest ancient cities like Ur[uk] that Abram/Abraham and Sarai/Sarah had the courage to leave.

Once needing to be migratory and nomadic to avoid Egypt and Assyria, people became more and more settled as the political situation changed, crumbled. Archaeologists Israel Finkelstein and Neil Asher Silberman report that in 1200 BCE, as Egypt and Assyria were failing, "a dense network of highland villages" (*The Bible Unearthed*, p. 107) emerged that much later became 'Ancient Israel.'

Who exactly were these people? Perhaps some of those shepherds avoiding empires, disbanded mercenaries for hire, rebels from other kingdoms/systems, farmers looking for safety and richer soil, and more. Maybe even an ecstatic/prophet or two who got tired of bordercrossing, wandering, living wherever the wind blew.

These once-unaffiliated people of the Levant moved — with each generation of new stability — from tents anywhere they could survive, to joining their tents with others in tent-circles on highlands, to more permanent stone-houses on those highlands, to stone-houses with additions built onto them as families grew, to entire villages growing on tops of hills and mountains with every passing generation.

Rather curiously, these highland-villages had no government buildings, no spaces for worship of any kind. Not for many generations.

Finkelstein and Silberman note that in 1200 BCE there were 250+ settlements, each settlement having about 100 total people living on about an acre of village-land plus about 800 surrounding acres of land growing all the food each highland-village needed, using/storing all the water needed, and caring for all the animals needed to survive, even thrive, in each highland-village.

It's curious to me that there's very little indication of any religious practice or even art in these highland-villages. Maybe their lives felt full with responsibilities, no time to create. Or perhaps like a number of Appalachian friends have shared with me, there's no need to create when people are living their art — one's life as art — or perhaps these highland-villagers had grown tired of all that organized religion and art with Egypt and Assyria. Or perhaps these highland-villagers' art was in stories, in a well-told tale with humorous, style-rich word choices.

In these highland-villages excavated by Finkelstein and Silberman and their colleagues, there's a very occasional altar within a home but no dedicated public worship space within a village — no temples, etc. Also no city walls or weaponry have been found with this era of the villages. What was found there by archaeologists? Practical and non-artsy tools for growing and harvesting and storing grain, wine, water. It was a subsistence economy, undisturbed by the Canaanite neighbors down below these highland-villages. There are no signs of attacks or violent ends of any kind by these neighbors, by anyone. After all, when you have the high-ground, it's much easier to defend oneself — just roll things down the hill at invaders. Such a threat is real to anyone living down below and climbing upward.

There are also no signs of trade with other highland-villages. Also, no signs of stratification or hierarchy within the village — that is well worth paying attention to. A similar circular, non-hierarchical, equal-status economy is what I've found to be animating 1 & 2 Samuel, the prophet-guild tales of Elijah and Elisha in 1 & 2 Kings, the band of YAH's stories in Genesis too, and even much later Jesus' sayings and parables.

Life in these highland-villages sounds simple, and yet perhaps purely abundant, the beauty that comes with work and rest, with the slowed down life of waiting...shepherding, planting-growing, being very in touch with the elements and yet sheltered and safe too, the time and the mind to feel the wind, to know in every way the elemental-forces that feed you and your family. The only thing differentiating these highlanders from their neighbors in the valley or from highland communities in other regions was a complete absence of pork in the region that became 'Ancient Israel.' No pig bones were found there. The archaeological record offers no reason, of course. The insistence on avoiding pork that we find in the Torah comes centuries later, perhaps even seven centuries after this 1200 BCE layer from which Finkelstein and Silberman write in *The Bible Unearthed*.

It's important to note that there were very few of these highland-villages in what we today call Ancient Judah in 1200 BCE or the centuries immediately after. The geography of Judah/Jerusalem made it very difficult upon which to farm and live and even navigate with its often steep, rocky terrain and lack of rain. It's not until the 8th century BCE that Jerusalem seems to become much of anything, long after the supposed 1000 BCE that we used to associate with the rise of King David and the so-said founding of Jerusalem as the capital of the United Monarchy of Ancient Israel/Judah.

The only 'United Monarchy' could have been the political-immigrants running from Assyria and eventually settling in and around Jerusalem/Judah. All the highland-villages of Judah grew with the citizens and royal-court of Ancient Israel seeking asylum from Assyria's rising from its near-collapse in 1177 BCE. In 722 BCE, Assyria regained its footing and attacked Ancient Israel. And places like Jerusalem began to grow and thrive for generations until Babylon rose and conquered Assyria and then soon after that Ancient Judah/Jerusalem in 597 BCE.

But those places like 7th century BCE Jerusalem and Assyria and Egypt and Babylon 'thrived' often at the cost of their citizens' freedom — and that's what 1 & 2 Samuel continually points out. Monarchy has a significant cost to it. Every system — every way of organizing communal life — has a cost to it no matter if it's a monarchy or dictatorship or capitalist-democracy or socialist-democracy or some kind of combination of those ways of organizing communal life, the social-contract that keeps people from harming/killing each other. If the citizenry gets to shape that social-contract and the system that governs that agreement, it's more likely that the system will last.

Of course, monarchy or dictatorship or capitalist-democracy or socialist-democracy are not the only ways to organize or live communally. The ecstatics/prophets on the mountaintops seem to subscribe to a life ordered by the wind, and the wind alone — not by any ruler, not by any king or general or mayor or *messiah*, not by anyone...at least as the band of X stories go in 1 & 2 Samuel, 1 & 2 Kings, and the portions of Genesis crafted by the band of YAH. A life dependent on the wind up on a mountain or any out-of-the-way place is far different than city life, for sure.

Systems can grow life and take it away; the wind does too — but not at the command of any human authority.

When it comes down to it, it's how humans organize their system (government, religion, family, team, corporation, etc.) that determines the health and happiness of its citizens/people. Systems that forget how power really flows often collapse — no human system can exist without the wind, the rain or rivers, the earth, perhaps fire too. We can see why the ecstatics/prophets continually remind people — especially in cities — to put their faith in YAHWEH alone, the ancient storm-divinity who controls wind and rain...the forces that govern life.

But instead...

...we often get distracted by the big, pretty buildings and a story we tell ourselves that we really haven't examined carefully.

Many today — too many scholars and religious-believers alike — see in David and Solomon a Golden Age of Ancient Israel/Judah — the supposed builders of Jerusalem in 1000 BCE and after. But at that point, Jerusalem was just a scrubby little tent-camp. Jerusalem didn't emerge as a city of any size or power until after the kingdom of Israel's citizenry from the north immigrated there in the years leading up to 722 BCE.

Some scholars and religious-believers purposefully ignore the archaeological record and assume that if it's written in the Bible it must have happened that way — they also refuse to deal with differing and competing versions of stories in the same Bible. This is highly frustrating.

Some scholars and religious-believers note the lack of archaeological evidence for David/Solomon but still see in 1 & 2 Samuel and 1 Kings a supposed Golden Age of Ancient Israel/Judah with the great kings of David and Solomon — but these scholars and religious-believers clearly are not reading what's there in those biblical texts. David and Solomon come off as fools in 1 & 2 Samuel and 1 Kings. These scholars are likely reading the David and Solomon of the Psalms and Chronicles onto the David and Solomon of 1 & 2 Samuel and 1 Kings. This is very frustrating too.

I suspect most of these scholars and religious-believers do this to support their religion — Judaism, Christianity, Islam. They refuse to give up their narrative for one that would likely give them and others even more life and love and freedom/personal-choice — a narrative that the ecstatic/prophetic imagination supports. But instead these organized religious-believers hold onto a narrative and belief that not only does not match 'what was' but that kills others or stands by as others are killed in the name of their narrative, in the name of their God.

If we are honest about our organized religions and the narratives they employ, we must admit that organized religion is often fascist in the way the system gets organized. Fascism attempts to control. We religious-believers of each generation have allowed fascistic tendencies to grow without calling them out nonviolently. Instead of sensing for oneself what is right, we give our power over to authorities who decide for us and who cloak their decisions by saying "God says this" — and these same authorities are the ones benefitting financially, politically, and prestigiously from the religion and the narrative. It happens within Judaism, within Christianity, within Islam — the three organized religions who trace their roots in the Bible. Just look at the wars happening as I write this in 2024 — wars led by religious-believers thinking "God" is on their side as they kill people in the name of their "God" and in the name of the the biblical texts they use to support their decisions.

I suspect it happens in every organized religion eventually... within any system that creates an 'us' and 'them' dynamic: saved/lawful vs. unsaved/heretic. Heretic, by the way, is a Greek word that simply means 'one who chooses for oneself' — someone choosing not to go along with the empire and the emperor's demands. Ecstatics/prophets and any bordercrossing wanderer chooses differently. With the ecstatic/prophetic viewpoint where the wind rules and enlivens all humans and all creatures, there can be no 'us' and no 'them' — instead, only THE ALL — all of us figuring out how to live in an ever-expanding universe.

I was born and baptized into Christianity. Even though I've swum away from the shipwreck of Christianity, I still find Jesus' parables/sayings intriguing, not to mention his way of life as a wanderer filled with wonder. Anyone who finds Jesus interesting and wants to follow him in some way would never in their right mind call him *"Christ."* Look that term up, research it completely as I've begun to do in this and the next volume...you'll never call Jesus that if you love him.

Most scholars and religious-believers fail to read 1 & 2 Samuel carefully — a text that likely is making fun of the notion of *messiah/christ.* The Samuel-saga was told so stylishly and cleverly to make ancients and moderns alike question the whole system of monarchy/dictatorship and even the whole system of organized religion — and with a laugh — if you dare listen to the sounds of the Ancient Hebrew.

These stories of 1 & 2 Samuel are ecstatic and epic in every way, crafted by ecstatic-minded poets who chose carefully the words and even the sounds to communicate something that very well could be the greatest story ever told...

if you have the ears to hear.

A Few Notes on My Translation
of 1 Samuel from the Biblical Hebrew

...as it's my intent to avoid having to dance one's eyes all over the place with footnotes and to barge very little into the story unfurling itself in 1 Samuel so that the 21st century reader can catch the subtle differences that the band of X intends for us to catch...

(xx)...indicates I've added this to explain an assumption that the band of X has about life in the ancient world of what is now called Ancient Israel/ Palestine, the ancient trade routes of the eastern Mediterranean seaboard, the Levant

xxx xxx xxx...underlining indicates my efforts to highlight a clever pun that appears in the Ancient Hebrew text

x...a single italicized word indicates something that has been borrowed from Ancient Hebrew or Ancient Greek and brought into English...a word that might be wise to note its divergent roots *xxx xxx xxx*...italicized whole sections indicate an addition by the later Deuteronomistic editors, mostly likely the post-exilic generation of Deuteronomists trying to sew an overarching thread through their vast work of Deuteronomy/Torah through Joshua, Judges, 1 & 2 Samuel, and 1 & 2 Kings (more on how and why they do that later)

I have also capitalized divinities with their assumed vowels included for ease of reading — for instance, YAHWEH instead of YHWH and ELOHIM instead of AHLHYM. This whole business of ELOHIM in the Bible is tricky...could be translated as God, gods/goddesses, divine/divinity. These might be controversial choices for a number of reasons, though I believe you'll come to discover it makes for ease of reading for a wider audience. I have retained only the 'original' consonants-only versions of non-divinity words — for instance, GLH instead of GaLaH or GeLaH or something of that sort. More details on this system can be found in **Hebrew Alphabet - transliterated** and **Major Characters** in the *Resources* near the back of the book.

Trying to bring forward the flexible style of Ancient Hebrew verbs, English verbs like 'climb' and 'style' — for example — are used transitively and intransitively, even sometimes when not appropriate in modern English usage. Try it out. Play along.

here begins
a translation
from the 'original' Ancient Hebrew
of the first scroll of Samuel...

chapter 1

And so —
there once was this guy from The Heights,
the one full of Honeycomb where wild honey floods the area,
from Ephraim, the tribe of Ancient Israel from the mountains
known for being fruitful.

His name was Elkanah-Divinity-Creates.

(You see, this guy was named after EL, some understanding of
'divinity.' "EL" is a tricky word in Ancient Hebrew. It can mean
the chief god/divinity that people of this Canaanite area had
worshipped for centuries. Later, the ancient Levitical priests
pluralize EL to ELOHIM to denote 'God of all divinities'...'the
One <u>God</u>'...though ELOHIM can also mean 'the divinities'
or 'gods and goddesses' — as in non-Hebrew/non-Israel
divinities — both in the Bible and elsewhere.

And Ephraim? It's north of The Heights. So we have a
story of a northerner who migrated to the south...perhaps as
Finkelstein and Silberman have posited people began to do as
Ancient Israel fell to Assyria.

And Honeycomb? That's TSUP...same sounds as 'Sufi'...known

today for their whirling turns of phrase, a clever style all their own.

Needless to say, this is no gentle beginning...it's power-packed!)

This guy was from quite a line of people...
  he was son of Womblike-Compassion,
  who was the son of That's-My-EL-Divinity,
  who was the son of Humble-Guy,
  who was the son of Honeycomb...
  the guy from Ephraim, the tribe from the mountains known
    for being fruitful.

And (Elkanah-Divinity-Creates) had two wives.
The first one's name was Hannah-Bend-Down.
The second one's name was Power-Jewels.

Power-Jewels had children.
Hannah-Bend-Down had no children.

And this man would climb up from his city year after year —
to bow down
and to butcher and burn up animals (wealth)
for YAHWEH of-the-Big-Armies-Who-Require-Service —
at A-Quiet-Place, He-Whose-It-Is.

(As the story plays out, we'll discover that 'A-Quiet-Place,
He-Whose-It-Is'/Shiloh is imagined here as a smallish
highland-village with a tent-temple...about 25 miles from
Elkanah-Divinity-Creates' home, a rugged, uphill, multi-
day adventure...this divinity YAHWEH has a tent-temple, yet
most divinities like EL would have a temple made of stone...)

It was there that Climb-Up's two sons —
Two-Fists and Snake-Mouth —

were YAHWEH's priests (responsible for the expensive and profitable butchering and burning of animals for YAHWEH). And so it was — time for Elkanah-Divinity-Creates to butcher and burn an expensive animal for his wife Power-Jewels and portions for all her sons and daughters.

And for Hannah-Bend-Down,
(Elkanah-Divinity-Creates spent more money)
and had a portion offered (to YAHWEH) —
his nostrils flaring, out of his anger and his resolve —
because it was Hannah-Bend-Down he loved.

You see, YAHWEH had shut up her womb.

(That's to say, she was not able to have children.

Now when a man in the ancient world had two wives — or often more wives, depending on his wealth — you can imagine that there would be a rivalry for both affection and time with one's husband for intimacy, for sex...as a woman of the ancient world wouldn't consider herself complete until she had children, especially a boy-child who would keep the family-line going through the next generation. All of this, of course, flies in the face of the 21st-century, post-industrial-world's values, but we need to keep it all in mind if we're to understand the landscape and inner life of these ancient biblical characters and stories so that we might come to know our own, ourselves.

So Hannah-Bend-Down had a rival, a rival-wife in Power-Jewels.)

And her rival (Power-Jewels) would provoke her anger —
even <u>crossing over so far as</u> to purposefully make her angry
and tremble like <u>thunder</u>
about YAHWEH shutting up her womb.

(AYBOR/'crossing over so far as' is from the same word-family as AYBR/'bordercrosser, wanderer' from which we get the word 'Hebrew';

HRAYMH/'thunder' sounds similar to HRMH/'The Heights' in/on which Hannah-Bend-Down and her family live.

And all this 'climbing up'/AYLH calls us back to the character they are climbing up to see at the tent-temple, Eli-Climb-Up/AYLY, the priest with the nasty named sons.

Little giggles would probably be heard in the crowds first hearing these tales offered by the band of X, already styling out their clever style.)

And just like this, she would do this, year after year,
whenever she climbed-up to YAHWEH's house,
(Power-Jewels) would provoke her to become angry
so much so that (Hannah-Bend-Down) would weep and not eat.

And her husband Elkanah-Divinity-Creates would say to her,
"Hannah-Bend-Down!
Why do you weep?
Why don't you eat?
Why is your heart all shaky?
Am I not better for you than having ten sons?!"

And (so this time) Hannah-Bend-Down stood herself tall
after she ate
in A-Quiet-Place, He-Whose-It-Is —
and after she drank.

And Climb-Up — the priest responsible for butchering and burning animals — was sitting on the special seat by the doorpost of YAHWEH's palace-temple.

And she was so bitter — (Hannah-Bend-Down was!) —

her living-breathing-body so out of sorts —
she prayed, she put out there her desires and hopes —
upon YAHWEH.

And she <u>wept, wept, wept</u>!
And she <u>vowed, vowed, vowed</u>!

And she said,
"YAHWEH!
Of-the-Big-Armies-Who-Require-Service!
How is it you can't see
the absolute oppression —
humiliation —
torment —
of your woman-slave!?!? of me!!!
Remember me!
Don't forget your woman-slave!
Give your woman-slave seed-of-men/people (offspring)
and I will give (the boy-child) to YAHWEH —
all the days of his life —
a razor will not climb upon his head — ever!"

(Now this whole 'not cutting one's hair' was very serious business in the ancient world. A special vow, it was an outward sign of an inner reality, what is not cut outside oneself is uncut within oneself, as in one's tether and relationship to EL or YAHWEH or to any god(dess) / power. The wildness of such hair, such relationship....

And as for 'wept, wept, wept' and 'vow, vow, vow'...there's a style in Ancient Hebrew to double verbs, to repeat them but conjugate them just slightly differently, usually with an aim to say 'look I *mean* this!'...as I did in *A Wildly Sensual YAHWEH*, I triple the doubled-verbs both to reveal the style of the 'original' text and to make it clear that it's not a typo on my part in the English translation.)

And it came about like this —
as she carried on in her praying, in her putting out there her
desires and hopes right there in front of YAHWEH's face,
(the priest) Climb-Up was watching her mouth very carefully,
protectively.

And as for Hannah-Bend-Down,
well, she had a special style of speaking in her own heart —
only her lips quivered.

Her voice could not be heard.

(See, it was customary during this time to pray in such a way
that one's voice *could* be heard. One usually prayed out loud
in the ancient world — and loudly enough for any ELOHIM
to hear, whether that ELOHIM was 'God' or any and all 'gods
and/or goddesses'...as ELOHIM, recall, can mean both.)

And Climb-Up figured she was drunk,
and Climb-Up said to her,
"How much longer will you be drunk?
Turn away from — leave off your wine!"

And Hannah-Bend-Down responded and said,
"No, my boss!
A woman (suffering) with a terrible/stiff-necked wind/spirit —
that's me!
And as for wine and liquor — I haven't had anything to drink —
I'm spilling out my living-breathing-body —
in front of YAHWEH's face!
Don't make your woman-slave — me! —
out to be a good-for-nothing cheating daughter
because of the abundance
of my musing-babble
and my being provoked to anger
that I styled into speech all the way to right now!"

(Did she forget she had had something to drink just before this?? Did she lie?? Whatever the case, she's certainly speaking with some 'style'/DBR...MRB/'many, great, abundance...also the name of a character in 1 Samuel, Merob' and SYCH/'to complain, to muse, babble, talk it out out loud'...and a circling back and hinting to what her sister did to her, to what that wind is that stirs within her.

Later, a key character will suffer with a 'bad wind/spirit' but here it's QSHT/'terrible, stiff-necked'...the same adjective to describe the Israelites during the Torah/Exodus story.

Note how Hannah-Bend-Down deals with her 'terrible wind'... she belts out her feelings, she prays.)

And Climb-Up responded and said,
"Go in peace and health!
And may Ancient Israel's ELOHIM/God-or-the-gods-and-goddesses give you what you asked for,
whatever you asked from (ELOHIM)!"

(As mentioned before, this whole business of 'EL' and 'ELOHIM' can be confusing in 1 Samuel. We're never quite sure which 'EL/ELOHIM' is intended...the name of the Canaanite godhead, the generic name for the One God of Ancient Israel, an indefinite way of saying 'gods and/or goddesses.' When the very specific name 'YAHWEH' is used, we know for sure that we're not talking about other gods and goddesses. We should assume that the priest Eli-Climb-Up would be referencing the One God as Eli as priest serves at YAHWEH's footstool, the ark, the place to which people climb-up to worship. But we should not be so sure that every time Eli says 'ELOHIM' that he means the One God. Soon in our saga the asked-for head of the nation of Ancient Israel will be interested in other ELOHIM than the One God.

And all of this in mind as we consider the name of the nation Eli-Climb-Up references here — Ancient Israel — with its famous origin story....its national hero who wrestled EL, got groped and penetrated by EL, and still won. What's more than a little interesting is that Eli-Climb-Up here asks EL/ELOHIM to grant Hannah-Bend-Down's wish, not specifically YAHWEH. Note that the character Eli-Climb-Up, the priest, is the one calling the divine 'ELOHIM' though most of the time going forward the narrator will prefer 'YAHWEH.'

And to make matters interesting, <u>SHLTC</u> and <u>SHAHL</u> both have to do with 'asking' which will be important to the plot of 1 Samuel as well, foreshadowing perhaps about being smart/careful what we <u>ask-for</u>.)

And she said,
"May you find your successful-child-bearing-woman-slave — me! — <u>charming-and-grace-filled-so-much-so-that-you'd-kneel-down-to-me</u> — in your eyes, from your viewpoint!"

(You see, she had given herself a promotion by what she had said here, by giving herself the same status as her rival-wife who has children. Just a few minutes ago Hannah-Bend-Down spoke of herself as a 'woman-slave'/AHMH...and now she speaks of herself as a 'woman-slave who has already successfully borne children'/SHPCHH. Wives had rank within families of the ancient world, based on how they were married...slave or 'free' and then later based on whether they gave their husband children. It's the hierarchical-mindset of their world, which might get us wondering about our own assumptions about who we value more and less than oneself.

Such trust she has that YAHWEH already had given her man-seed/descendants through her asking!

And note the clever plays on the names already...Hannah-

Bend-Down/CHNH hopes to be found 'worthy and charming, enough that a superior might kneel down to an inferior'/ CHNN, here in this hierarchically-minded society. And in front of whom does Hannah-Bend-Down/CHNH make this plea, who witnesses her plea? In front of Climb-Up/AYLY, the guy everyone climbed up to for his priestly butchering-and-burning animals/wealth to ELOHIM. Welcome to the style of the band of X that most translators of 1 Samuel ignore.)

And the woman went on her way and ate.

And as for <u>Power-Jewels</u> (her rival wife), (Hannah-Bend-Down) was not hers anymore.

(I suggest that there has been a copyist error in the Masoretic text and have adjusted for that. The Masoretes have PNYH/'her face' but I think it's probably supposed to be PNNH/Peninnah/Power-Jewels. It's basically the difference of an apostrophe being lengthened into a line. Without that adjustment, the text as it has been received makes no sense grammatically or in the present context.)

And they got an early start in the morning,
bowed down in worship before YAHWEH's face,
returned,
and <u>(fuck) entered</u> their house in The Heights.

And Elkanah-Divinity-Creates <u>knew intimately —</u>
<u>had sex with</u> — his wife Hannah-Bend-Down,
and YAHWEH remembered her.

(Here are the old friends so often punned upon by the band of YAH in Genesis:

BOAH/'to enter, arrive, bring, fuck' and YDAY/'to know in all ways, including sexually.' Every time an ancient would hear either of these two words they'd be wondering which way these words explode, which direction the meaning goes. Often, it's both. Every time BOAH is used in 1 Samuel, I'll often translate it as *(fuck) entered* or *(fuck) went* or *(fuck) arrived* or *(fuck) brought* so that we moderns too can climb into the ancient hearer's listening-imagination and wonder with them. Not every BOAH means 'fuck' but often somewhere nearby there's something that leans in that direction or even makes sense as we use 'fuck' today in expressions of anger or wonder or curiosity. 'Oh fuck, would you look at that tree on top of that car!')

And so it was —
the days circled around
and Hannah-Bend-Down was pregnant
and gave birth to a son!

And she called out his name,
"Samuel!
(which means 'named for EL/the divine')
because it was from YAHWEH that I <u>asked for</u> him!"

(Notice how she freely connects EL with YAHWEH. And note how she asked for a child from YAHWEH, and YAHWEH delivers. Later, her nation will ask for something from YAHWEH that will set them up for trouble....)

And her husband Elkanah-Divinity-Creates and everyone from his house/family was climbing up (to A-Quiet-Place, He-Whose-It-Is, where YAHWEH's tent was) to butcher and burn up expensive animals for YAHWEH as they did every year

— it was his vow.

But Hannah-Bend-Down didn't climb up (with them),
see...she said to her husband,
"Not until the boy/slave finishes up weaning...
I'll (fuck) take him
and <u>he'll be seen</u> in front of YAHWEH's face —
and (the boy/slave) will stay there forever!"

(This whole business of 'seeing'/RAHH foreshadows the
boy Samuel's future role as 'seer'...one who sees into things.
NAYR/'boy' can also be 'boy-slave' which also has something
to do with his future role...his mother vowed to dedicate him
as YAHWEH's slave. In the saga here and elsewhere in the
biblical tradition, the character YAHWEH seems to be taking
on some of BAAL's importance/attributes in this era of the
ancient world of the Levant. BAAL was previous generations'
storm-god symbolized as an erect penis inserted into the
ground to fertilize land and people...thus taking care of the
two greatest concerns of any ancient person: having enough
to eat and having descendants to carry on the family-line.)

And her husband Elkanah-Divinity-Creates said to her,
"Do what's good in your eyes...
stay until you've weaned him.
One thing's for sure:
let YAHWEH stand up tall —
erect Its own style!"

And the woman stayed home and nursed her son until she
had weaned him.

And she climbed him up with her,
just after she had weaned him,
with three bulls
and a whole lot of flour
and a large storage jar — a <u>stupidly-large</u> amount — of wine.
(All of this worth a lot of money.)

And she (fuck) brought him to YAHWEH's house
in A-Quiet-Place, He-Whose-It-Is.

And the boy — he was just a boy!

And they killed and cut up a bull.

And they (fuck) took the boy to Climb-Up.

And she (Hannah-Bend-Down) said,
"In me — oh my — my boss —
alive — your living-breathing-body — you live —
my boss —
I am — I'm the woman who stood her ground with you
right here
to pray, put out my desires and hopes to YAHWEH —
for this very boy/slave — I prayed for him,
put out there my desires and hopes for him —
and YAHWEH gave me what I <u>asked for</u> —
exactly what I asked from It!
So, I — that's right! — *I* am <u>asking-him-back</u> (lending the boy/
slave) for YAHWEH!
All the days he lives he will be <u>asked-back</u> for YAHWEH!"

(Now, this was an ancient woman offering her child — not
the husband who had rights to the child. This is surprising
speech in the ancient world — not to mention a strange way
of putting it!

In Hebrew, the words 'ask' and 'lend' are from the same word...
SHAHL...the same 'ask' Hannah-Bend-Down had made to
YAHWEH earlier. Perhaps we readers/hearers are being
<u>asked</u> to differentiate <u>asks</u> in this saga...?

Two upcoming characters' name in the saga have been
mentioned here as woven into the plot...NBL/'stupid'/Nabal
and SHAHL/'asked-for, lend'/Saul. This is something that the

band of X tends to do, something to which we can circle back later after these characters make their appearances.)

And they bowed down right there to YAHWEH.

chapter 2

And Hannah-Bend-Down prayed, put out her desires and feelings and said,

"My heart rejoices in YAHWEH —
 my powerful horn gets high with YAHWEH!
My mouth opens wide in a smile over my enemies
 because I cheer at Your rescuing me!

There's nothing so honored as YAHWEH
 because there's nothing besides You —
 and there's no sheltering cliff like our EL/divine!

No more styling on and on —
 higher-and-haughtier, higher-and-haughtier!

Let something brash come from your mouths —
 because EL's/divine's sexual, intimate, in-all-ways knowing
 is YAHWEH,
 and by It (YAHWEH) offensive, piercing, profane things are
 measured!

The champions' weapon is broken
 and they who once stumbled now strap on a powerful force!

Those who've had their fill of bread (or fighting) now have to
hire themselves out
 and those who were hungry aren't anymore!

Even the barren-wombed give birth seven times
and the one with many children withers away!

YAHWEH makes death and makes life...
makes people go down into death's pit
and makes them climb up!

YAHWEH seizes people's wealth,
and makes others rich,

humiliates people
and — of course — raises them up,

makes the powerless stand up tall from the dust —

from the garbage-dump (YAHWEH) picks up the needy
to make them sit with the upperclasses
and make them inherit seats of greatest honor!

Because the deepest pillars of the earth are YAHWEH's
and It has set the continents upon them!

The feet/testicles of Its loyal-ones (YAHWEH) protects
and those who act in wicked ways become silent in the
darkness!

Look, it's not by human-power that someone becomes a
champion —
YAHWEH sinks deeply into the sore spots of Its contenders
— It thunders through the skies against them!

YAHWEH sails a straight course — acts as judge — to the ends
of the earth,
gives real-strength to Its king,
and raises high the powerful horn
of Its *messiah*, Its specially-selected-and-ointment-smeared-
leader!"

(Now this is a highly complex and stylized poem — out of the mouth of this woman from the hill-country, from The Heights!

And not only that — it would have toppled the expectations of every person in her time...the lowest at every turn becomes the greatest?!?

YAHWEH can make people poor? If YAHWEH is the wind — and even a wild wind like a tornado or storm — that could make a rich person poor in an instant, especially in a world without insurance. That very wind could kick up ancient wealth/animals and deposit them on someone else's land, or kill them. As just mentioned, YAHWEH there were other storm divinities...including BAAL, a Canaanite god. Storm/wind divinities controlled everything in the ancient understanding...breath, wind, rain to make crops grow, too much rain to destroy, fertility of land and even fertility of human beings. Nearby nations all knew about BAAL and its seductive power and its sexual rituals used to conjure BAAL's interest in raining/ejaculating on the land. But something new is being imagined here, a new EL/ELOHIM...ah, the nature of the wild wind — YAHWEH — the new storm divinity on the ancient block!

And our character-poet Hannah-Bend-Down would know something of how quickly YAHWEH can flip expectations and personal value and social standing...YAHWEH took this woman who styled out a quivering, silent-like prayer, this woman all Bent-Down by the weight of not being able to have children, this woman who was roused to anger by her rival-wife, who now celebrates her victory of not only being able to have a child but also to be able to dedicate her child to YAHWEH, to ask little boy/slave Samuel back to YAHWEH.

Such is the cleverness and profound nature of the band of X and their tales. Some scholars have suggested that Hannah's poem was added to 1 Samuel much later in the text's development. That is entirely possible, and actually strengthens the idea that these tales that became 1 & 2 Samuel were told and re-told over generations and, in my opinion, played with a certain few key words and ideas, a style that could riff a new story in the saga every night, a style that was seeking to influence the emerging group-think of the time.

Here are a few of those style-rich ideas and style-rich word choices...

Hannah's from-the-middle-of-nowhere-hometown 'The Heights'/RMH gets raised up and punned upon four times in this pretty short poem...'gets high/RMH & 'raises them up'/ ROMM & YRYM/'thunders' which happens up there in any heights, the realm of the divine & 'raises high'/YRM...all of these sound similar and descend from the same family of words having to do with 'up/high'

and yet this 'highness' will often be differentiated from GBH/'high-and-haughty, arrogant'...two characters will be described this way, one will be king (1 Sam 9) and one will be passed over as king (1 Sam 16)

'bread, fighting'/LCHM...as we'll discover about midway through 1 Samuel, a certain key character comes from a city named for bread or fighting...and in most instances in 1 & 2 Samuel we never really know which LCHM — 'bread' or 'fight' — is intended...in their world, it seems one must often fight to get to eat one's daily bread due to the systems of government/ religion people have chosen for themselves...and we often choose poorly when we do not let ourselves acknowledge that the current system we've chosen doesn't need to be this way... we can conceive of completely different systems with even a little imagination

'feet, testicles'/RGL...this is one of the great puns within 1 & 2 Samuel — better versions coming soon — and *Strong's Exhaustive Concordance* among most others notes well that the Hebrew word for 'foot'/RGL is also a euphemism for 'testicles/genitals' just as YD can mean 'hand' or 'penis'...like any good horn that points up, up, up, that gets high, like here in the poem.

And note the clever way the character Hannah-Bend-Down brings it back to the very nature of her nation..."YAHWEH sinks deeply into the sore spots of Its contenders"...the nation/people Israel, after all, earns its name from that likely very memorable mythos/story of Jacob wrestling YAHWEH, when YAHWEH gets on top of Jacob and YAHWEH gropes Jacob between the legs in his tender spots — genitals and asshole — and then penetrates Jacob right into that tender hole...until Jacob reverses the situation and tops YAHWEH. In Hebrew, the name Israel = 'the one who tops EL/divinity.'

And here's our first mention of *messiah*...MSHYCH/'*messiah*, specially-smeared-with-oil'...as if Hannah-Bend-Down is foreseeing what is on the horizon for Ancient Israel, this *messiah*, this *christ*, the Greek form of the Hebrew word *messiah*. And it has nothing to do with Jesus.

This is quite a poem, quite a prayer...what had gotten into Hannah-Bend-Down in that moment of, of...of...ecstasy?)

And (Hannah's husband) Elkanah-Divinity-Creates went back toward The Heights, toward his home.

And the boy/slave (Samuel) became a special-server for YAHWEH, right there in front of Climb-Up, the priest.

And Climb-Up's sons — they were wicked and worthless sons — they didn't know YAHWEH in every way...personally, sexually, intimately.

And this was the legal-decision of the priests (like Climb-Up and his sons) with the people:

any man/person offering one of their animals for butchering

and burning with some devotion toward EL/divine —

(an expensive affair since one's animals were one's liquid-wealth in that day, land being solid-wealth) —

the priest's boy/slave would (fuck) come — just as the meat was boiling — and a three-pronged fork in his hand/penis/phallic-control,

and he would stick it (that fork, we can only guess, into the meat dedicated to EL/the divine at any point in the process):
on the platform
or in the small cooking-pot,
or in the large cooking-pot,
or the very large earthenware pot —

everything that the fork climbed up, the priest took for himself!

This is what they did for all of Ancient Israel who (fuck) came to A-Quiet-Place, He-Whose-It-Is.

Even before they let the best fat go up in smoke (ancient divinities were usually understood to be in the sky/heavens, where smoke drifts), the priest's boy/slave would (fuck) come and say to man/person offering their expensive animal for butchering and burning,
"Give the priest some meat to roast (for himself)!
He won't take meat from you that's already been boiled
— only living (raw meat)!"

(In the ancient world, the fat was usually considered the best part. A live animal, of course, was worth money, was money in the ancient world, especially the fat that hadn't melted away and become smoke. And just to clarify again, 'boy/slave'/NAYR in the ancient world could denote a young male not yet of marriageable age and/or a slave, much like the Jim Crow South with its hierarchical assumptions about worth...something the band of X plays on to challenge those assumptions...priests and kings have NAYR/'slaves, boys' and prophets, we'll see, consider themselves YAHWEH's NAYR, and no anyone else's.

'the small cooking-pot'/DOD...the same letters for a certain character named David we will meet in the middle of 1 Samuel, who will also face a powerful someone trying to stick his hand/penis or sharp stick into him...there seems to be a trend here in foreshadowing future characters' names in the early plot of the saga...

AYLH/'climb up' is used to describe what a priest like Eli-Climb-Up/AYLY would do with the meat on his fork...more style-rich sounds elucidating meaning in our saga.)

And the man/person would say to him,
"Smoke, smoke, smoke it up!
Today - right now! The fat!
And then after that take for yourself as much as your living-breathing-body desires!"

And (the priest's boy/slave) would say,
"No — give it over now or else I'll take it by force!"

And so it was —
the terrible offense of the boys/slaves —
huge, I mean, very huge! —
right there before the face of YAHWEH...
you see, the men/people were treating with complete disrespect the gift offered to YAHWEH.

And Samuel, the one named after EL/divine, was serving right there in front of YAHWEH's face —

a boy/slave —

and he'd girdled on the special, priestly straggly-yarned underwear.

And a robe — she made for him a very short sleeveless robe
that covered him up a bit —
his mother did! —
and she'd climb up to him year after year —
climbing up with her husband for the annual butchering and
burning of expensive animals.

And (the priest) Climb-Up would bring (Samuel's parents)
Elkanah-Divinity-Creates and his wife to their knees into
abundance and say,
"May YAHWEH put in place for you a seed, a descendent,
from this woman
all because of the ask-back — the loan —
of what she asked of and loaned to YAHWEH!"

And they'd go back to their place in the world.

You see, YAHWEH <u>had been visiting</u> Hannah-Bend-Down,
taking up her cause —

and she became pregnant
and gave birth to three sons
and two daughters!

(This whole business of 'visiting'/PQD is always used in
strange ways, both here in 1 Samuel and throughout the band
of YAH's Genesis stories. PQD can certainly mean 'visiting,
taking care of' but it can also mean 'mustering/counting' or
even 'punishing'...and *Strong's Exhaustive Concordance* notes
that all of these could be "with friendly or hostile intent." PQD
is also the verb used when YAHWEH 'visits' Sarah and she too
becomes pregnant in Genesis 21, and when the guys 'visit' the
often-naked Joseph in the Genesis stories...catch the mystery,
perhaps the strangeness of YAHWEH from the viewpoint of
the bands of X and YAH...!)

And the boy/slave Samuel grew up with YAHWEH.

And Climb-Up was getting very old,
and he heard about all that his sons had been doing
to their entire nation of Ancient Israel —
that they had been <u>sleeping with — having sex with</u> —
the women who had been drafted and forced to serve
by standing at the opening of the <u>knowing/sexy</u> tent —
the tent where people could come face-to-face with YAHWEH.

('sleeping with, often implying sex'/SHCB and likely here is
not talking about how Climb-Up's sons are taking naps with
the women who likely have no choice about their service at
the tent dedicated to YAHWEH...so yes this is tragically more
like a rape-scenario...and rather strangely it's where we're told
Hannah-Bend-Down uttered her prayer...

and likely the band of X is making a statement here as AHHL
MOAYD is used 34 times in Exodus and 42 times in Leviticus —
these two priest-composed books that create an air of holiness
around this 'meeting-tent.' But what we often forget is that
MOAYD derives from YDAY/'to know something or someone,
often sexually.' And here we have the band of X crafting stories
about the priest Eli-Climb-Up's sons sleeping with and having
sex with women — probably by force — inside the opening of
the 'meeting-tent' which could very well be translated as the
'sexy-tent' and here most certainly seems to be. The band of X
seems to tease all the trappings of priestly-power in 1 Samuel.
And we haven't seen anything yet!)

And he said to (his sons),
"Why do you do these things in your own style?!
I've heard — I have! me! — about your specially-styled ways
of dealing with things — awful things —
from all of these people!

Not my sons!!

Because the report's not good —

I hear that you are <u>bordercrossing</u> YAHWEH's people!

If a person/man makes a terrible offense against a man/person,
ELOHIM/'God-or-the-gods-and-goddesses' can pray and judge and intervene...

but if it's against YAHWEH that a man/person makes a terrible offense...
who can pray and judge and intervene for that person?!"

('bordercrossing'/AYBR...a curious choice of words as Climb-Up knows that his sons have been knowing these women, crossing the borders of what's right and just both regarding these women-servants and YAHWEH...AYBR is also the word for 'Hebrew'...even Climb-Up seems to have some style in his way of speaking.)

And (his sons) didn't listen to their father's voice —
you see,
YAHWEH would take great pleasure in murdering them.

And the boy/slave Samuel was growing up —
in stature and in goodness,
with YAHWEH and with men/people.

And a ELOHIM's-man/person (fuck) went to Climb-Up and said to him,

"Here's what YAHWEH says:

'Did I <u>strip, strip, strip myself naked like an exile or slave is forced to do</u> —
did I strip myself naked for your father's house/family

when they were in Suffering-Egypt, when they were owned by Pharaoh-Negligence's house?!?

(I did!)

Did I choose him for myself from among all branches, all the tribes of Ancient Israel to be the priest

to climb up to my butchering-and-burning table?!

to make the smoke smoke on up to me (after the animals are butchered and then when the animals burned)?!

to lift up the special priestly underwear — errr, carry and wear it — for my face, for me?!

(I did!)

Did I give your father's house
all that was offered/burnt by fire by Ancient Israel's children?

Why did you kick and despise those things butchered and burnt for me?!
And those things offered to me?!
About which I shouted out orders from my room (where we cohabit and do our marriage duty of making children)!

You're making your sons more important than me!

You've fattened yourselves up
with the very best of all the offerings of Ancient Israel...
they are my people!

So this is the way it is...

YAHWEH whispers and hisses...

the EL/God of Ancient Israel (the nation named after the

hero who wrestled me — EL/divine — and got groped and penetrated, and still topped EL — me)...

I said it once, I said it twice, I said it over and over again —

"Your house and your father's house would walk
right there before my face forever!"

— but now —

YAHWEH whispers and hisses...

disrespect me...pierce and profane me...make me worth nothing —
look — whomever honors me, I honor!
and whomever despises me will be made into nothing!

Listen here —
days (fuck) are coming —
I will cut down your seed — your descendants —
and the seed/descendants of your father's house —
from ever having an old man/person in your house!

(Remember, old age revealed one's status for good-living in the ancient imagination.)

You will look and see an opponent in my room (where we cohabit and do our marriage duty of making children) —
and in everything (the opponent) will do good for Ancient Israel —

but there won't be an old man/person in your house/family all of those days!

But one man/person I will not cut off for you from my butchering-and-burning table —

I'll do it to ravage your eyes —
to grieve your living-breathing-body!

All the abundance of your house will be murdered —
the men/people!

And this will be a sign for you,
that (fuck) comes for your two sons,
Two-Fists & Snake-Mouth:

in a single day they will be murdered — both of them!

And I'll make stand up for me
a <u>completely reliable</u> priest —
<u>the kind of person that makes anyone want to stick around,</u>
<u>to drive in their tent-stakes in fertile and peaceful ground</u> —
whatever's in my heart and in my living-breathing-body he
will do!

And I'll build for him a completely reliable house/lineage —
the kind that makes anyone want to stick around, to drive in
their tent-stakes in fertile and peaceful ground —
and he'll walk on and on right there in front of me —
my *messiah*, my specially-selected-and-ointment-smeared-
leader —
every day — forever!

And so it'll be —
anyone left from your house/lineage
(fuck) will come bow down in worship to him
for a small coin and <u>a loaf of bread</u>,
and that person will say,
"Please scrape out a job (for me) among the priesthood so I
can eat <u>a bit of bread</u>!"""

(You see, just to <u>live</u> they would have to beg for a lower position
their relatives once 'hired' boys/slaves like Samuel to do.

Like Hannah-Bend-Down's very stylized poem/utterance, this random, unnamed ELOHIM's-man/person speaks with a style and even a comedic/dramatic tone that would have stopped any ancient hearer in their tracks...especially as we listen carefully and deeply to a few Hebrew words that most translators skip right over....

GLH is used 24 times in Leviticus and every time it gets translated as something like "uncover the nakedness" of someone, usually a relative...the Levitical laws prevent, wisely, the stripping naked of one's relative with such 'stripping' usually implying sex to follow, and with a power differential, with the one doing the stripping having more value/power in their society than the one being stripped. GLH implies an ownership of one over the other, a hierarchical move of demonstrating one's power over the other. The same verb GLH is used 21 times in 1 & Samuel, and every time translators will choose 'reveal' for GLH and shy away from the nakedness that is explicit in the priestly Leviticus text. And while stripping someone does reveal their nakedness, just saying 'reveal' loses most of what is being assumed with the verb GLH. That's why I've translated GLH as 'strip someone naked like an exile or slave is forced to do'...but note here in the ELOHIM's-man/person's poem that it's YAHWEH stripping Itself, on Its own, for Its human creatures. Hmm. I'll have more to say about this as the saga unfolds.

SHBT is usually translated as 'tribe' or 'scepter/club' and *Strong's Exhaustive Concordance* notes that it comes from a word meaning 'branch'...and here in this stylish speech it seems that the poet/ELOHIM's-man/person is insinuating that YAHWEH should hit the misbehaving tribe with a club/branch to get them to wake up and behave. We might be wise to read any prophet's poems with that in mind when SHBT is used.

AYLH/'climb up' is used again in this speech addressing AYLY/Climb Up. Funny.

NSAH/'lift' will be used often in 1 Samuel, and often in comedic ways, this time referring to the straggly-yarned *ephod* that the priests wore...lift it up and one's genitals would slip out, and if the wearer got excited, those straggly-yarns would certainly be lifted up from within.

MAYON/'room or dwelling-place, where partners cohabit and do their marriage duty of making children'...*Strong's Exhaustive Concordance* notes AYONH is from an unused root "to dwell together; sexual (cohabitation) — duty of marriage"...and this seems to work in that the meeting-tent was where the people met YAHWEH/ELOHIM in the priestly imagination...though in the priestly imagination only the priest can present himself in front of YAHWEH to do his service for YAHWEH...and of course the prophets play on this marriage of YAHWEH and Ancient Israel and how Israel was the unfaithful bride often going off to have affairs with the other ELOHIM/'gods-and-goddesses.'

NAHM/'whispers and hisses' is a word usually associated with the Bible's ecstatics/prophets regarding their way of speaking, of spinning forth the next thing needing to be heard, spun out in this prophet's wild-visioning as we'll soon discover....

NAHMN/'to confirm, support' derived from AHMN/'to turn to the right, go the right way' and from where we get the word *amen*...in a wanderer-culture, when needing to move herds every day for reasons of food or safety, one would not probably drive in their tent-stakes often, especially if you've ever tried to extract an unruly tent-stake from the deep and grabby earth...though when finding fertile ground where humans and animals would feel safe and where one would want to stay awhile, one would drive in their tent-stakes in this reliable and supportive and dependable place of safety... and so too of divinity and even of wanting to anchor onto trustworthy people...it's worth noting that Leviticus has no use for this word though the rest of the Torah does, and while that might be a coincidence, it could also be yet another way the band of X is differentiating themselves from the Levitical priests, as they do so here with this ELOHIM's-man/person coming to Levitical priest Eli-Climb-Up to tell him his line is doomed and that YAHWEH seeks someone more 'completely reliable'/AHMN than Eli-Climb-Up and his line/family.

As I mentioned before, when LCHM is used in the context of 1 Samuel, it's often challenging and punny to figure out whether the band of X means 'bread/food' or 'fighting'... especially when the so-called hero/warrior to come hails from a city of LCHM, which could be <u>bread</u> and it could be <u>fighting</u> and it could be both. But here we have CCR LCHM/'a loaf of bread' and PT LCHM/'a bit of bread' to make it clear here that in these two cases it is not 'fighting' the ELOHIM's-man/person is talking about.

The ark was considered holy, holy, holy to the Levites. The whole priestly livelihood centered around the ark and its cultic and expensive butchering and burning of animals in front of it, something it seems that Climb-Up's sons were accustomed to doing, the role where they were stealing the best of the sacrifices for themselves. You'd think that only the top-notch priest would be allowed in there with the ark, with YAHWEH, as Leviticus 16 recommends...but here, as we continue our saga, note who sleeps in there with YAHWEH....)

chapter 3

And the boy/slave Samuel (named after EL/divine) was serving YAHWEH, right there in front of Climb-Up.

And YAHWEH's style was precious in those days —
visions and revelations didn't burst forth.

And so it was —
on that day that (the priest) Climb-Up <u>was lying down</u> in his place and his eyes had become worthless, <u>dim</u> —
he could not see.

And there was ELOHIM's candle/light —
before it went out on its own —
and Samuel (the guy named after EL) was lying down
in YAHWEH's palace-temple,
where ELOHIM's ark was.

(This word ARON is a bit tricky...usually it means 'ark' or 'chest'. In Genesis 50, ARON means 'coffin' referring to Joseph's burial in Ancient Egypt.

Through the diverse biblical tradition, usually ARON comes to be known as...

the 'Ark of Testimony'/ARON HAYDOT or ARON LAYD(O)T in Exodus and Numbers and once in Joshua,

or 'Ark of the Covenant'/ARON (H)BRYT in Numbers and Deuteronomy and Joshua and Judges,

and as 'Ark of YAHWEH'/ARON YHVH in Joshua,

and in 1 & 2 Samuel we get a new understanding: 'ELOHIM's ark'/ARON (H)AHLHYM though 1 & 2 Samuel also has 'Ark of the Covenant'/ARON (H)BRYT and 'Ark of YAHWEH'/ARON YHVH...curiously the same three uses of ARON that also appear in 1 & 2 Chronicles, priestly texts. We'll have to see what kinds of stories we get with ARON/'ark' in 1 & 2 Samuel.

ARON is used only once by any prophet — Jeremiah — and he seems to be making fun of the whole ARON BRYT business in envisioning a day when it will never be talked about again... just after talking about how Ancient Israel had been whoring around with other ELOHIM.

In the ancient priestly imagination, this ARON/'ark' acted as the footrest for YAHWEH /ELOHIM when YAHWEH/ELOHIM came down from the heavens/sky to stay awhile, to make a visitation.

Eli-Climb-Up was SHCB/'sleeping, lying down, sometimes implying sex' in his place — the same thing his sons were doing with/to the women stationed by the tent — but here it seems Eli-Climb-Up is all alone? And then we learn that young Samuel was also SHCB in the palace-temple. Near Eli-Climb-Up, the guy in charge of him? Isn't that where the head-priest should be, his place, close to the ark? Or has he let a not-yet-a-full-fledged-priest boy/slave taken over that role? As we will often in 1 Samuel, the band of X teases priestly/ Levitical expectations that appear in the priestly Torah.)

And YAHWEH called out to Samuel and said,
"Listen up! I'm over here!"

And he ran to Climb-Up and said,
"'Listen up! I'm over here!'
You called out to me?!"

And he said,
"I didn't call out for you —
go back, lie down!"

And he went and lay down.

And once more YAHWEH called out — yet again! —
"Samuel!"

And Samuel stood himself up tall
and went to Climb-Up and said,
"Listen up! I'm over here!
You called out to me?!"

And he said,
"I didn't call out for you, my son —
go back, lie down!"

And Samuel had not yet known YAHWEH intimately, sexually,

completely. It had not yet stripped Itself naked like a slave or exile is forced to do, YAHWEH's style.

(Well, well, well...sexy YAHWEH! And note that what the ELOHIM's-man/person said about YAHWEH is becoming real...where he said YAHWEH would make a completely reliable person stand up tall...and that's what Samuel is now doing, 'standing up tall'/QUM.)

And YAHWEH called out "Samuel!" a third time.

And he stood himself up tall and went to Climb-Up and said,
"'Listen up! I'm over here!'
Look — you called out to me!"

And Climb-Up figured it out, he understood —
YAHWEH was calling out to the boy/slave!

And Climb-Up said to Samuel,
"Go on, lie down!
If it happens that someone calls out to you, you say
'Speak in your style, YAHWEH!
Your slave — me! — is listening!'"

And Samuel went to lie down in his place.

And YAHWEH (fuck) came
and took Its stand
and called out
just like the times before...
"Samuel! Samuel!"

And Samuel said,
"Speak in your style!
You slave — me! — is listening!"

(Note the ironies and layers of meaning here...MSHRT/'serving' is the word used to describe Samuel's role earlier and NAYR/'boy, slave' and AYBD/'(man)slave' and GLH/'to strip oneself naked like a slave or exile is forced to do'....it's always a question of positions in Ancient Hebrew...a question of who's on top of whom....)

And YAHWEH said to Samuel,
"Listen up!
I — me! — I'm bringing forth some style in Ancient Israel —
something that when everyone listens,
their two ears will rattle-and-ring!

On that day,
I will stand myself up tall to (the old priest) Climb-Up —
all that I've styled-out about his house —
the disrespect
and the end of it!

I've announced to him
that I — me! — will be acting as judge
for his house
forever
about the crookedness that he knows about — in every way
anyone can know...relationally, intimately, sexually —
because they have made themselves worthless —
his sons have! —
and he didn't dim them down.

(Note, this is the same word — CHH/'dim' — used to describe Climb-Up just a few lines ago regarding his vision, his eyesight...worthless and dim!

The band of X thrives on juxtapositions, on sitting this near that and letting their starknesses intensify, even when it's the same word used just slightly differently. Notice the distinctions being made here between YAHWEH revealing Itself before the boy wearing special priestly underwear and the judgment upon the sons who have not simply looked at the women working at the meeting tent but have used their hierarchical privilege and power to use these working-women for sex.

YAHWEH continues speaking to young Samuel:)

So this is the way it is —
I swear against Climb-Up's house/family...
that the crookedness of Climb-Up's house cannot be made right
by butchering and burning expensive animals
and by gifts/offerings
— forever — !!!"

And Samuel, the guy named for EL/divine, was lying there until morning.

And he opened the doors of YAHWEH's house.

And Samuel was afraid to report to Climb-Up
what he had seen.

(YRAH/'he's afraid' and HMRAHH from RAHH/'he sees'... as we continue through the saga, we will note the band of X playing on the similar sounding and often confusing similar conjugations of these two words that normally, in context, one could perceive their differences...but the band of X thrives on playing with sounds, and with us.)

And Climb-Up called out to Samuel, and said,
"Samuel! My son!"

And he said,
"Listen up! I'm over here!"

And he said,
"What's the style that It styled out to you?
Please don't hide/destroy from me here
what ELOHIM/God-or-the-gods-and-goddesses did to you —
and even more so don't hide/destroy from me anything of
the style
of all that the style that was styled out to you!"

(There are many words for 'hiding' in Hebrew...usually STR/'to hide, as in behind a rock, or to hide from someone so as not to be seen' and CHBAH, which we will soon meet — ah yes, a very different kind of hiding — but here the band of X puts into the character Climb-Up's mouth CCHD, the kind of 'hiding' that can also mean 'destroying'...essentially what was predicted by the ELOHIM's-man/person about Climb-Up's very house/family and was indeed shared with the young character Samuel, about which he's afraid to tell his boss Climb-Up the very bad news which Climb-Up already knows from the ELOHIM's-man/person and has not done much about.)

And Samuel, the guy named for EL/divine, reported to him
everything that was styled-out —
and he didn't hide/destroy anything from him.

And (Climb-Up) then said,
"YAHWEH —
whatever is good in Its eyes
It's going to do!"

And Samuel was growing up,
and YAHWEH was with him.

And he didn't toss to the ground — take for granted — all that
had been styled-out for him.

And all of Ancient Israel knew intimately, personally — from the inside-out, all there was to know about —

all the way from the most just places...
   from Dan, the tribe known for offering clear judgements,
to the just-right places...
   to Seven-Wells, a southern city,
from the northern-most reaches of Ancient Israel to southern-most reaches,

Samuel having proven himself as completely reliable —
as an ecstatic of YAHWEH, a prophet of YAHWEH.

And YAHWEH continued to let Itself be seen
in A-Quiet-Place, He-Whose-It-Is —
you see, YAHWEH had stripped Itself naked like an exile or slave is forced to do — YAHWEH did this for Samuel —
in A-Quiet-Place, He-Whose-It-Is
in YAHWEH's style.

chapter 4

And so it was —
Samuel styled it out for all of Ancient Israel.

And Ancient Israel went to call out the Dust-Rolling-Philistines for a <u>fight</u>.

And they <u>bent-down and camped</u> upon the Rock of Help, while the Dust-Rollers <u>bent-down and camped</u> in a fortress.

(MLCHMH/'a fight, battle, war' and though from LCHM/'fight or bread' it's clearly a 'fight' in this usage.

CHNH/'bend down, encamp' and also recalls Hannah's name, same word.

Now it's helpful to recall what the hearers of this saga would think of the name 'Israel' and 'Philistines'...Ancient Israel's enemy in 1 Samuel, the 'Philistines' would have sounded like the word for 'mourning, rolling in the dust/ashes as one would do in mourning/grief'/PLSH...and let's recall that 'Israel' is the nation taking its name from Jacob, the hero who wrestled EL/divine, got groped and penetrated and then topped EL and won....)

And the Dust-Rolling-Philistines put themselves into battle formation to call out Ancient Israel,
and Ancient Israel joined the fight and were pounded to the edges —

Ancient Israel was struck down in defeat right in front of the Dust-Rollers.

They killed the whole front-line on the (battle)field — about 4,000 men/people!

And the people (fuck) arrived in the camp
and the old men/people of Ancient Israel (likely the veterans of battle) said,

"Why did YAHWEH strike us down with defeat today —
right there in front of the Dust-Rollers?!

Let's go fetch for ourselves the Ark of YAHWEH's Covenant from A-Quiet-Place, He-Whose-It-Is!

(YAHWEH, via the ark) (fuck) could come into the midst of us and rescue us from being in the grip of our enemies!"

And the people sent to A-Quiet-Place, He-Whose-It-Is so that they would lift up and carry away from there the Ark of YAHWEH's Covenant...where The-General-of-the-Big-Armies sits upon the terribly-scary-sphinx-guards (on top of the ark).

And there — Climb-Up's two sons with the Ark of ELOHIM's Covenant — Two-Fists and Snake-Mouth.

And so it was —
when the Ark of YAHWEH's Covenant (fuck) came into the army's camp, they shouted out the war-cry — all of Ancient Israel — with great whelping and shouting and commotion. The earth was moving, in an uproar!

And the Dust-Rollers heard the sound of the whelping and shouting and commotion, and they said,
"What's this? This great whelping and shouting and commotion from the Bordercrossers' army-camp?!"

(Recall 'bordercrossers' is a name for the larger family that comprises those that live in and around Ancient Israel — often transliterated as 'Hebrews'/AYBRYM.)

And they knew in every way that the Ark of YAHWEH's Covenant had come into the army's camp.

And the Dust-Rollers were afraid,
because they said,
"ELOHIM/God-or-the-gods-and-goddesses (fuck) came to the army-camp!"

And they said,
"Oy! Woe is us! It wasn't like this three days ago!
Oy! Woe is us!
Who could ever snatch us away from the hand/penis of ELOHIM?!
These are the Mighty Ones!
They are the ELOHIM who hit the Egypt-Sufferers
with all the death-blows in the wilderness!
Be strong! Be like men/people, Dust-Rollers!
Or else you'll become slaves to the Bordercrossers

just as they've been slaves to you!
Be like men/people and fight!"

(Note well...at first we're not sure what the band of X has the Philistines mean by 'ELOHIM'...those letters could mean 'many gods and goddesses' or 'God'...as in the One God. EL is the Philistines' godhead, head of all gods and goddesses/ ELOHIM.

And it's possible the band of X is using ELOHIM in this text to put down the priestly use of ELOHIM to mean the One God in Leviticus/Torah. The band of X and the band of YAH prefer to name this One God..."YAHWEH." The use of 'ELOHIM' is quite confusing.

The first usage involving ELOHIM's 'hand or penis'/YD could mean ELOHIM as in the One God. But after that 'these' instead of the singular 'this' clarifies that ELOHIM probably means 'gods and goddesses.' When the priests use ELOHIM to mean the One God, they usually use a singular verb with that plural subject ELOHIM.

But whatever the intention, the band of X has these Dust-Rolling characters clearly expressing their faith in — or, at the very least, fear of — Ancient Israel's ELOHIM, with a reputation for having freed small-Israel from giant-Egypt's power, and — note very well — with no mention of Moses.)

And the Dust-Rollers fought,
and Ancient Israel was struck down in defeat —

and every man/person fled to his tent.

The death-blow was big — very much so —

30,000 foot-soldiers (sometimes: testicles) from Ancient Israel fell,

ELOHIM's ark was taken,

and Climb-Up's two sons were murdered —
Two-Fists and Snake-Mouth.

And a man from Benjamin, the small tribe known for its powerful children, ran from the battle's front-lines and (fuck) arrived that day at A-Quiet-Place, He-Whose-It-Is.

And his clothes were torn,
and dirt was on his head.

(Now his appearance of course could have happened in battle for sure, though any ancient person would interpret this as signs of mourning, outer signs of one's inner reality...torn, messed up, dirty. This might be important, a message in itself to anyone who saw him...even though Climb-Up was not able to see so well, as the band of X folded into the story earlier.

30,000 dead — imagine it! And we're told they were RGLY, usually translated as 'foot-soldiers' though in a few chapters we'll get a story where RGL indeed means 'testicles,' just like YD can mean 'hand' and 'penis' depending on the context... though the band of X often tries to blur the context so that both work...words that explode with meaning are a hallmark of the ecstatic/prophetic tradition.)

And he (fuck) had arrived,
and there was Climb-Up sitting on his special-chair —
he'd been wounded on the roadside as he kept watch over it all.

You see, his heart was trembling with distress,
all because of ELOHIM's ark.

And the man (fuck) came to reported the news throughout the city, and the whole city cried out.

And Climb-Up heard the sound of the outcry, and he said,
"What's this sound, this roar?!"

And the man hurried,
and (fuck) went and reported to Climb-Up.

And Climb-Up was a son/child of 98 years of age,
and his eyes stood firm — he wasn't able to see.

And the man said to Climb-Up,
"I — (fuck) having come from the battle's frontlines —
I — from the battle's frontlines — I fled today —"

And (Climb-Up) said,
"What's with the style, my son/child?"
And the <u>cheerful-news-bearer</u> responded and said,
"Ancient Israel fled from facing the Dust-Rollers —
it was a slaughter among the people —
and your two sons were murdered —
Two-Fists and Snake-Mouth —
and ELOHIM's ark was taken —"

And so it was —
just as he was made to remember ELOHIM's ark,
that he fell backwards from his special-chair
onto the hand/penis of the city-gate
and his neck was broken
and he died —
you see, he was an old man and heavy.

(Remember, he'd been getting fat on the fatty offerings made
to YAHWEH that his sons had been stealing for him.

And note the word describing the man with the news —
HMBSR. *Strong's Exhaustive Concordance* notes that the
word carries with it a sense of being 'fresh' and 'rosy' and
'cheerful.' Again, quite stylish of the band of X. And there's

that YD again...'hand, penis' or perhaps 'handle' here referring to the city-gate near where the elders sat...but with it being YAHWEH's palace-temple it could indeed be a penis on the city wall, YAHWEH being the storm-divinity and controller of fertility as the Canaanite storm-divinity BAAL was also symbolized as a penis. We'll soon learn what YAHWEH does with Its penis. But first we need to hear what happens to Climb-Up's family after his death.)

For a very long time — 40 years! — (Eli-Climb-Up) had acted as judge and leader of Ancient Israel, the nation taking its name from the hero who wrestled EL, got groped and penetrated and still won.

And his daughter-in-law, Snake-Mouth's wife, was pregnant, about to give birth —
and she heard what there was to hear —
that ELOHIM's ark had been taken,
and that her father-in-law was dead — and her husband —
and she crouched down
and gave birth —
you see, the messenger and the pangs had overtaken her.

And just as she was dying,
the woman stationed nearby her styled-out,
"Fear not!
You gave birth to a son!"

But she didn't respond —
her heart paid no attention.

And she called out the name for the boy,
"No-Honor!"

as she said,
"The honor has been stripped naked from Ancient Israel
like exiles or slaves are forced to strip
because ELOHIM's ark has been taken!"

And because of her father-in-law and her husband.

But really all she said was
"The honor has been stripped naked from Ancient Israel
like exiles or slaves are forced to strip
because ELOHIM's ark has been taken!"

(Ha! Welcome to the imagination of the band of X — hilarious!)

chapter 5

And the Dust-Rolling-Philistines took ELOHIM's ark and (fuck) brought it from Rock of Help toward one of its well-known, powerful cities known for its cruel violence and ravaging other civilizations.

And the Dust-Rollers took ELOHIM's ark and (fuck) brought it to DAGON's house, and they set it down near DAGON, with the intention that it would remain there permanently.

(DAGON is one of the ancient gods of this region; they worshipped EL as the chief god. In addition to DAGON, this region also worshipped DAGON's son BAAL and BAAL's wife ASHERAH/ASHTAROTH. It's likely too as all the storm-god powers of BAAL were transferred by 'believers' to YAHWEH that some YAHWEH-worshippers saw BAAL's old wife ASHERAH as YAHWEH's wife...but for the biblical prophets, the 'wife' of YAHWEH is human beings, no matter their gender. Bucking the gender-norms of these ancient days — and maybe even our own 21st century too — the character-YAHWEH even has a proclivity for sex/breath with boys and men, we'll see here in 1 Samuel and in the band of YAH's stories in Genesis.

Each one of these regional god(desses) had something to do

with fertility, with providing rain or grain or sea-storms —
ultimately the elements to survive. DAGON's name either has
something to do with 'fish' or 'grain'...food. While BAAL was
the big god of the region, the Philistines taking YAHWEH's
ark to BAAL's father DAGON's temple is a bit like getting to
the heart of the matter...not to mention the double-entendre
of 'bringing/fucking it into DAGON's house'....)

And the people from this Dust-Rolling-Philistine city known
for its cruel violence and ravaging other civilizations woke up
early the next day and —
yikes! —
DAGON had fallen on his face,
down onto the ground facing YAHWEH's ark!

And they took DAGON
and returned him back to his place.

And they woke up in the morning of the next day and —
yikes! —
DAGON had fallen on his face,
down onto the ground facing YAHWEH's ark!

And DAGON's head and the two palms of his hand/penis
(from which the Dust-Rollers received so much!)
had been cut off over by the snake-like threshold.

Only DAGON was left behind down there.

(Well! We could assume that this refers to DAGON's torso
being all that was left, or it could be the understanding of
DAGON...all that was left of DAGON with his head and palms
of his hand/penis chopped off was, well, DAGON. DAGON
might have been symbolized as a fish? Keep in mind that
while the ark symbolizes YAHWEH for much of Ancient
Israel, the ark itself is not YAHWEH...just YAHWEH's footstool

or resting place...especially if indeed YAHWEH is the wind, the essence of life. And as for what YAHWEH had done in the night to DAGON there face-down on the ground with his head off and his hand/penis off, it does indeed look like a wrestling match gone awry. Or a rape. Ancient Israel would have known something of YAHWEH's raping/wrestling ways through the legend of Jacob and how the band of YAH's character Jacob earned his nickname "Israel." As we'll soon discover, YAHWEH has a way of sticking Its hand/penis into whomever It chooses....)

For this reason,
all the way to this day (this story was first composed),
DAGON's priests and all who (fuck) come into DAGON's house
do not tread on DAGON's snake-like threshold
in the Dust-Roller city known for its cruel violence
and ravaging other civilizations.

And YAHWEH's hand/penis was heavy and severe on/in the people of this Dust-Rolling-Philistine city —

and (YAHWEH) stunned them —
and attacked them with <u>swelling sores in their assholes</u> —

from the Dust-Roller city known for its cruel violence
and ravaging other civilizations and all the way to its border
on the coast!

And the men/people of this Dust-Roller city saw that this was the way it was,
and they said,
"The ark of <u>ELOHIM</u> of Ancient Israel will not stay here with us —
Its hand/penis has been hard upon/within us
and upon/within DAGON, our <u>ELOHIM</u>!"

And they sent it away.

(Some Hebrew Bibles have AYPLYM/'tumor, mound' from AYPL/'to swell, be elated' as *Strong's Exhaustive Concordance* notes and some Hebrew Bibles have TCHRYM/'anal tumors/ hemorrhoids'.

It is curious that we have such different words here in different texts — perhaps an effort to cover up what must have been embarrassing for the prudish...that YAHWEH would stick Its penis into people in such a heavy-handed way. And yet YAHWEH — the wind — does this with every single human being...YAHWEH breathes life into us. But here YAHWEH seems to prefer assholes over noses and mouths, Dust-Roller ones at that. And YAHWEH's 'hand, penis'/YD is said to be 'hard, severe, fierce'/QSHH. Yikes. Inside those assholes. Yikes.

The use of the preposition AYL/'within, upon' after YD/'hand, penis' is curious, especially twice.

Note too the use of ELOHIM in those sentences said by the Dust-Roller characters...if indeed the band of X is questioning the priestly preference for 'ELOHIM' as the name to describe Ancient Israel's divinity, these recent sentences support that notion. 'ELOHIM' is generic, and while it's clever on the priests' part to use ELOHIM to say that any name or divinity/ELOHIM falls within the One God/ELOHIM, it gets rather confusing to figure out which use of ELOHIM is intended, when 'ELOHIM' to a non-Israelite means 'gods or goddesses.' The band of X and the band of YAH and anyone else using 'YAHWEH' as the name of the One God makes these understandings clearer...even when the priests will later outlaw anyone saying 'YAHWEH' out-loud through their Torah, perhaps to distance people from the prophets/ ecstatics.)

And (the Dust-Rollers) sent for and gathered together all the Dust-Rollers' city-bosses to. themselves, and said,
"What are we to do with the ark of ELOHIM of Ancient Israel?"

And they said,
"To the city with the wine-press and their drunken concerts —
the ark of ELOHIM of Ancient Israel is to be led away!"

And they led away the ark of ELOHIM of Ancient Israel.

And so it was —
after they led it away —
there was YAHWEH's hand/penis —
on/in the city —
against the city
a huge uproar, confusion —
very much so —
and (YAHWEH) attacked the city's men/people —
from the smallest person all the way to the greatest person —

and swelling sores broke out in their assholes!

And they sent ELOHIM's ark onto the city known for things
pulled up by the roots, for childlessness (perhaps a city where
DAGON was never able to get fertility going).

And so it was —
just as ELOHIM's ark (fuck) was arriving into this pulled-up-
by-the-roots city
that the people of that city cried out together, saying,
"They've led the ark of ELOHIM of Ancient Israel to us —
to murder me and my people!"

(You see, word had gotten around about the power of the
ELOHIM of Ancient Israel. And note these non-Ancient
Israelites have a great deal of trust in this foreign ELOHIM's
power. The Philistines had their own ELOHIM-plural-
divinities...but here again, the Philistines are expressing
faith/fear in the ELOHIM-Ancient-Israel's-One-God...a
juxtaposition that the band of X will often use to make the
Ancient Israelites look not nearly as faithful to their own
ELOHIM/One God compared to Ancient Israel's enemies.)

And they sent it away and they gathered all the Dust-Rollers'
city-bosses and said,
"Send away the ark of ELOHIM of Ancient Israel —
lead it away to its own place —
so that it doesn't murder me and my people!"

You see, there had been a deadly uproar and confusion
throughout the entire city —

ELOHIM's hand/penis was very heavy there.

And the men/people who weren't murdered were attacked
with swelling sores in their assholes —

and the city's shouting climbed up to the skies/heavens.

> (We need to remember that the skies/heavens, the celestial
> realm, was the world of the ELOHIM/'God-or-the-gods-and-
> goddesses' in nearly every ancient culture...very different
> from we moderns conceive of "heaven" as a place we might
> hope to go after death. In the ancient imagination, the dead
> lived below ground in Sheol, with its long benches where the
> dead given good burial slept their eternal sleep.
>
> And if YAHWEH / Ancient Israel's ELOHIM listens to the
> cries of the Dust-Rollers, will YAHWEH listen to the cries
> of Ancient Israel? That would be a question a hearer of
> Ancient Israel would probably ask — and then there are those
> 'swelling sores in their assholes'/AYPLYM or TCHRYM —
> depending on the manuscript, though both mean essentially
> 'hemorrhoids' or 'ass-sores' — with which the Dust-Rollers
> were contending, brought on by YAHWEH's 'heavy, huge,
> rich, serious, honorable, burdensome'/CBD + 'hand, penis'/
> YD...yes, all of that. This fiction is meant to be ridiculous,
> ridiculously funny. Thankfully even Holladay's usually pretty
> conservative *A Concise Hebrew and Aramaic Lexicon of the Old
> Testament* does not shy away from mentioning either of these
> 'asshole abscesses' or 'penis' euphemisms.)

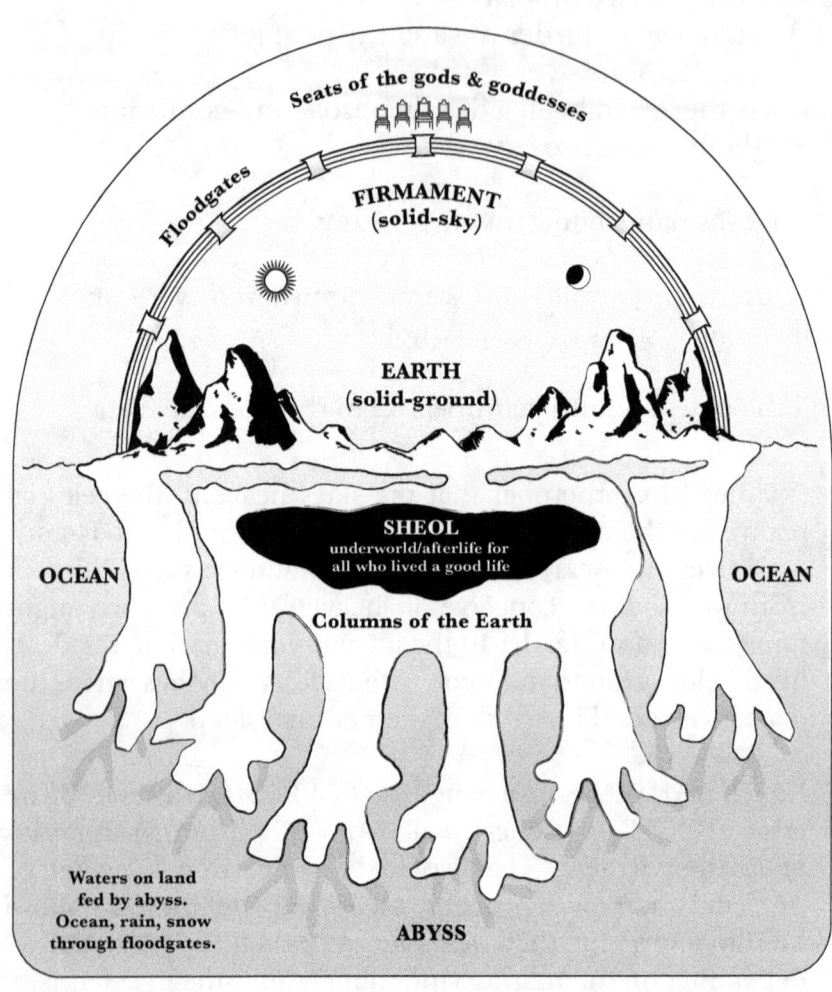

an ancient view of the world

chapter 6

And so it was —
YAHWEH's ark was out in Dust-Rolling-Philistines' open-country for seven months.

And the Dust-Rollers called out
to the priests
and
to those who <u>divine-the-future (who try to make ELOHIM/
divine speak by throwing dice or reading from magical scrolls/
books)</u>, saying,
"What should we do with YAHWEH's ark?
Make it known to us in every way —
with what should we send it back to its place?"

(You see, they were trying to figure out what to do to get
the curse off their backs, conscience...these 'death-blows' or
'plagues'/MGPH. Much will be said about this whole business
of 'divining-the-future'/QSM later in our saga.)

And (the priests and diviners) said,
"If you're going to send away the ark of ELOHIM of Ancient
Israel,
don't send it back empty, with nothing —
but return, return, return it to (Ancient Israel & their ELOHIM)
with something to make up for your offense & guilt,
then you will be healed —
and it will be made known to you in every way
just why Its hand/penis hasn't been turned away from you."

And (the city-bosses) said,
"What kind of offense & guilt offering should we send back
with It?"

And (the priests and diviners) said,
"Count up one for each of the five Dust-Roller city-bosses —

five sore assholes made of gold —

and five mice made of gold —

one for each of the <u>death-blows/plagues</u>
on all of them
and on your city-bosses —

and make the models of your sore assholes
and the models of your mice ruining the land —

give <u>seriously-heavy-glory</u> to Ancient Israel's ELOHIM —

and maybe It will soften Its hand/penis upon you and upon
your ELOHIM and upon your land.

Why would you <u>seriously-heavy-with-glory</u> your hearts
just like the Egypt-Sufferers
and their <u>Pharaoh-Negligence</u> <u>seriously-heavied-with-glory</u>
their hearts?!
Didn't (Ancient Israel's ELOHIM) overdo it on them, abuse
them,
and then (the Egypt-Sufferers) sent off (the Ancient Israelites)
and off they went!

Now fetch things and make a fresh, new wagon
— just one —
and two <u>young cows that are nursing</u>
and <u>that's never climbed up upon them — a yoke that is</u> —

and hitch the young cows onto the wagon
and <u>return back</u> their children, back toward their home —

and take YAHWEH's ark
and give it over to the wagon —

and all the gold gear
which you are <u>returning back</u> to It —
the things you're to make for your offense & guilt —
put them in a box next to it

and send it all away —
and off it goes! —

and then you'll see...

if it climbs up the road toward its own border,
toward the House of the Sun,
then (Ancient Israel's ELOHIM) has done to us this great, bad
thing —

but...

if not,
then we'll know in every way
that it wasn't Its hand/penis that beat us up —
that all of it just happened by chance, by some accident!"

(There's a great deal of comedy here, and a great deal of
thoughtful differentiation through juxtaposition. We'll need
to recall that these tales were heard, listened to, not likely
read or intended to be read to oneself in Ancient Hebrew like
most scholars or Ancient Hebrew readers today do. And with
that spoken aloud hearing, the sounds come alive — as if the
images themselves aren't enough!

The people ask, and the solution offered is quite hilarious...
"make models of five golden assholes — right where YAHWEH
had been nibbling at you with Its YD/'hand or penis' — and
make models of five golden mice — that nibble the land into
complete decay — and send off the ark with them and see
where it goes — just make sure you send it all off on a one-
way, one-lane road!"

Soon, we'll discover that the people of Ancient Israel will also ask their leaders for something, with much more tragic results than the Dust-Rolling-Philistines.

Note that the Dust-Rollers' priests and dice-rollers have no trouble calling Ancient Israel's ELOHIM 'YAHWEH'...though Ancient Israel's Levitical priests seem to have a problem with that, at least in the traditions of the Torah that go back to them. The Dust-Rollers' priests and dice-rollers even insinuate that the milking-cows being sent back with the ark are YAHWEH's to begin with...in that these cows were being 'returned'/SHUB with YAHWEH, to YAHWEH and YAHWEH's people of Ancient Israel. Such faith on the Dust-Rollers' part — a faith Ancient Israel just can't seem to mimic. And that's precisely the style of the band of X. And that's not the only style here on their part....

CBD and CBOD, both mean 'seriously-heavy-with-glory,' one as noun and one as verb, and used so close together and yet so differently in the speech/plot here.

PRAYH/'Pharaoh'...though that Egyptian word sounds like 'negligence' in Hebrew and followed by AHT then plays with PROT AYLOT/'young cows that are nursing'...

'that's never climbed up upon them — a yoke that is'/AYLH AYLYHM AYL...it's a mouthful of up-up-up/AYL...

all of this to say that even these enemy priests and dice-rollers have some style in their manner of speaking, yet no one yet can match Hannah-Bend-Down and the random ELOHIM's-man/person in the wit and wisdom they've brought forward in their own style, in their style of honoring YAHWEH in their ecstatic speeches...precisely what the band of X makes clear throughout their saga.)

And the men/people did all of this exactly —
they took two young cows that were nursing,

hitched them to a wagon,
and they shut up their children at home.

And they set YAHWEH's ark onto the wagon
with the box with the gold mice
and the models of sore assholes.

And the young cows picked the right road to take,
the road up to the House of the Sun —
by that one direct turnpike, they went, went, went.

> (More ancient comedy here...there was only one way! And
> the cows pick the 'right way'/YSHR...something Ancient Israel
> seems to have trouble with...they marched YAHWEH's ark
> into battle led by Climb-Up's stupid sons, and this won't be
> Ancient Israel's first fatal screw up in this fictional saga.)

And they moo-ed
and they didn't turn right or left.

And the Dust-Rollers' city-bosses went right along after them,
all the way to the border of the House of the Sun.

And the House of the Sun was cutting and gathering the
wheat-harvest in the valley
and as they lifted their eyes,
they saw the ark
and they rejoiced when they saw it.

And the wagon came to the hero-rescuer's field in the House
of the Sun,
and it stood still there.
There was a great big rock right there.

And they split the wood from the wagon
and they climbed up the young cows
and burned them up as an offering to YAHWEH.

And the Levites, the tribe known for being attached to the ark,
took down YAHWEH's ark
and with it the box and all that was in it —
the golden gear!

   (Nothing better than receiving a box with five golden sore
   assholes and five golden mice — and out of nowhere!

   Levi is from a Hebrew word that means 'attached.' Interesting
   that with all the ark-scenes so far the Levites are not named
   in 1 Samuel until here, as the Levites are 'traditionally' the
   caretakers for the ark...but not mentioning them until now
   — and even putting them in a foolish light, as we'll soon
   see — would not be so surprising if indeed the band of X
   crafted 1 Samuel to stand up against the Levites' and royalist-
   Deuteronomists' Torah, five books designed to make the
   prophets seem unnecessary to life. And note with all the
   mentions of the Exodus story, still no mention of Moses...!)

And they put them (most likely 'the golden gear') on the great
big rock,
and the men/people of the House of the Sun burnt them up
as offerings
and butchered and burnt animals/wealth that day to YAHWEH.

And the five Dust-Roller city-bosses saw all of this —
they returned that day to the city of their nation, the city
known for things pulled up by the roots, for childlessness.

And as for these golden ass-sores
which the Dust-Rollers had been returned
to make up for their offense & guilt to YAHWEH...there was...

   one for the Dust-Roller city known for its cruel violence and
   ravaging other civilizations,

   one for the Dust-Roller city known for its strength,

one for the Dust-Roller city known as the bank for weighing produce & wealth,

one for the Dust-Roller city with the wine-press and their drunken concerts,

one for the Dust-Roller city known for things pulled up by the roots, for childlessness.

And as for the golden mice —
they were numbered for all the Dust-Rolling-Philistines' cities —
for the five city-bosses —
from the most-protected and most-fortified cities
and all the way to the unwalled, peasant-villages
and all the way by the great <u>meadow</u> on which they laid down
YAHWEH's ark —
all the way to today (at least when this story was crafted thousands of years ago) —

out in the open-country, the middle of nowhere, the field of the hero-rescuer of the House of the Sun.

And It attacked the men/people of the House of the Sun because they looked inside YAHWEH's ark — It attacked 70 men! And then another 50,000 men!

And the people <u>mourned</u> because YAHWEH attacked the people with such great death-blows.

And the men/people of the House of the Sun said,
"Who is able to stand at attention before YAHWEH...this <u>extraordinary</u> (holy, scared) ELOHIM?
Who will it be? Who will climb up for us?"

And they sent ambassadors to the inhabitants of the town in the honey-combed forest, and said,
"The Dust-Rollers made it return — YAHWEH's ark —
come on down — then climb it on up with you all!"

(Both 'meadow' and 'mourned' include AHBL within them...
more style through similar sounds.

Apparently, they were trying to pass the curse of caring for
the ark onto some city they did not like...this honeycombed
town not even close to Shiloh / A-Quiet-Place, He-Whose-It-Is,
where we might expect the ark to return. In other saga material
edited by the Deuteronomists — Joshua & Judges — Shiloh is
said to be home to the ark, it seems, for many generations.

Pay attention to this whole business of 'extraordinary, holy,
sacred'/QDSH as it unfolds here....)

chapter 7

And the people of the town in the honey-combed forest —
they (fuck) went and climbed up YAHWEH's ark
and (fuck) brought it into the house of Patriarchy-Volunteers-
for-War, on the hilltop.

And they made his son EL's-Helper <u>extraordinary</u> (holy,
sacred) to protect YAHWEH's ark.

What is 'holiness'/QDSH as a system?

Now this whole business of making someone 'extraordinary,' to make someone stand out from the rest, to make someone 'sacred or holy'/QDSH...let's contemplate the assumptions here a bit.

Trying so hard to be 'holy' is an interest and habit of the Levitical priests who shaped much of the Torah with the help of the Deuteronomistic scribes. The Levites would tell you that Leviticus is essentially a book about how to become holy, make things holy, and how to maintain one's holiness. The scribes' book of Deuteronomy has much of the same...though not everything that is holy/unholy to the Levitical priests is holy/unholy to the Deuteronomistic scribes.

Even today, priests and their religious-followers seem to have the need to make things and people and occasions holy and sacred. Why? Because they experience their Universe as split between sacred and profane/not sacred, between holy and unholy. Some things are just better than others, in their view of the world. It's a hierarchical vision.

From the same QDSH/'holiness' comes the name for the 'holy prostitutes' in the Jerusalem temple dedicated to the priestly/Deuteronomistic version of YAHWEH — a different understanding from the band of X's YAHWEH and most of the ecstatics-prophets, it seems. Never heard of the holy-prostitutes? Better check out 2 Kings 23. 'Holy prostitutes'/QDSHYM is a plural-masculine word, which in ancient languages like Hebrew means it includes at least one male. So there were male prostitutes in the Levitical temple in Jerusalem — and we with our 21st century idea might think, well, at least women could purchase a male prostitute. Fairness. Albeit, a sick fairness. But women had no such power in ancient societies like Ancient Israel/Judah. The male 'holy prostitute' would be available for rental by a male client — all so that they could make the client's life more fruitful and fertile through their sex with each other inside the holy temple kept up by the Levitical priests. I guess as long as it's blessed by the Levitical priests — and Deuteronomic scribes/royals too — then such slavery/prostitution is okay...?!

'Holiness' and all that goes with it is a very problematic vision. Whose vision decides what is holy and what is not? 'Holiness' is a vision that is teased by the biblical prophets, it seems. Certainly here in 1 Samuel. Even Isaiah of Jerusalem, priest of the temple, teases the people's visions of 'holiness.'

'Holiness' and 'making something sacred' is a forgetting who you are, what you are, and who/what you will always be...

at least according to a biblical ecstatic/prophet.

In the midst of ecstasy, in the midst of lovemaking, in the midst of beholding something amazing, do you divide everything you're experiencing into 'good' and 'bad'...into 'sacred' and profane'...into 'pure' and 'impure'? Do you try to figure out where one begins and where the other one ends?

Of course not. The rush of ecstasy often invites a vision of wholeness, an indivisibleness, a 'neither-this-not-that' kind of imagination. THE ALL, all at once.

In an ecstatic vision, no one can make anything or anyone any more 'holy' than they are. Everything already is 'holy' and 'extraordinary' (QDSH) in an ecstatic's vision.

Why?

YAHWEH. Breathe in and out and you too will know.

It surrounds us all, yes?

There is no separation with the wind, right? It oozes into enclosed places. It permeates everything...even those things and people we think are profane or wrong. It enlivens us.

The same breath that nourishes you nourishes me...and anyone we think of as an enemy.

From an ecstatic's point of view — a prophet's point of view — we exist in QDSH...everything exists in QDSH. No one can go make anything else any more QDSH than it really is, than it already is, because YAHWEH breathes life into all, surrounds us all. You can feel It on your skin, no? in your mouth and nostrils and throat and lungs, no?

DBR's super style

I've been translating DBR in the text as 'style, to style something out.' Most translators opt for 'say or speak.' But there's already a word for that in Hebrew: AHMR.

Every time 'style'/DBR appears in the Ancient Hebrew, note what follows. It's often clever, pun-rich, playing with similar sounds, playing with meanings that explode in different directions.

DBR is almost always an awakener in Ancient Hebrew storytelling and speech...as if to say "Listen up!" or "Catch it from the beginning!" or the centuries-old "Hear ye, hear ye" meant to quiet a crowd before the days of electronics and sound systems. DBR..."catch the style coming up!"

Such is the ecstatic/imagination...to help the listener uncover the true Power that no temple or ark or throne or palace can house. The cleverness of human-ecstatic language should help to uncover the opportunity of the moment — one that only the Creator of the Universe rules. Only YAHWEH, the lifegiver, the One in whom we have our being.

A prophet/ecstatic worth their salt styles with the hopes that they themselves and those who hear stop in their tracks and notice, do nothing, drop all offense and all defense, be. YAHWEH...from the verb 'to be.'

Where has Samuel been?   And what has YAHWEH's style been doing within him and others?

Where was Samuel during this whole time that the ark was in enemy-territory?

Where was young Samuel while YAHWEH was giving sore asses to all the Dust-Rolling men, while YAHWEH demonstrated Its YD/'penis, hand, phallic-control' over/in them?

Did Samuel stay in the empty tent at Shiloh / A-Quiet-Place, He-Whose-It-Is?

Did he continue to wear the straggly-yarned priestly underwear that Eli-Climb-Up made him wear? Or did he prefer the robe his mom had made for him?

Did he leave all that behind, especially when the ark was no longer there for him to care about?

Did he continue to get blissed out on YAHWEH's style, on the way YAHWEH styled things out for him?

That 'styling-out' by YAHWEH sounds like it's quite powerful stuff — and even appears to be styled-out not by priests, not by city-bosses, not by any usual authority...

after all, YAHWEH's style came out of Samuel's mom's mouth...

and then some random dude (a 'ELOHIM's-man/person') who shows up and tells Eli-Climb-Up the way it is...

and YAHWEH even speaks to a boy...Samuel...

...when boys were worth nothing (besides labor) in the ancient world until they were marriageable, until puberty, until they were worth enough to stand on their own in this ancient economy...when boys are no different than slaves in the ancient parlance, as the same Ancient Hebrew word NAYR/'boy, slave' denotes them both.

Consider to whom and through whom it is that YAHWEH speaks, in Its own style. It's never to or through whom we might expect. Surprisingly, the old priest Eli-Climb-Up receives no message from YAHWEH spoken directly to him. Messages from YAHWEH were rare, X tells us. But they're beginning to become quite frequent so far in the story, yes?

YAHWEH speaks, so far, to and through a brash woman, through a random dude, to Samuel — and in YAHWEH's special-style. Poetry. Song. Rap. Wordplay. Humor. Irony. Read 1 & 2 Samuel carefully and you'll note that there's a huge difference between AHMR/'to say, to speak' and DBR/'to style it out.' Most translators opt for 'to speak' with DBR. They do not differentiate between AHMR and DBR — sadly. But the band of X sure did. In 1 Samuel, what follows DBR is usually something pretty clever out of the mouths of the band of X's characters. What follows AHMR in 1 Samuel is pretty plain speech. It's as if the band of X was warning their audiences when they used DBR, "Listen up! Catch it from the beginning! Here it comes!"

Remember too: the word 'prophet' is the same word for 'ecstatic' in ancient Hebrew. The prophet spits rhymes and raps and poems and songs and gets It through some ecstatic experience, or at least we can assume so far.

Consider that as you read and play with this text and perhaps any and all biblical texts and let it/It style-forward your own imagination into ecstasy as a fellow prophet/ecstatic.

After all, it seems that's what the ancient biblical storycrafters like the band of X and the band of YAH are after...to get the hearer/reader in touch with the experience of the prophet, the ecstatic.

And such experience is mediated by no one, it seems, except YAHWEH. Such ecstatic experiences come and go. Like one's breath. Like the wind. It's pretty easy to miss the wind, the gift of life in breathing. It's constant, after all. Perhaps that's what 'style'/DBR does...it wakes us up to what is.

Ecstatic experiences can be constant when we realize the world in which we live, a world that feeds us breath and through that motion of breathing, the ecstasy of sensation.

YAHWEH. Say it/It out loud a few more times. Sense the way that sound — YAHWEH — moves through your mouth, through your whole body.

And linger with it/It. Linger with your own experience. And you too will know...hopefully for far longer than the length of time Samuel had no role with the ark, as YAHWEH was demonstrating the power of Its mischievous YD/'hand, penis' in enemy territory and then hanging out around Its ark in the honey-combed forest.

How long was it/It?

I mean — how long was that length of time? Listen well here...

And so it was —
from that day on, the ark remained in the town in the honey-combed forest.

And the days multiplied —

it had been there twenty years!

And the whole house of Ancient Israel groaned and wailed after YAHWEH.

(Now this is a very strange construction...VYNHU AHCHRY. And quite wishy-washy, likely on purpose. VYNHU derives from NHH/'to lament, groan, wail' — VYNHU/NHH is used only three times in the entire Hebrew Bible. And never followed by AHCHRY, which can mean 'after' but can also mean 'away from' or 'back from behind.' AHCHR means 'the hind part, one's behind.'

At the very least, the band of X makes it quite unclear Ancient Israel's devotion to YAHWEH. And based on what follows here, we can catch a whiff of just how not devoted to YAHWEH Ancient Israel must be if Samuel must step into the fold and say what he does....)

And Samuel (the guy named after EL/divinity) said to the whole house of Ancient Israel — the nation taking its name from the hero who wrestled EL/divinity, got groped and penetrated and then topped EL/divinity...

saying,

"If you all would return
with your <u>hearts</u> back to YAHWEH
and <u>turn away from — behead</u> — the foreigners' ELOHIM/
divinities from among yourselves —

and the ASHTAROTHS —

and <u>firm up</u> your hearts for YAHWEH

and be slaves to (YAHWEH) <u>alone</u>
and (YAHWEH) will snatch you away from the hand/penis/
phallic-control of the Dust-Rollers (who strip you and plunder
you for your wealth)!"

And the children of Ancient Israel <u>turned away from —
beheaded</u> — the BAALS and the ASHTAROTHS, and they
slaved away <u>only</u> for YAHWEH.

(Hmm...and this is supposed to be 'plain speech'/AHMR
without any DBR/'style' from our character-Samuel who has
clearly changed since his boyhood days of serving the priest
Climb-Up and the ark!

Samuel recommends Ancient Israel 'firm up, erect, prepare'/
CUN their 'hearts'/LBB for YAHWEH 'alone'/LBDO and to
SUR/'turn away from, turn aside from, behead, pluck out' the
foreigners' gods and goddesses/ELOHIM. Well, if you know
what these gods and goddesses are about, that style spoken so
plainly here will begin to make some sense.

Like DAGON, the BAALS and the ASHTAROTHS were some
of the ELOHIM/divinities of their neighbors, the nations like
the Dust-Rolling-Philistines who tried in this fictional saga
to conquer Ancient Israel. EL was the chief of the Canaanite
ELOHIM/divinities. DAGON was the father of BAAL.

BAAL was a penis-pole; ASHTAROTH was his wife in some

stories. Catch a whiff of what SUR/'behead' would have done in the ancient hearers' imaginations? Ahem...

Depending on the region, ASHTAROTH went by Asherah, Astarte, and ISHTAR...from which we get Easter, the time, at least in the Northern Hemisphere, that is Spring, when things spring back to life. Many know Easter as a time of fertility, symbolized with Easter eggs, bunnies, new life. Easter. Ishtar. ASHTAROTH. In the Canaanite pantheon, some stories have ASHTAROTH married to BAAL. In some of the early YAHWEH traditions, YAHWEH had a wife too named ASHTAROTH. See Thomas Römer's *The Invention of God* for a survey of the archeological research supporting this.

From many of the prophets' standpoint, YAHWEH marries the nation of Israel alone...with YAHWEH as groom and Israel as bride...perhaps playing on the YAHWEH topping and getting topped by the Genesis character Jacob...the sexual wrestling match where Jacob gets 'ribbed' just like the mud-creature was in the Eden story.

There are some curious things about this speech the band of X inserts into character-Samuel's mouth. ASHTAROTH is the first of the foreign ELOHIM/divinities mentioned by Samuel — and not BAAL or DAGON. Perhaps the band of X is pushing against the temple-version of YAHWEH that has YAHWEH marrying ASHTAROTH, the version of 'YAHWEH-as-the-storm-divinity' that took on all of BAAL's attributes, including BAAL's marriage to ASHTAROTH, and including the 'male and possibly female holy prostitutes'/QDSHYM available for purchase even, at one time, in the Jerusalem temple built for YAHWEH, at least if we trust 2 Kings 23.7. Perhaps this whole 'holy prostitutes in the temple' business — from which the Levitical priests were likely enriching themselves — is one of the significant impetuses for the Deuteronomists to enact their religious/state reform of the temple by cleaning out these 'holy prostitutes.' The Deuteronomists enact this reform through their raised-and-reared Josiah, King of Judah.

"BAALS" usually refer to their statues — wood-resembling-erect-penises stuck into the ground to be worshipped and danced around to encourage and excite BAAL to ejaculate into the earth to guarantee another year of eating food from the earth. Such a dance around BAAL was also said to promote personal fertility, to grow one's own family. When the Number One concern(s) in the ancient world included having food to survive and having children — especially boys — to keep the family-line going, it becomes easy to see how people would fall into BAAL-worship and fascination. Fertility of land and family were critical, indeed were essentially one and the same.

BAAL and ASHTAROTH were fertility-gods, fertility-ELOHIM/divinities. For Ancient Israelites of all persuasions — the band of X & the prophets, the Deuteronomists, the Levitical priests — YAHWEH was the fertility-God of all gods and goddesses.

The significant question we might ask, knowing what BAAL and ASHTAROTH were as fertility-ELOHIM, is just what is this YAHWEH as a fertility-ELOHIM? How was this (new) Power any different from the old Powers of BAAL and ASHTAROTH worshipped by Ancient Israel's neighbor-nations? And how is X's version of YAHWEH different from the versions of YAHWEH that essentially projected all of BAAL's and ASHTAROTH's traits onto their version of YAHWEH? X is quite subtle in these differences — at least to our modern ears that often want to lump it all together.

And from X's standpoint, what did one need to do to interest or excite YAHWEH? Is it the same dance around BAAL? Hannah-Bend-Down simply powered out her guts to YAHWEH and she got what she wanted. Maybe it's as simple as feeling one's life and giving voice to one's feeling?

In any case, ancient practitioners of BAAL-religion and ASHTAROTH-religion thought that their dancing around the penis-pole in the ground guaranteed grain, food, children, life.

Recall too the famous 2 Samuel story of nearly-naked King David dancing at the dedication of Jerusalem as his capital city and how afterwards he gives out a feast of food to every subject...many resemblances to BAAL/ASHTAROTH there.)

And Samuel, the guy named for EL, said,
"Gather together all of Ancient Israel at the watch-tower
and I'll pray, put out there my desires and hopes and dreams,
on your behalf,
to YAHWEH!"

(If we do trust that these locales are real locations — and more will be said about that — the watch-tower was not close to where the ark had been resting — at least 10 miles away.)

And they gathered together at the watch-tower.

And they drew water

(perhaps not an easy thing to do up in those heights where the watch-tower would be in the mountains / hill-country, unless there is a spring up there, and if there is a spring on top of a mountain, such a place would be considered a very special place),

and poured it out before YAHWEH's face.

And they kept their mouths covered, didn't eat any food that day, and they said there,
"We're guilty!
We've offended YAHWEH terribly!"

And Samuel acted as mediator and dispute-decider
with the children of Ancient Israel at the watch-tower.

And the Dust-Rollers heard that the children of Ancient Israel had gathered at the watch-tower, and the Dust-Rollers' city-bosses climbed up to Ancient Israel.

And the children of Ancient Israel heard of it, and they were afraid to face the Dust-Rolling-Philistines.

And the children of Ancient Israel said to Samuel,
"Don't just sit there in silence —
for us — cry out to YAHWEH — our ELOHIM/divinity!
It might rescue us from the Dust-Rollers' hand/penis!"

And Samuel fetched a young, fat lamb and climbed it up to butcher it and burn it —
whole — (unlike how Climb-Up's foolish sons did it) —
to YAHWEH.

And Samuel cried out to YAHWEH
on behalf of Ancient Israel —

and YAHWEH answered him!

And so it was —
Samuel was climbing up (the lamb) to butcher and burn it
and the Dust-Rollers were getting closer
to fight with Ancient Israel...

that YAHWEH <u>thundered</u> —
in a loud voice —
on that very day —
upon the Dust-Rollers!

And (YAHWEH) threw them into a confusion, a panic —they were gored, struck down right there in front of Ancient Israel!

And the men/people of Ancient Israel went out from the watch-tower,
and they chased after the Dust-Rollers and attacked them all the way to the pasture-house in the Dust-Rollers' land.

And Samuel, the guy named for EL, took a rock — one rock
— and set it up between the watch-tower and the overhanging
crag of rock and called out its name,
"Rock of Help!"
and said,
"Now this is the place where YAHWEH helped us!"

(You might recall that Ancient Israel had lost to the Dust-
Rollers/Philistines the last time they took their stand at a
place called Rock of Help...where they had lost the ark. Note
also the whole business of it being one rock to commemorate
YAHWEH's victory...Joshua 4 has the story of a rock set up for
each tribe. And setting up a phallic rock into the ground is
usually associated with BAAL and ASHTAROTH — but here
Samuel dedicates the rock to YAHWEH.

And earlier, YAHWEH 'thundered'/RAYM...Samuel hails from
Ramah/The Heights/RMH.

And recall that these Dust-Rolling-Philistines were considered
Canaanites...people known for their 'humble-trading'
prowess...Canaan being from the verb CNAY/'to be humbled.')

And the Dust-Rollers were humbled —

never again would they (fuck) come into the Ancient Israel's
territory
and YAHWEH's hand/penis/phallic control was on/in the
Dust-Rollers all the days of Samuel.

And they were returned! —
the cities that the Dust-Rollers had taken from Ancient Israel —

to Ancient Israel:

from the city we heard about earlier...known for things pulled
up by the roots, for childlessness,

all the way to another city we heard about earlier...the city with the wine-press and their drunken concerts,

and the territories around those two cities.

Ancient Israel stripped and plundered from the Dust-Rollers' hand/penis.

And so it was —
a lasting-peace between Ancient Israel and the braggarts, those who talk and talk and talk.

And Samuel, the guy named for EL, acted as mediator and dispute-decider all the days of his life.

And he went from year to year,
and circled around the cities named
Divinity's-House and Stone-Wheel and Watch-Tower.

And he acted as mediator and dispute-decider for Ancient Israel in all of these places.

And his return was always to The Heights
because his house was there,
and he mediated and decided disputes there for Ancient Israel,
and he built there a butchering-and-burning table
for YAHWEH.

(Now this is noteworthy...because the ark is still in the town in the honey-combed forest, but Samuel is not there, and doesn't seem to have any interest in the ark. Samuel has no claim to the ark, nor does he care to. After all, YAHWEH responds to Samuel even without the ark and even without the title of 'priest'...without the family-lineage of a Levite, the keepers of the ark and the temple-cult. YAHWEH thunders in response to Samuel's prayer...this is how they talk with one another...and YAHWEH successfully takes on the enemies of Ancient Israel, even when there is no leader of Ancient Israel but Samuel, even when the Ancient Israelites do not notice they are being attacked. YAHWEH is indeed storm-divinity and more. Note well who else in the Bible talks to YAHWEH/ELOHIM through the thunder...? Moses, of course. And as many times as Israel-being-led-out-of-Egypt has been mentioned in 1 Samuel, still no mention of Moses. Curious, yes?)

chapter 8

And so it was —
when Samuel, the guy named for EL, grew to be old,
he put his children in the role as mediators and dispute-deciders
for Ancient Israel...the nation taking its name from the hero who wrestled EL, got groped and penetrated and still won by topping EL.

And so it was —
the name of his first-born son was YAHWEH-is-EL,
and the name of his second was Patriarchy-is-YAHWEH.

And they acted as mediators and dispute-deciders in the most perfect place on earth — in Seven-Wells!

(Notice...Samuel is covering most of the nation while his sons hang out in the southernmost paradise, a place that has seven wells! Seven! The perfect number of wells! And note Samuel's dedication to YAHWEH in the names he chooses for his children. We will need to hold that dedication up alongside other characters who will name their children in this saga....)

But his children didn't walk in (their father's) ways.

And <u>they stretched themselves out — turned</u> themselves after dishonest gains, sometimes made through violence, and took bribes, and <u>stretched themselves out, turned themselves</u> away from the role of being mediators and dispute-deciders, away from justice.

(Samuel's sons NTH/'stretched themselves out, turned toward something perverted, unjust' in the same way the character Judah did in Genesis 38, that hilarious story of Judah stretching himself out and buying some sexual time with a prostitute...only later when she'd become pregnant did he discover that this was actually his daughter-in-law! There's Judah living up to his name YHUDH from YDH/'to throw out one's hands/penis in praise'!!)

And every old and wise man/person of Ancient Israel gathered themselves together and (fuck) went to Samuel in The Heights.

(Notice...the people have <u>some</u> power to gather themselves together when they need to...they don't always need a 'leader' to gather them...)

And they said to him,
"Listen up!
You are — you're growing to be an old man
and your children don't walk in your ways —
now put in place for us a king! —
to mediate and settle disputes for us —
just like all the foreigners have (their own rulers/kings)!"

And the style was very bad (in poor taste) in Samuel's eyes, when they said "Give us a king to mediate and settle disputes for us!"

And Samuel prayed, put out there his hopes and dreams and desires to YAHWEH.

And YAHWEH said to Samuel,
"Listen to the people's voice —
to all that they've said to you —
you see, it's not you they're <u>casting away</u> —
it's me they're <u>casting away</u> from being king over them!

Each and every <u>casting</u> (as in sculpting BAAL) they have made
since the day I climbed them up from Suffering-Egypt...
all the way to today —

they've abandoned me —

they've been slaves to other <u>ELOHIM</u>/gods-and-goddesses!

And just like that...they're doing the same to you.

Now — listen to their voices

yes —

you are to repeat, repeat, and repeat again —

you are to be completely out in front with them — be clear —
about a king's arrangements of mediating and settling disputes
— the king who will royally-rule over them!"

(Note the clever style with 'casting away as in rejection'/MAHS
with the similar-sounding 'casting as in making something'/
MAYS...such is the exceedingly clever style of the prophets,
words that play with one another and explode in many
directions and do something within the hearer, something
that awakens. And note here the character-YAHWEH talking
about the Israelites slaving away for other ELOHIM — and
YAHWEH is not referring to Itself here as 'ELOHIM'! And let's
be mindful of all the plays on the people's SHAHL/'asking'...
and who they get from that 'asking.')

And Samuel said all of YAHWEH's stylings-on
to the people who <u>asked</u> for a king from him, he said,
"This is the arrangement — the way of mediating and settling
disputes — for how a king will royally-rule over you:

As for your sons —
he will take them,
and put them for himself in his own chariots and on his own
horses —
and some will have to run in front of his chariots
(and often be the first in battle to die, either at the hands of the
enemy or from being run over by the king's chariots).

He will put in place for himself...

      officials over groups of a thousand
      and officials over groups of fifty...(a hierarchy)

            to plow what needs plowing,
            to harvest his harvest,
            to make his gear for battle
            and his gear for his chariots.

And as for your daughters —
he'll take them as perfumers, as cooks, as bakers.

And as for your fields and your vineyards and your olive
groves —
the best of them he'll take and give to his slaves.

And the seed you sow and your wine —
he'll confiscate one-tenth of them
and give them to his slaves and his eunuchs (special-slaves
whose testicles have been removed at the king's request so that
they might have no sexual-desire for the king or his family).

And as for your slaves
and your female-slaves who can bear children

and your <u>choicest young men</u> — the best of them! in the prime of their adolescence! —
and your valuable male donkeys —
he'll take them and put them to work for himself.

(Notice the hierarchy of life being envisioned here by Samuel as he lays out the huge problems with having a ruler, a king. When a group has a ruler who gets put on a pedestal, higher than everyone else, then everyone else is lower. And people — at least most of us — don't like to be lower than everyone, so we create ranks...'I'm better/more valuable than this person, this other person is better than me.'

And one more thing...this is a rather strange place to put 'your choicest young men'/BCHURYCM among the other human-property that any wealthy man of the ancient world would have or purchase for himself and the growth of his family — women to give birth to children, women who will rank lower than his first-wife and his second-wife.

We'll have to see how this plays out with these 'choicest young men,' perhaps strengthening Dr. Jennings' theory of Ancient Israel's pedaristic military-training he lays out in *Jacob's Wound*. In just a few more sentences, we'll meet a particular 'choice young man'...and we'll have to study what happens to him....)

And your sheep and goats —
he'll confiscate one-tenth for himself.

And as for you all —
you'll be his slaves!

You'll cry out on that day —
because of your king whom you've chosen for yourselves —
and YAHWEH won't respond to you on that day!"

And the people completely refused to listen to Samuel's voice,
and they said,
"Not so!
Because if we have a king over us,
then we'll be just like all the foreign-nations —
our king will act as mediator and dispute-settler for us —
he'll go out ahead of us and fight our fights/battles!"

And Samuel listened to all the people's styles,
and he styled them out into YAHWEH's ear.

And YAHWEH said to Samuel,
"Listen to their voice!
You are to king them up a king!"

And Samuel said to the men/people of Ancient Israel,
"Go — every man/person to his own city!"

chapter 9

And there was a man <u>from Benjamin</u>, the small tribe known
for its powerful children, and his name was Set-a-Trap,
son of Patriarchy-is-EL,
 who was the son of Bundle-Grain,
 who was the son of Choicest-Born,
 who was the son of Breathe-and-Blow,
 who was <u>a son of man of the right hand</u>
— a seasoned warrior.

(This is a curious way of putting it. BN AHYSH YMYNY/'son
of a man of the right hand', which is far different from
MBNYMYN/'from Benjamin.' In the ancient world, the right
hand was the hand of honor...used for fighting and especially
for wielding a weapon, for reaching out to make deals because
handshakes or arm shakes showed you were not armed. The
right hand was also used for eating, especially because the left

hand was used for wiping one's rear end, in an age without toilet paper. The left hand was less valued and used for defense like holding a shield if you didn't have a gear-lifter/shield-bearer, for holding the cup for drinking because one didn't want to mix one's feces with their or anyone's food. All of ancient Mediterranean society was organized in this way. The effects of this left-right taboo seems to have lasted into the 20th century with teachers of my parents' generation tying kids' left hands behind their backs to make them use their right hands for key school tasks like writing if a kid was more naturally inclined to use their left hand. The horror!

There might be one more thing for which a right hand could be useful...his YD on his YD. And based on what's to come, that could be what the band of X has in mind here, especially for a BCHUR/'choice young man'...especially one who is so good looking....)

And (Set-a-Trap) had a son named <u>Saul</u>, a name which means Asked-For —
a <u>choice young man</u> — one who's good, handsome —

there wasn't a single man/person
among the children of Ancient Israel
as good or handsome as he was —

from his shoulders climbing upward he was <u>higher-or-haughtier</u> than any of the people.

(These are some very stylishly chosen words. GBH can mean 'higher and taller,' and it can mean 'haughty and arrogant, thinking oneself better than others.' We'll have to found out which meaning is intended here based on what we discover about this boy named Saul/Asked-For/SHAHUL.)

And the valuable female donkeys of Set-a-Trap, Saul's father, were lost — lost as in probably dead and gone.

And Set-a-Trap said to his son Saul,
"Take with you one of the boys/slaves
and stand yourself up tall
and go search for the valuable female donkeys!"

And (Saul) <u>crossed the border</u> into the mountains of Ephraim, the tribe known for being fruitful —
he <u>crossed the border</u> in that land three times! —
but he didn't find (the donkeys).

And he <u>crossed the border</u> into the land of <u>the foxes and jackals</u> — nothing.

And he <u>crossed the border</u> into the land <u>of the right hand</u> but he didn't find them.

> ('crossed the border'/AYBR...the same word from which we get 'Hebrew,' the people probably known for their bordercrossing ways, for wandering, for shepherding...and Saul is definitely wandering, and seemingly off course...
>
> and SHAYLYM/'foxes and jackals' — animals known for hunting prey — when spoken out loud sounds almost exactly like Saul's name SHAHUL...playfully punny...and in this self-discovery journey of being lost, Saul must find his way to what his father wanted — find the family wealth that's lost and likely dead and gone — and return home alive himself from this quest......
>
> and then we get that curious YMYNY again...'of the right hand')

And they (fuck) entered to the land of the <u>Honeycombs, where wild honey gushes,</u>

and Saul said to his boy/slave who was with him,
"Come on,
let's go back,
otherwise my father'll stop caring about the donkeys
and become anxious about us!"

(DAHG/'to be or become anxious' foreshadows a character
by the same name who will be important in Saul's life...using
characters' names early on in the saga seems to be something
that this text does a lot of...perhaps an argument that these
tales were so popular and well known that hearers would catch
the hint after just another re-telling and play along with more
and more wrinkles and clever folds in the story by the band of
X seeking to awaken people to the choices they were making
politically and religiously, organized religion is essentially
using one's cosmology politically. Organized religion is
politic, is about deciding how power will be directed to flow...
far different from the prophets who know the real power
cannot be contained, crosses all human-made borders, gives
life and takes it away.

And the land of the 'Honeycombs, where wild honey gushes'/
TSUP sure sounds like a sweet place on a quest...a place to
discover one's way...maybe with a quip of poetry...a place that
sounds just like 'Sufi'....)

And (the boy/slave) said,
"Listen here — there's a ELOHIM's-man/person in this city —
and the man enjoys great respect —
all that he styles out (fuck fuck fuck) comes, comes, comes
about —
now let's go there —
maybe he can tell us which way we should go!"

And Saul said to his boy/slave,
"Listen here — we can go

but what can we (fuck) bring the man?
The bread/fight is gone from our gear —
we don't have a song/gift
to bring the ELOHIM's-man/person —
what do we have with us?"

And the boy/slave continued responding to Saul and said,
(you see, he's answering as if he's an equal)
"Listen here —
I found here in my hand a coin that's barely worth anything —
I'll give it to the ELOHIM's-man/person —
and he'll tell us our way!"

Ages ago in Ancient Israel,
a man/person going to seek out something from ELOHIM/
God-or-gods-and-goddesses would say:
"Come on! Let's go to the one who sees!"

You see, today's ecstatic/prophet was called "a person who
sees" ages ago.

And Saul said to his boy/slave,
"Good styling on your part!
Go, go, go — let's go!"

(Lots of potential 'fucks'/BOAH/'coming and going' here —
and this whole business of 'a song-gift'/TSHURH has scholars
stumped so they infer it's 'a gift' from the context. *Strong's
Exhaustive Concordance* sees it related to SHUR/'travel about
(as a harlot or merchant' and then wonders if it's related to
SHYR/'to sing.' Saul's response that they don't have any
'bread, fight'/LCHM is a curious response. Why would a
ELOHIM's-man/person accept crumbly bread — or a fight —
from lost travelers who brought it from home days ago? Why
might he accept a song? or a worthless coin?

When did we last hear of a 'ELOHIM's-man/person'? When

Samuel was a youth in the service of Eli-Climb-Up and the ark...and the random man showed up and spat out some wild rhymes and styles to Eli-Climb-Up as a warning about his sons' bad behavior in fucking the slave-girls behind YAHWEH's tent....

Is this TSHURH a song they must sing to be able to entice the ELOHIM's-man/person to hear their request? Does this visit have something to do with a harlotry, religious prostitution? If so, who's getting fucked? Is that part of 'seeing'?

And as for 'boy/slave'/NAYR, we're never quite sure if the guy accompanying Saul is a boy or a slave who is the age of a boy — though he sure seems to know something about the ELOHIM's-man/person in these distant parts....)

And they went to the city
where there was a ELOHIM's-man/person.

They climbed up — they did — the steep path of the city, and they found — they did — some slaves/girls going to draw water,

(...now in the band of YAH's Genesis stories, this is where a young man would meet a young woman whom he would soon marry — but here...?

These two guys whom the band of X points out twice here as 'they'/HMH is unusual...when in Hebrew no extra pronoun is needed since the pronoun is included in the verb...perhaps it's as if an ancient reader/hearer might assume that the master would not climb up to a holy place with a slave at his side... but here in 1 Samuel both Master Saul and Slave/Boy go together...)

and they said to them,
"Is the one who sees here?"

And (the girls) responded and said to them,
"There! Look! Right there in front of you!
Hurry now — because today he (fuck) came to the city
because there's a butchering-and-burning up of valuable animals
today — for the people — up on the high place!

Now as soon as you both (fuck) enter into the city,
sure thing, you'll both find him
before he climbs up to the high place to eat
— you see, the people won't eat until he (fuck) arrives
because he'll bring people to their knees into abundance
as part of the butchering-and-burning-up of valuable animals —
and afterwards, they eat — <u>all those who've been announced
and invited — the important people</u>!

Now climb up there
because this is the time you'll both find him!"

(Note...these girls see the boy Saul and his slave/boy —
essentially a term for property in most ancient cultures,
whether he's a purchased-slave or a boy-not-yet-a-man — as
if the two of them are the same class. The girls do not address
Saul directly — the girls speak to the two boys in the plural.
This whole scene is unusual and perhaps jarring in the ancient
world, in a world ordered by hierarchical social importances.
Maybe Saul did not stand out as being very different from his
slave/boy, despite his being GBH/'tall or haughty.'

In more ways than one, this story does not go the way of
the typical boy-meets-girl-at-the-well-and-marries which
is certainly the default storytelling line in the band of YAH's
Genesis stories. Here, in the band of X's story, the girls point
the way to a man and the boys walk onward — they are to
BOAH/'enter or fuck' just like the ecstatic-seer does, this well-
known and well-respected one who will QRAH/'call out, greet,
invite' these boys who have been traveling and are probably a
mess — Samuel will QRAH them just like the important guests.)

And they climbed up to the city —
(fucking) entering into the middle of the city — they were —
yikes! — and there he was — Samuel!!!

He was coming to <u>call out to them — to greet, to announce
and invite them, just like important people</u> — on the climb
up to the high place.

(You see) YAHWEH had <u>stripped Itself naked like an exile or
slave is forced to do, revealed Itself</u> directly to Samuel's ear
one day before Saul had (fucked) entered by saying,

"At about this time tomorrow,
I'm sending to you
a man from Benjamin, the small tribe known for its powerful
children.

You are <u>to smear him with oil,</u>
<u>to make him my *messiah* by anointing him</u> as a <u>front-man, a
leader</u> over my people, Ancient Israel.

He's going to rescue my people from the hand/penis/phallic-
control of the Dust-Rolling-Philistines...

because I see my people —

because their crying-out has (fuck) come to me!"

(There's our old, strange friend GLH/'stripped Itself naked
like an exile or slave is forced to do, revealed' Itself...YAHWEH
again doing the self-stripping to ecstatic/prophet Samuel.

MSHCHTO/'to smear someone with oil, to make someone
messiah by anointing'...remember, the people asked-for it!

NGYD/'front-man, a leader'...this is the same word from the
Eden story — a band of YAH story also lampooning leaders

set up to do one thing but instead do another — where a NGD was made for the mud-creature, a NGD who disregarded YAHWEH's rules and gave birth to wisdom through her curiosity to know the lusty fruit of the tree, which nudged her to know the mud-creature through the way of hiding within and in one another...lovemaking.

We'll have to see what this *messiah* or any *messiah* — any NGYD/'front, leader' — does in the Samuel-saga.)

And Samuel saw Saul, the young man whose name means 'Asked-For', and YAHWEH responded,
"Look — there's the man about whom I spoke to you —
this one will <u>hold back and shut up</u> my people —
errr, <u>recover and lead</u> them!"

(Another very strange verb choice out of the character-YAHWEH's mouth...AYTSR...used in Deuteronomy and Numbers for things like 'holding back plagues' and 'shutting up the heavens to prevent rain,' in Genesis for 'shutting up wombs.' Is that what a *messiah* will do to Ancient Israel...? The *messiah* will shut up the heavens and cause drought for the people of Ancient Israel? AYSTR can mean 'to retain/to recover, as in lead'...but notice how the verb is an unclear/ambiguous choice here...we might expect a word like MLC/'to royally-rule' or SHPT/'to mediate and settle disputes, to judge' as we've had earlier...but the band of X has the character-YAHWEH playing with us, X's hearers, throughout 1 & 2 Samuel with a comedic, double/triple-entendre style. And note this boy, this <u>choice young man</u> Saul about to be anointed as *messiah*/ MSHYCH/'oil-smeared' often has a military understanding to it — a bit different from what Christians will hear in their *messiah/christ*. Who would be mentor to the boy-become-king — especially if the arrangement of older-warrior-mentoring-younger-warrior is the way of warriors in Ancient Israel? Would the mentor be the wind/YAHWEH? Samuel? a military-commander from one of the tribes? Who?!)

And Saul drew nearer to Samuel,
right in the middle of the city-gate, and said,
"Tell me please...
where is the house of the one who sees?"

And Samuel answered Saul, and said,
"I am the one who sees!
Climb up in front of me to the high-place —
and you both'll eat with me today —
I'll send you off in the morning...

and all that's in your heart...
I'll tell you — you alone....

And as for your valuable female donkeys that were lost — as in
dead and gone — three days ago,
don't set your heart on them —
they've been found.
For whom is all the delight and desire of Ancient Israel?
Why not for you — you alone?!
And for everyone in your father's house/family?!"

(Notice the ways Samuel sometimes speaks to Saul and his
boy — the two of them — and sometimes to Saul alone.)

And Saul, whose name means 'Asked-For,' answered and said,
"Am I not a son of the right hand?
Me? From the smallest of tribes of Ancient Israel?
From the least significant family — even including the
extended family with maid-slaves — from among all the
extended families of Benjamin, the small tribe known for its
powerful children?
Why style-out for me style like this!"

(More style here for sure in Saul's response to the style-rich
Samuel as Saul plays with BN-YMYNY/'son of the right hand'

and BNYMN/'Benjamin'...the difference between the two being a hyphen and pause between words that could make all the difference to an ancient hearer. The last Y in YMYNY is curious though — possibly euphonic, possibly a scribal error, possibly something else.)

And Samuel, the guy named for EL, took Saul and his boy/slave
and (fuck) brought them into the big rooms
and gave them the place at the head (the most honorable place)
among all those who had been announced and invited —
about 30 men/people!

And Samuel said to the butcher/executioner,
"Give over the portion
that I gave you earlier,
the one about which I said,
'Keep it with you!'"

And the butcher/executioner <u>lifted up</u> (for everyone to see)
the meat-abundant-leg and all that went with it...tail, genitalia
(ancient delicacies)...
and put it in front of Saul, and he said,
"Look here —
what was <u>swollen — errr, set apart and left behind</u> — for you —
eat it —
you see, for a special time it has been protected for you, saying
'The people — I'm inviting them!'"

(More of the clever speech that makes this book so curious... SHAHR can mean 'to remain, to leave (behind), to set apart'... and *Strong's Exhaustive Concordance* notes that SHAHR is from a root meaning 'to swell up'...this meaty leg and all that goes with it, the genitalia, the tail...the delicacies of the ancient world. And such a special piece of meat is reserved for a boy — a boy and his slave-boy at the head of the table among dignitaries, a boy and his slave who just showed up after a long journey.

YRM/'lifted up' from RUM...from the same word as RMH/'The Heights' where they all are right now, Samuel's hometown on the mountain.)

And Saul ate with Samuel on that day.

And they went down from the high-place of the city, and Samuel styled it out with Saul up on the <u>top/roof</u>.

(GG/'roof/top' and *Strong's Exhaustive Concordance* notes that GG is likely from or related to GAHH/'to rise up, to mount, to rise, to be majestic'....

Ahem.

No mention of where Saul's slave was.

In a world before air conditioning, a rooftop would be a great place in the house to sleep and rest, the coolest spot, the most hospitable spot, where the wind blows....)

And they woke up early in the morning —
it was as the red light of dawn was climbing up —
and Samuel called out to Saul on the <u>top/roof</u>,
"Stand yourself up tall!
I'll send you off!"

And Saul stood himself up tall, and they went out —
the two of them —
he and Samuel —
<u>outside</u>.

(Remember, the band of X is crafting a fiction and choosing words that — umm — explode with meaning in their hearers' imaginations. And not only that — playing with similar sounds of words...CHUTSH/'outside' and QTSH/'edge, extremity'...all part of the entertaining, ear-friendly style of the band of X....)

And they — they did — went down to the <u>edge</u> of the city, and Samuel said to Saul,
"Say to the boy/slave,
'Pass on by us!' —
he's to go on ahead and you stand here a little longer —
and I'll make you hear the style of ELOHIM/divine."

chapter 10

And Samuel took <u>the flask of oil</u>
and <u>poured it out on his head</u>
and <u>kissed him...</u>

(PC HSHMN VYTSQ AYL RAHSHO/'(took) the flask of oil and poured it out on his head' and then kissing him is quite wild in and of itself...though any ancient hearer would hear even more than that.

I would have thought that PC HSHMN/'flask of oil' would be a common thing in the Hebrew Bible but it is only used three times and only by the band of X in Samuel/Kings.

Strong's Exhaustive Concordance sees PC as coming from PCH/'to trickle.' And SHMN usually gets translated as 'oil or fat or grease' but if you say it out loud sounds just like our modern word *shaman*, one who is in touch with some of the deeper elements of life and death...no scholar I know makes such a connection though Wikipedia notes that Mircea Eliade observed the similar-sounding Sanskrit word *śramana* has made its way through many cultures, though even he does not seem to make the connection with the Hebrew word for oil and smearing oil on someone to put them in some kind of trance, as a shaman might. And here in our saga our character Samuel certainly sends young Saul off on a shamanic, trance-inducing journey/experience, as we'll soon hear.

Strong's notes that SHMN pointed/voweled differently can also mean 'to grow fat, bigger' or even 'to shine' and all that very well could be happening to Saul with what Samuel and he did together on the roof or to what he's in the process here of doing... with something of Saul growing bigger and shining forth...Samuel YTSQ/'poured' the oil on Saul's 'his head'/RAHSHO and *Strong's* notes that YTSQ can also mean "to melt or cast as metal; by extension, to place firmly, to stiffen or grow hard" and even "to overflow" — and note this usage of YTSQ/'pouring out to cast metal, something hard' happens in the priestly text Exodus 25-26 and Exodus 36-38 at the same time the usage of the same word with different meaning YTSQ/'to pour out (oil on someone's head' is used in Exodus 29 — all of that to say that an ancient hearer would probably note both the flowing-quality and hard-quality of YTSQ.

Then Samuel performs the grand finale of all those rich words...Samuel YSHQHO/'kisses him'...and that word is a loaded word for sure...if you take YSHQH from NSQ/'to burn, kindle, catch fire' or from CHZQ/'to become firm, to grow strong, to fasten on, to seize, to become courageous' or even CHSHQ/'to become attached to, to cling, to love'...all noted by *Strong's* because when conjugated they all sound similar to any hearer — and any hearer would be craning their neck to wonder what's happening here in the saga.

And that whole scene with pouring oil on this boy's head and making him hard and strong and courageous and kissing him follows upon YAHWEH telling Samuel to do these very things for Its *messiah* — to anoint this boy the king, this boy who can't find his family's lost wealth — indeed, the wealth for which he himself was probably irresponsible and somehow lost. But first Samuel wines and dines this boy Saul and gives him the seat of honor and lets him sleep on his roof. Talk about a story that explodes with meaning! Such is the hallmark of the prophets, the Bible's ecstatics, the NBAHYM...and we can hear some of that style now in the speech from Samuel to Saul to explain why he's done all of this and what Saul is to do....)

and (Samuel) said to him,
"Why not?!
After all, YAHWEH specially selects you
and smears you with oil as *messiah*
over Its inherited property, Its wandering stream through a valley —
to be Its front-man, Its leader!

In your leaving me here today — you alone —
you'll find two men/people beside Rachel-Little-Lamb's-famous-gravesite

> (Jacob's wife, Jacob being the hero from which we get the name 'Israel,' the hero who wrestled EL and got groped and penetrated and still won)

right there at the border (of your own home-region) Benjamin,
the small tribe known for its powerful children,
in a place where the light dazzles among the shadows —

and they'll say to you,
'The valuable female donkeys have been found,
the ones you went after to search for them —
and listen up —
your father has stopped styling-on about the valuable female donkeys
and is <u>anxious</u> about you both, saying,
"What am I to do about my son?"'

And you'll slide on by through from there — you alone —

and a little further you'll (fuck) arrive at the great, broken tree,
and there they'll find you —
three people climbing up to ELOHIM/God-or-gods-and-goddesses
to Divinity's-House —
one will be carrying three baby goats,
one will be carrying three large round loaves of bread,
one will be carrying a large storage jar of wine —

and (to you, Asked-For/Saul) they'll <u>ask for</u> your peace —
whether you are well, healthy, at peace...the formal greeting —
and they'll give you two loaves of bread,
and you're to take it from their hands/phallic-control.

Now, after that, you'll (fuck) arrive at the hill of ELOHIM/
God-or-gods-and-goddesses—
you alone —
where the Dust-Rolling-Philistines have an armed military post —
and so it will be — just as you (fuck) arrive there in the city
you'll get caught up in <u>a band of ecstatics</u> —
they'll be going down from the high place
and right in front of them leading the way
with a wine-jar-turned-into-guitar
and tambourine
and flute
and twangy-harp
— they will <u>be in ecstasy</u>—

and It will <u>rush upon you and push you forward and prosper
you</u> — you alone —

YAHWEH's wind will —

and you'll become ecstatic along with them —
you will be turned this way and that — overthrown within
yourself —
turned into another man/person!

And so it will be —

when these signs (fuck) come to you — you alone —
let be done for you
whatever your hand/penis/phallic-control finds
because ELOHIM/divinity is with you!

And you're to go down ahead of me to the city of wheels,
where the wind wheels and whirls around —
listen up! —
I myself will come down to you
to climb up (on a hill/slaughtering-altar) and butcher and
burn up some valuable animals as peace offerings.

For seven days you are to wait patiently
until I (fuck) come to you
and I'll make known to you in every way
what you are to do."

(Ah...the ways of the NBAHYM...we have much to discuss, and
soon! But first...

TSLCH/'to rush upon, push forward, perhaps to penetrate...all
in some way that has to do with prosperity'...a word found in
two band of YAH stories about that dress-wearing Joseph and
about Abraham's slave sent off to find a wife for Isaac — both
of whom are unlikely people upon whom YAHWEH would
rush. And here too with this young man Saul from the least
significant family in the smallest tribe all proud of all they can
do with their right hands (Benjamin = 'son of the right hand,
son of the power hand, son of rightness'), YAHWEH seems
to have a habit of rushing upon and prospering seemingly
insignificant people.

Here's another instance mentioning a character's name in the
story before the character appears...DAHG/Anxious....usually
translated as Doeg, who will influence Saul's journey down
the road too.

It's interesting this 'band of ecstatics'/CHBL NBYAHYM...
CHBL can mean 'band' or 'company of people' but, besides this
use in 1 Samuel 10, CHBL always has a negative connotation...
as in 'destruction' or 'birth-pang' or 'pain/sorrow' elsewhere in
the Hebrew Bible...CHBL perhaps could be understood in the
ancient world as a 21st century nineteen-year-old announcing
to his parents "I've quit my job/school and joined a band!"
Can you hear the groans about his choice of joining a CHBL?
And thus we might get a glance at what the ancients thought
of these CHBLs of ecstatics on the mountaintops...especially
with their wild vision-inducing and poetry-spitting ways....)

And so it was —
when he turned his shoulder to leave from Samuel,
ELOHIM/divinity turned him this way and that — overthrown
within himself —
turned into another heart,
and they (fuck) came to pass — all those signs did — that day.

When they (fuck) arrived there on the hill —
listen up! —
a band of ecstatics called out to him,
and ELOHIM's/divinity's wind rushed upon him and pushed
him forward and prospered him —

and he was ecstatic right there in the middle of them!

And so it was —
everyone who knew him three days ago and saw that —
hear this —

right there among the ecstatics, he was ecstatic —

and the people said —
one man/person to his friend/neighbor —
"What's this that has come upon Set-a-Trap's son?!
Even Saul is among the ecstatics?!"

And one man/person from there responded and said,
"And who is their father?!"

> (What an unusual question and response! Does the question
> imply their wildness and perhaps sexual licentiousness made
> it difficult to know who might be the father? Or is it a question
> that gets at roots, that the roots of whatever these ecstatics are
> about are elusive? Or that this group has no patriarchy, no
> descendants from a particular father? Or no patriarchy as in
> no hierarchical system of worth based on a father's pedigree?)

So that's how it came to be —
that tricky, playful, clever little saying that messes with your
imagination and invites mastery within oneself:

"Even Saul is among the ecstatics?!"

And when he'd finished acting ecstatically,
he (fuck) went to the high-place.

> (This 'high-place' may or may not be the particular place
> where Samuel had told young Saul to go after his experiencing
> ecstasy....)

And Saul's <u>beloved</u> said to him and to his slave/boy,
"Where did you go?!"

And (Saul) said,
"To look for the valuable female donkeys —
and seeing they weren't there, we (fuck) went to Samuel."

And Saul's <u>beloved</u> said,
"Please tell me
what Samuel said to you both!"

And Saul said to his <u>beloved</u>,
"Well, he told, told, told us
that the valuable donkeys had been found!"

And as for the stylings-on about the kingship...
he didn't tell him what Samuel had said.

(Note the contrast of this story about Saul's ecstatic-experience
and not telling his 'beloved' about it with the earlier story where
Samuel has an experience of YAHWEH and tells Climb-Up all
about it when Climb-Up asks him for details. Seems that young
Saul not only doesn't follow Samuel's advice about where to go
after his ecstatic experience, young Saul isn't completely clear
with his own 'beloved' about any of his experiences while away.
What kind of 'beloved' this is, we'll have to see...'beloved'/DOD
can be 'relative, uncle, lover'...all the same word in Hebrew...
and the same letters for the name 'David' as well...perhaps the
clever way X foreshadows Asked-For/Saul via Hannah-Bend-
Down's/Hannah's request for a son and now X foreshadowing
David/'love-boiling beloved' via Asked-For's/Saul's beloved.
There is something peculiar happening with the names in
this text being used as regular words long before the character
shows up with the same name....)

And Samuel cried out with the people to YAHWEH at the
watch-tower,
and he said to the sons/children of Ancient Israel,
"This is what YAHWEH says!
ELOHIM of Ancient Israel!
'I — I was the one
who climbed up Ancient Israel out of Suffering-Egypt —
I snatched you all away — stripped and plundered you away —
from the hand/penis/phallic-control of the Egyptian-
Sufferers
and from the hand/penis/phallic-control of every royal-
nation oppressing you!'

(Again, no mention of Moses! Samuel continues, this time speaking for himself:)

And you all today cast away your ELOHIM/divinity
who was the one who rescued you
from all the terrible things done to you
and from all your tight and terrible spots!

And you all say to (your ELOHIM),
'A king!
Put one over us!'

So now,
take your stand, your position
right here before YAHWEH's face
by your tribes
and by your groups of thousands!"

And Samuel got nearer to all the tribes of Ancient Israel...
and Benjamin, the small tribe known for its powerful children,
was <u>captured</u>!

(This is a strange way of putting it...'capture, catch, ensnare'/
LCD is usually used in war/conquest, as in capturing a town
in war. We might usually expect LQCH/'take, choose' here...
but that assumes that a tribe would want a king to come from
them...or perhaps such 'capturing' expresses what the band of
X really thinks about this whole system of monarchy....)

And he got nearer to Benjamin,
the small tribe known for its powerful children,
to their tribe's extended families (made larger by the maid-
slaves),
and the family from the place where the heavy-rains happen
was captured!

And <u>Saul</u> was captured — the one whose name means <u>Asked-For</u> — Set-a-Trap's son!

And they looked around for him,
but he couldn't be found.

And they <u>asked for</u> it again
from YAHWEH,
"Has he (fuck) arrived here yet? The man!"

And YAHWEH said,
"Look —
there he is — <u>making love with himself, hiding himself</u> there
in the gear/baggage!"

And they ran —
and they fetched him from there!

And he took his stand there in the middle of the people,
he was higher-or-haughtier than all the people —
from his shoulders and upward!

And Samuel said to all the people,
"Do you all see him?!
The one whom YAHWEH has chosen by Itself!
There's no one like him among all the people!"

And all the people shrieked out their approval and said,
"Long live the king!"

(Umm — 'making love with himself, hiding himself'/CHBAH — talk about an interesting verb-choice again by the band of X, one that is X-rated and ecstatically-inspired about what kind of hiding our young-king Saul was doing. And even the reflexive/*niphal* voice! STR is the usual word for 'hiding' — as in hiding behind a rock. But here we get CHBAH, the kind of 'hiding' that Mud-Creature and Woman were doing in knowing each other just after eating from the Knowing-Tree in the Eden Story, the band of YAH's story eventually placed in Genesis. But here with the reflexive/*niphal*, Saul is CHBAH-ing himself! And why wouldn't Saul be off making love with himself, back where the slaves hang out with the baggage? He just came down from his ecstatic-experience with YAHWEH, when YAHWEH had rushed upon him, with that band of wild ones coming down the mountain and playing all their instruments, an experience anyone and everyone can have, even among the slaves and baggage. Ecstasy, after all, is a non-hierarchical experience — ecstasy blows up hierarchies. And surely now that he's been exposed and brought before all the people as their king, Saul is standing up there all firm and tall before the people, head and shoulders above the people — ahem. The band of X's saga of 1 & 2 Samuel is highly stylized comedy, some of the best fiction out there lampooning people's desires for royalty/hierarchy, when all the royals want to do is hide themselves and make love to themselves and be paid for it by their hardworking subjects... and, soon, this oil-smeared king will even have the gall to build specially-shaped trophies to himself with his subjects' hard-earned wealth....)

And Samuel styled-out to the people
about the custom of kings
about the ways things would be mediated and disputes would
be settled under the king's royal-rule
and wrote it on a scroll
and placed it right there in front of YAHWEH.

(Perhaps at this momentous occasion for this growing-up nation of Ancient Israel, the priests had brought the ark, YAHWEH's footstool, and Samuel places this scroll in front of the ark or even in the ark. If that's the case, notice that the Levites — Samuel's old boss Eli/Climb-Up's tribe — seem to have no audible/visible importance in this public choosing

of the king. The Levites and the ark are not mentioned here,
only a reference to placing a scroll 'in front of YAHWEH'...the
clever way the band of X downplays this priestly-people who
clamp down on the ecstatic-prophets with their Levitical-laws
that kill.)

And Samuel sent all the people —
every single man/person — to his own house.

And even Saul, the one named Asked-For —
even he went to his own house up on the hill,
and an army went with him,
men/people whom ELOHIM/divinity had struck their hearts.

And sons of good-for-nothing cheats said,
"What?! He could rescue us? This guy?!"

And they despised him,
and they didn't (fuck) bring him a gift.

And so it was —
silence and secrecy...like holding their tongues....

Ecstasy and ecstatics — in the Bible?

In the 21st century, nearly everyone translates NBYAH as "prophet" and not "ecstatic."

Why? Well, it goes back to the creation of the Septuagint in the 3rd or 2nd century BCE in Greek-speaking Egypt by 70+ Jewish scholars.

Why did these scholars choose prophet — *prophetēs* — as they translated the Hebrew Bible into Greek? Perhaps it's what these scholars thought would best fit for NBYAH, the Hebrew word for 'ecstasy' — it's not an easy word or concept to translate.

Or...could it be that these Jewish scholars who created the Septuagint wanted to cover up what the NBYAHYM were up to in their ecstatic ways?

It's hard to say for sure, unless we study just what seems to be coming through from the Hebrew text that we have received through the ages. This whole business of NBYAH — of ecstasy — might surprise us 21st century readers/hearers. (More will be said soon about this Septuagint Hebrew-to-Greek translation.)

There are 24 references to any form of the Hebrew word 'ecstatic' (NBYAH) — either as verb or noun — in 1 Samuel.

We've already heard 12 of them in these first 10 chapters of 1 Samuel:

- once in Chapter 3: referring to Samuel as being an ecstatic and reliable...the word 'reliable'/AHMN is the same from which we get the word 'amen'

- once in Chapter 9: when the band of X explains that in olden days ecstatics were referred to as 'seers'...people who see things

- three times in Chapter 10: just after Samuel smears Saul with oil and kisses him and tells Saul that he'll get caught up in a band of ecstatics as part of his journey homeward, his inner quest

- five times in Chapter 10: when the band of X describes Saul's experience with this band of ecstatics

- twice in Chapter 10: in quotes/sayings of the people about Saul being associated with the ecstatics — which seems to be a marvel to the people of Ancient Israel

So what can we glean from these 12 times 'ecstatic' is used in these chapters of 1 Samuel so far?

In that first appearance of the word 'ecstatic' at the end of Chapter 3, we are told that Samuel is an ecstatic for all the people of Ancient Israel but more than that...our first clue about what being an ecstatic is all about. Samuel is said to be reliable...trustworthy...dependable...in the right. Amen!

And in the next line after that, we get something rather unusual...that YAHWEH continued 'to strip Itself naked as a slave or exile must do when in captivity, what one does under the thumb of an oppressor'/GLH. And that YAHWEH chooses to do this for young Samuel.

Does this have something to say about being an ecstatic?

Is such self-stripping required for someone to be 'in the right,' to be moral and trustworthy? There is no way to hide yourself or anything — no weapon — you're carrying when you're naked. One's whole self is exposed, after all. Young Samuel before the ark was not completely naked himself —

he was wearing the *ephod*, the stringy, strangly-yarned, open-aired thing that priests or their assistants wear to minister to YAHWEH, the One who self-strips. Hmm.

Is the relationship between YAHWEH and young Samuel like lovers, what lovers do, how lovers are? Is that what it means to be a prophet/ecstatic?

What indeed is it to reveal one's whole self to someone, as lovers do so easily later in their relationship and so timidly at first?

This is a wild idea in 1 Samuel — and it is reiterated throughout the text. Sit and imagine it awhile — YAHWEH stripping Itself before Samuel, and a young Samuel at that!

Way different from the Torah!

Note the divergence here from the Torah-saga where YAHWEH shows Moses only his backside and in just a fleeting moment (Exodus 33).

Note too in the Torah-saga (Exodus 3) when Moses encounters ELOHIM/divinity in the burning bush, ELOHIM invites Moses to take off only his sandals — not his whole wardrobe. And the verb the Levitical priests use is NSHL/'to pluck off, remove.' This is a big reduction from the Samuel-saga where YAHWEH takes off Its clothes and in such an unusual way: GLH...'by stripping them off, forced to do so as a slave or exile would when captured.'

Seems extreme, yes? YAHWEH stripping Itself, especially in this way...!? And YAHWEH does this with a young boy, Samuel, who wears the special strangly-yarned underwear before YAHWEH.

But maybe not so strange if we have any sense of history...

consider the later traditions which come from 1 Samuel and perhaps flow from 1 Samuel and all that it espouses:

- the multiple Bible-based traditions within Judaism that recognize the spousal relationship between groom-YAHWEH and bride-Israel,
- prophetic witness throughout the Hebrew Bible, including Jeremiah accusing YAHWEH of seducing him,
- the mystics of the Christian tradition who experienced ecstatic-union in prayer...it's not a short list of men and women saints and even the rather stern Ignatius Loyola whose followers educated me was said to have quite a mystical side, which we get a taste of in his Autobiography,
- the Sufis and their knowing God as beloved / lover (especially Rabi'a). And these ancestral Sufis might even be referred to in 1 Samuel — TSUP/'Honeycomb' — where words and language are stylish, style-rich, sweet and sometimes salty.

Perhaps erotic love between human beings and YAHWEH is not so strange, hmm, if we pay attention?

Self-stripping before a lover...offering oneself as a slave to the other, that one could do what one wants to do in the throes of passion...it's the stuff of life, isn't it? Lovers offer themselves to each other — to be ravished. Lovers offer themselves to each other — to remember their wholeness and the wholeness of the Whole World, THE ALL, in their ecstasy with one another.

Such relational-ecstasy has everything to do with YAHWEH, if you know what YAHWEH is. If indeed YAHWEH is the wind, the atmosphere, it must be taken in and released out by creatures like you and me and the character Samuel. Not only for love but for life. You and I are penetrated by the wind with every breath. This is life.

Breathing and sex and love and relationship and intimacy can be mundane, hum-drum, "I've seen it all before."

But breathing and sex and love and relationship and intimacy can be ecstatic too — especially when we pay attention, when we feel, when we let all of our senses take in the experience, when love swells within and beyond us. You've known this before, yes? Even in your fantasies, if not in living life...?

Our Pungent Roots

These are the roots of the biblical imagination — ecstatic relationship with YAHWEH, and so far our character Samuel is the model for it. Like the 'seers' of olden days, Samuel can see into a future for Saul where this young man Saul too will get caught up with a band of ecstatics and be changed by them, by the ecstatic-experience. Perhaps Samuel or any ecstatic can see into any human's future that the wind — knowing what it/ It is we're breathing — will change us.

If Saul had stayed with this ecstatic experience he knew with the band of ecstatics instead of very soon in our saga building penis-shaped trophies for himself as king of Ancient Israel, I suspect the story of the kingship of Ancient Israel would have played out quite differently. And that is the band of X's point, I think.

X is not trying to give us a history of the roots of the kingship of Ancient Israel. Finkelstein and and Silberman and many archeologists' work make it clear — 1 & 2 Samuel and much of the Kings-saga are fictions. There is no archeological evidence to support the establishment of an early empire of Ancient Israel joined with Ancient Judah — a United Monarchy — at least as we have it in these stories and at least at the year supposed (just before 1000 BCE is often offered as the best guess for the beginning of Saul's rule of Ancient Israel — no archeological evidence exists to support that date or Saul's story).

The Samuel-saga is not a history to be studied and enshrined as much as it is a great and wise fictional-story — an inner map — for us to study power, love, and what really matters in life, in one's heart...ecstasy, knowing THE ALL. Can ecstasy be contained in such a thing as a kingship? in a throne? even in an ark dedicated to YAHWEH? We'll have to see. Maybe ecstasy can only be 'contained' in the One who self-strips, in YAHWEH alone — this YAHWEH who was storm-divinity for the ancient people. After all, YAHWEH could be found in breeze and in storm. YAHWEH was the very essence of life. Breathe in and know...and be known, even and especially in the Ancient Hebrew sense.

Perhaps through 1 Samuel, the band of X might be envisioning in their fiction how real life prophets — the ecstatics of their age(s)...Amos and the Isaiahs, Jeremiah and so many — emerge, and how we too might step into the role of prophet in our time.

It is a wild, ecstatic life it seems. And a life that power-brokers fear....

What do the power-brokers do with the band of X's stories?

The power-brokers — Levitical priests and Deuteronomistic scribes — who colluded to assemble the Torah and much of the Hebrew Bible appear to fear ecstasy and such relationship with YAHWEH as the character Samuel has with YAHWEH. The Deuteronomistic scribes do indeed include 1 & 2 Samuel in their emerging Bible...though at a time long after the royalty was dead and yet these later-generation scribes still edit some of the band of X's Samuel-saga to suit their own power-grabbing needs. They even add a whole chapter coming soon, a whole long-winded speech that doesn't match at all the imagination of the rest of the book. More on that to come.

And both the Levitical scribes and the Deuteronomists of every generation rally around their Moses-character to prop him up to be better than what the prophets were doing. But truly, all that they set up Moses to be can't hold a candle to the wild ways of the ecstatics — the wind enlivens such candles, and It can extinguish them too.

The hero of the Torah — Moses — doesn't have this kind of naked-relationship or lover-relationship with YAHWEH...at least not as Samuel or any ecstatic does. Just seeing someone's backside — as the Levitical priests and Deuteronomists celebrate their Moses-character doing — is not the same as being naked together, nowhere near the same as making love together.

Why wouldn't the power-brokers who assembled the Torah want their main character (Moses) to see the full-throttle nakedness of YAHWEH? And especially why would they shy away from having YAHWEH use a verb (GLH) that has to do with slavery, with oppression in their version of the story with YAHWEH and Moses? In 1 Samuel, YAHWEH acts — at least for a moment — like a slave! With a human-lover! With the character Samuel! Even with the character Saul! With all who hold It in even for a second! For all who are breathed by It! And not just once — repeatedly! Imagine it!

So it appears that the Levitical priests and Deuteronomistic scribes — at least in the Torah — dampen down the ideas of YAHWEH exposing Its naked self to anyone and of YAHWEH acting like a slave and of ecstasy with YAHWEH and of personal relationship with YAHWEH...and opt instead to have Moses mediate any kind of experience between YAHWEH and the people. Moses acts as priest, as arbiter between Ancient Israel and YAHWEH. Besides Moses, YAHWEH doesn't speak directly to the people in the Exodus story, the Torah-saga. YAHWEH speaks through Moses alone, sometimes with Moses' side-kick Aaron.

But in 1 Samuel, YAHWEH appears to speak through Hannah-Bend-Down — a woman! And through some random dude who shows up — ELOHIM's-man/person — to warn Eli-

Climb-Up about the doom coming because of Climb-Up's foolish sons and their father Climb-Up who must not be parenting well. And YAHWEH speaks to and through Samuel. And Samuel is from the middle of nowhere, The Heights. He's not from a priestly family — and yet YAHWEH speaks directly to and through Samuel. And there are thunder and storms to prove it.

Sure, there are storms and thunder and lightening in the Torah-saga, especially at Sinai/Horeb (Exodus 19). And the character Moses talks to YAHWEH's thunder and understands this primal language, like the character Samuel. But are there places where anyone besides hero-Moses speaks with YAHWEH or YAHWEH speaks through another human besides the band of YAH's characters in the Torah-saga? Perhaps through Miriam and her song after crossing the Sea of Reeds in Exodus — but she only gets a few lines, and nothing quite as profound as Samuel's mother's poem/song/rap that flips the world up-side down. Hannah-Bend-Down's poem/song/rap is wild — read it again!

In the hierarchical-priestly imagination, Moses must mediate such things that can get out of hand...like relationship with YAHWEH. Samuel does a bit of this mediating too, for sure. But he also sends Saul off to have his own experience of It with the band of ecstatics.

And that's just it. A priest/leader like Moses is very different from a priest/ecstatic/leader like Samuel.

Sending someone off to have an ecstatic experience with a bunch of ecstatics — how does one control such a thing? how does one make sure that 'the right experience' happens for someone?

Samuel wasn't there with Saul and the band of ecstatics.

Samuel trusts that the experience of ecstasy — of YAHWEH — will be reliable. Samuel trusts that YAHWEH will be reliable.

Amen! ('Reliability,' 'trustworthiness,' and 'amen!' are all from the same AHMN.). Samuel knows that YAHWEH will do YAHWEH's thing. As a reliable leader, Samuel or any ecstatic/prophet can certainly point things out to people to help them discern what's best, to help them discern freedom together as a newly emerging nation. Samuel does so in his speeches to the people and to Saul. Soon we'll discover through Samuel's vision, it's not in the butchering and burning up animals that YAHWEH is pleased. It's not in the roll of the dice to know the future, a priestly function. It's not in dancing around BAAL's penis-pole. But it is in relationship with YAHWEH, the one who strips Itself of Its clothes as a slave would do.

But in Moses' vision (and the Levitical priests who crafted most of the Torah-saga and the Deuteronomists who seem to rubber-stamp it), one finds freedom by following the 613 laws of the Torah.

Ecstasy...get it...It!

Ecstasy and prophetic imagination cannot be bound by laws, cannot be contained by commandments or boundaries. Ecstasy cannot be contained by a temple — just like YAHWEH cannot be contained by a temple or an ark or any building.

Ecstasy is an awakening to relationship — with everything.

Ecstasy awakens us to the Ultimate Reality...which I suspect is that there is no 'you' and no 'me' that seem separate from one another. Ecstasy strips off the blinders and foolish assumptions from our eyes and ears and hearts so that we know something different from our worn-out, caged, partial-truths. Ecstasy reveals that we're both — you and me — swimming in the larger ocean of THE ALL, the Infinite, the Inseparable. If you know something of the wind, the breeze, the atmosphere, then you know this to be true. If you know something of modern physics, perhaps even more so.

No priest or hierarch can offer such an experience of ecstasy. It must be discovered for oneself, within oneself. Can a friend like our character Samuel point out something important — *'have you ever looked over there?'* — or ask an important question that induces an experience on the noticer's own terms — *'what do you feel as you notice your foot on the ground?'* — or even offer a strange story or saying — *'the Reality of God is like farmers sowing dandelions in their fields'* — all to awaken, to invite a noticing of THE ALL right before one's own eyes...and within oneself?

Of course. But no 'special knowledge' is needed. No gnosis.

My modern-religion-following friends will surely push me here, "Can one have an ecstatic experience while a priest/religious-leader mediates it through some ritual or through some sermon?" Of course, I say. But do note that this is different than the wind coming upon you and taking your breath away when you least expect It.

Indeed, the wind is always doing that.

Those who know ecstasy with the wind just notice It more often, sometimes with every breath.

Feel the Rush...

Ecstasy involves feeling, sensing, and then a rush of excitement, a rush of...ecstasy.

What happens when you take your clothes off for the first time in front of someone? What was it like with your first lover?

It's a rush, yes? Often a nervous, anxiety-fueled excitement, yes?

Samuel never comes right out — at least not yet — to say what being an 'ecstatic' or being 'reliable' is...

and this is very much the style of the band of X in 1 & 2 Samuel and in 1 & 2 Kings, especially with Elijah and Elisha and the ecstatic-guilds. X never comes right out and says 'this is it!' but instead peels away the layers of what you think 'it' is and then you're left with something quite simple, beautiful, exquisite... something available to anyone and everyone. It. THE ALL.

We'll learn more about 'ecstasy' in the next installment of *The Naked Path of Prophet*, 1 Samuel 18 - end.

So let's watch together for the little morsels, the little breadcrumbs, the little hints of it here and there that the band of X places like breadcrumbs waiting to be found in the narrative, the ongoing Samuel-saga. One would think that the premier story of 1 Samuel is the building of this up-and-coming nation of Ancient Israel. But perhaps not. This new nation of Ancient Israel will fall, like every nation does. Ecstatics remain. Even when rulers and hierarchically-minded people will try to kill off the ecstatics as every empire attempts, ecstatics have a way of rising up into life. Breathe in and out and in and out and you'll know.

But that kiss! Does that have something to do with being a prophet, an ecstatic?

What to do with that kiss between Samuel and Saul? And for that matter, all the sexy talk?

Did they sleep together on the roof of Samuel's place? And if they slept together, did they sleep together?

There are some rather strange details in Chapters 9 & 10 — lots of double-entendre, and then some, surely very purposefully on the part of our band of X.

What's X's intention? Does an ecstatic's sexiness with YAHWEH imply a sexiness with all human-creatures, no matter their gender? Maybe. Maybe not.

Our character Samuel has sons — though we never hear about his wife. Maybe she died during childbirth...a commonplace tragedy of the ancient world. One thing's for sure... Samuel's sons were surprisingly rotten, maybe because he was never home and out on his circuit of towns acting as dispute-decider and trying to stir up people's affection for YAHWEH instead of BAAL & ASHTAROTH...instead of raising his sons to be decent human beings.

It sounds like quite a kiss, though, between Samuel and Saul — and the word for 'kiss'/NSHQ is also used later between allies/lovers David and Jonathan and then later between son-father Absalom and David.

Samuel and Saul's kiss could just be an ordinary kiss, or possibly something particular that is done when anointing kings, or it could be something of passionate love. In Genesis, NSHQ is combined with the verb for weeping when Esau and Jacob reunite; with Joseph and his brothers; between Jacob and Rachel, their love-at-first-sight...just to name a few. Rather strangely, in the priestly Chronicles, NSHQ has to do with bows and arrows, weapons...perhaps how closely you want your weapons kissing your body for surety of protection, or maybe the priests are trying to dilute the meaning of NSHQ away from the ecstatic/prophetic kiss-meaning. The Chronicler-priests do a lot of diluting 1 & 2 Samuel in their 1 & 2 Chronicles.

Are prophets/ecstatics sexy? Is YAHWEH really sexy — besides all that self-stripping?

What is it that ecstatics know that invites them to experience the world so differently and to choose from there — not based on someone else's code or law?

And does the vulnerability of nakedness have something to do with being able to behold a vision of the whole — more so than being clothed, no matter as a royal or as a peasant? Our clothes so often reveal our status, in the ancient world and today. Remove them and our equal-nature as living creatures, as human beings, becomes much more obvious. We are flesh.

Priests fear nakedness — even YAHWEH's nakedness — but prophets/ecstatics apparently do not.

Perhaps there's some wisdom in that...to not be afraid of one's own naked body or anyone else's...and to experience it all as holy and having no need to 'make holy' (QDSH) someone or something as priests want to do.

We'll just have to see where this 1 Samuel-saga leads us and adds to our data-base of what an ecstatic/prophet is — at least from the perspective of the band of X. Perhaps all those breadcrumbs will add up to some rich 'bread'/LCHM....or rich 'fighting'/LCHM. King Saul — long live?

chapter 11

And (that) Snake from the Inbred-Kinfolk second-cousins (the Ammonites who were related to Ancient Israel) climbed up and set up their army-camp on the city of the dry ground and heaped up stones, the city of their second-cousins, Ancient Israel's land.

(You see, this land was once important — heaped up stones indicate that as it takes a great deal of effort to heap up stones by human hand and seems to be a ritual, at least in the Book of Joshua. But now the land has become crumbly, dry, withered... and the people are likely hungry if they can't grow food or becoming poor if they must eat only their animals/wealth. It must look like easy taking for the Inbreds, relatives of Ancient Israel ready to attack and steal the wealth there for their own.)

And all the men/people of dry ground said to Snake,
"Cut a serious-agreement/covenant with us,
and we'll slave away for you!"

(These Ancient Israelites of the city of dry ground and heaped up stones did this, of course, without consulting their new king — Saul — without even thinking of asking him or the rest of their new Ancient Israel royal-nation for help — not to mention that the new king, we'll soon discover, doesn't even know when his country is being attacked! This story is communicating the 'state' of Ancient Israel at this point in the story, and it's not in a very good state at all...hardly acting like a state and even acting less united than the cities of the Dust-Roller/Philistine confederacy who worked together without a king, as we just saw a few chapters back. And before Ancient

Israel had a king, remember, YAHWEH protected Ancient Israel from the Dust-Roller's attack when Samuel had called upon YAHWEH for and with the people.)

And he said to them — Snake of the Inbreds did —
"On this I'll cut a serious-agreement/covenant with you...
to gouge out every spring of your right hand (or, right eye?) —
lay down some disgrace on all of Ancient Israel!"

(AYYN YMYN is quite euphonic — insert your own vowels and listen to it. And talk about an expression that explodes... AYYN can mean 'eye' but it also often means 'fountain, spring' and YMYN we've met before as 'right hand'...and as we know in the Ancient Hebrew imagination, 'hand' and 'penis' — both extending from one's torso — are often euphemistically one, YD. It's likely that the seemingly virile Snake is trying to insult the Dry Grounders here for their dried up 'springs' — even their pissers can't wet the land enough to bring it back to life.)

And the old men/people of the city of dry ground said,
"Slack back for seven days —
we'll send message-runners through the whole territory of Ancient Israel —
if there's no one to rescue us, we'll walk right out to you!"

And the message-runners (fuck) arrived on Saul's hilltop,
and they styled out the style in the hearing ears of the people.

All the people raised their voices and wept.

And listen here —
Saul was (fuck) coming in after his cattle from the open-country —

(Yes, that's right...the new king of Ancient Israel was out working in the fields!!)

— and Saul said,
"What's with the people?
Because they're weeping!"

And they recounted for him the stylings-on of the men/people of the dry ground.

And the wind of ELOHIM/divinity rushed upon Saul, pushed him forward,
when he'd heard these stylings-on —

and his face became red-hot with anger — so very much so —

and he took a pair of cattle and cut them into pieces at their joints —

and he sent them throughout every territory of Ancient Israel in the hand/phallic-control of the message-runners saying,
"Whoever isn't with us — coming after Saul and Samuel —
so will it be done to that person's cattle!"

(Note: earlier in his ecstatic experience it was YAHWEH's wind rushing upon Saul; now it's ELOHIM's wind. That might be significant later, and it might not. At the very least, note that young King Saul does not consult YAHWEH....)

And a dread, a terror of YAHWEH fell upon the people —
they came out — like every single man/person!

And he passed by them in review —
in a lightning flash —
300,000 sons of Ancient Israel —
and the men/people of Judah, the tribe known for throwing up their hands/penises in praise...30,000!

And they said to the message-runners who had (fuck) come,

"This is what you are to say to the men/people of dry ground
and heaped up stones:
'Tomorrow — you'll have for yourselves a rescue —
when the sun warms!'"

And the message-runners (fuck) went and told the men/
people of the dry ground —
and they were overjoyed and the men/people of the dry
ground said,
"Tomorrow, we'll go on out to you —
and you all do for us whatever seems good in your eyes!"

And so it was —
the next day Saul put three heads over the people,
and they (fuck) entered into the (enemy's) army-camp during
the morning-watch
and struck down and killed the Inbreds
until the warming of day.

And so it was —
whoever remained was scattered,
and no two of them remained together.

And the people said to Samuel,
"Who said,
'Saul will rule as king over us?!'
Bring these men/people to us and we'll put them to death!"

And Saul said,
"No! You're not going to put to death a single man/person
today —
because today YAHWEH has worked a rescue in Ancient
Israel!"

And Samuel said to the people,
"Come on! Let's get going to the city of wheels,
where the wind wheels and whirls around.
We'll repair the kingship there."

And all the people went off to the city of wheels,
where the wind wheels and whirls around.

And they made Saul king there
in front of YAHWEH
in the city of wheels,
where the wind wheels and whirls around.

And they butchered and burned up valuable animals as peace
offerings
to YAHWEH.

And he was overjoyed there —
Saul was —
and all the men/people of Ancient Israel even more so.

(Note...despite Saul's quick-witted military strategy which
worked and despite Saul's generosity in not killing off those
who had once bad-mouthed him, Samuel thinks the kingship
already needs repair...for a dry-withered city that refused to
defend itself and calls in the whole nation to protect it, for a
young nation whose cousins do not show respect and instead
attack, for a group of citizens who doesn't honor the new
king Saul, for a kingship where the king is out in the fields
while his own nation is attacked and hears about it after he'd
finished tending to the animals, as he'd been doing for his
father before his ecstatic experience brought on by losing
his father's animals and the quest to find them, just before
becoming king. This is the 'state' of this new nation at this
point...and not only that, to motivate everyone to help protect
their nation of Ancient Israel, Saul calls on the people to come
out for Saul and Samuel...as if Saul alone is not worthy on his
own for whom the nation should show up...and as far as we
know Saul had not consulted Samuel about the plan or about
using Samuel's name in the directive...such is the state of the
monarchy in Ancient Israel, reports the band of X in their
fiction here....

and a few tidbits of interest to note the spice within all this stylish storycrafting...every time we hear 'rescue'/TSHUAYH in the story, it's some form of YSHAY, the same name for Joshua, the military-general who took over the leadership of Ancient Israel from Moses in the Torah-Joshua saga. And speaking of Moses, note how he's not been present in any of the Samuel-saga — and for that matter neither has Joshua though we keep hearing versions of his name. And for that matter, note that the kingship was just 'renewed'/CHDSH in front of YAHWEH — even in the windy city of Gilgal — but again there's no mention of the ark or the Levitical priests. All of that...until strangely now, in the very next chapter. Most scholars recently point to this next chapter — Chapter 12 — as an interpolation, a later addition to the saga, likely to make 1 & 2 Samuel fit into the Deuteronomistic agenda of creating a history for Ancient Israel/Judah...and the Deuteronomists have no trepidation in including a total fiction in their history to build the tradition they envision. By the way, CHDSH is used only ten times in the Hebrew Bible and it sounds so very closely to QDSH/'to make holy' — that priestly thing again — and the way it is used each time makes me think, at this point of the saga, this 'renewal'/CHDSH is all about 'making holy'/ QDSH...or making something new or holy again...that vision of 'holiness' that religion/priests and state/Deuteronomists both cherish....)

chapter 12
a later interpolation likely <u>not</u> from X,
inserted by the Deuteronomists
generations after the band of X first told their tales

And Samuel said to all the people of Ancient Israel,
"Listen up —
I've heard your voices in everything you've said to me,
and I've kinged a king over you
and now, there he is —

the king walking around right here before you all —
and I am old and gray —
and my sons — look! — they're with you.

(This seems to ignore the earlier references to Samuel's
sons being corrupt, perhaps another signal that this is an
interpolation — or later addition — in the text. Or possibly
Samuel wants to ignore the foolishness of his sons.)

And I've walked right here before you all,
from when I was a slave/boy all the way until this very day.

Here I am!
Testify against me,
in front of YAHWEH and Its messiah, Its specially-selected, oil-
smeared leader (with YAHWEH and the messiah/king as judges):

about the ox I took for myself
or the donkey I took for myself
or whomever I oppressed or defrauded
or whomever I crushed
or from the hand/phallic-control of whomever I took a bribe
or hid my eyes (from seeing some wrongdoing and saying nothing
about it) —
   I will return it to you!"

And they said,
"You didn't oppress or defraud us!
You didn't crush us!
You didn't take anything from the hand/phallic-control of one single
man/person!"

And he said to them,
"YAHWEH is a witness against you —
and Its messiah, Its specially-selected, oil-smeared leader is a witness
today —

because you haven't found anything in my hand/phallic-control today!"

And (the crowd) said, "Witness!"

And Samuel said to the people,
"It was YAHWEH...
who made Moses & Aaron
and who climbed up your fathers/ancestors from the land of Suffering-Egypt —
now, take your stand —
I'm going to mediate and settle the dispute with you in front of YAHWEH,
about all of YAHWEH's right-and-just acts It did for you all and your fathers/ancestors!

When (your ancestor & national hero, your nation's namesake) Jacob (fuck) arrived in Suffering-Egypt and your fathers/ancestors cried out to YAHWEH,
YAHWEH sent Moses & Aaron, and they went out with your fathers/ancestors from Suffering-Egypt and made them live in this place.

And they forgot about YAHWEH, their ELOHIM/divinity —
and It sold them off into the hand/phallic-control of Sisera, commander of Settlement's army,
and into the hand/phallic-control of the Dust-Rolling-Philistines —
and into the hand/phallic-control of the king of (your own second-cousin) From-My-Father-Inbreds-from-Moab — and they fought them.

And they cried out to YAHWEH and said,
'We've offended you terribly —
we've left behind YAHWEH —
we've slaved away for the BAALS & ASHTAROTH —
now strip and snatch us from the hand/phallic-control of our enemies, and we'll slave away for you!'

And YAHWEH sent you all kinds of people:
(the old legends of Ancient Israel...) Jerubbaal, Bedan, Jephthah, and

Samuel (could be a scribal error and instead: Samson...unless the Deuteronomist interloper has the character Samuel bragging about himself)*!*

And (YAHWEH) stripped and snatched you away from the hand/ phallic-control of your enemies surrounding you — and you lived in security.

And you saw that Snake, the king of From-My-Father-Inbreds-from- Moab, was (fuck) coming upon you, you said to me,
'No! You see, a king will rule over us!'

And YAHWEH your ELOHIM/divinity was your king!

And now — look here — the king whom you've chosen,
the one whom you've <u>asked for</u>!

Look here — YAHWEH gave a king over you!

If you fear YAHWEH
if you slave away for It
and listen to Its voice
and don't get all bitter and rebellious against (what comes from) YAHWEH's mouth...
then even all of you and even your king who rules over you will continue to live...
by following after YAHWEH, your ELOHIM/divinity!

If you don't listen to YAHWEH's voice
and you get bitter and rebellious against (what comes from) YAHWEH's mouth...
then YAHWEH's hand/phallic-control will be upon you...as it was on your fathers/ancestors!

Now, stand up —
see this great style YAHWEH will do right before your eyes —
isn't your wheat ripe and ready to be harvested today?

I'll call out to YAHWEH
and It will give/offer Its voice —
and rain right on it
(to ruin the harvest and pelt the grain right into the mud) —
and you will know in all ways
and you will see just how terribly bad you are
in what you've done in YAHWEH's eyes
— to ask for a king for yourselves!"

(Remember...Saul's name means 'Asked-For'...so if this is indeed an interpolation by the later generations of Deuteronomists trying to sew a common thread of faithfulness to ELOHIM/ divine and the whole Moses/Egypt narrative as ELOHIM/ God's saving plan, then these later Deuteronomists are also preserving at least some of the clever style — 'asked for'/Saul — of their earlier storycrafters, the band of X. And at the same time, these Deuteronomist-interlopers preserve the tradition of YAHWEH as storm-divinity raining down on the wheat to ruin it, to demonstrate Its power.)

And Samuel called out to YAHWEH,
and YAHWEH gave Its voice — and rained! that very day!

And all the people feared YAHWEH and Samuel —
very much so.

And all the people said to Samuel,
"Make our feelings and hopes and desires known —
pray on behalf of your slaves to YAHWEH, your ELOHIM/divinity —
so that we aren't put to death —
because we've added onto all of our terrible offenses
the very bad thing of asking for a king for ourselves!"

And Samuel said to the people,
"Do not fear —
you've done all this bad stuff —

yet don't turn away from following YAHWEH —
slave away for YAHWEH with all your heart!
Don't turn away
because if you do go after completely worthless things that offer no
value, they won't strip and snatch you away (from the enemy)...
because they're worthless....

Because YAHWEH won't leave Its people
for the sake of Its great name —
because YAHWEH is pleased, willing to make you Its people....

Even so, how dare I even think about it — I would be making a
terrible offense against YAHWEH if I did! — to be flabby and stop
praying for you....

I'll point you to the good and right/smooth way....

Just this — fear YAHWEH and slave away for It
in a reliable way, with all your heart!

See what great things It has done for you!

But if you continue to do bad, do bad, do bad
both you and even your king will be scraped away!"

Chapter 12 is an interpolation?

I agree with Römer and biblical scholars who note well that 1
Samuel 12 bears the marks of a later Deuteronomistic editor
— the same ancient editor who most likely dropped similar
speeches into Moses' and Joshua's and Solomon's mouths
and even set out the cycle at the beginning of Judges...be
faithful to YAHWEH/ELOHIM and all will be well, abandon
YAHWEH/ELOHIM for other gods/goddesses and die. It's
also the message of the prophets. But for the most part, this
whole, very long speech inserted into the fictional-character

Samuel's mouth here is a gloss on the prophetic message without the ecstatic-style common to the prophets. More will be said about this Deuteronomistic speech-dropping later. This later Deuteronomistic editor also brings Moses and the Law into the picture, something most of the prophets have little use for.

You see, for a prophet — and later, Jesus and Paul — it's the Law that kills. The Spirit — YAHWEH — gives life, and life in abundance. The Spirit — the wind we breathe — provides ecstasy, nourishes us with all we need, something a Law only hints at.

And that's the big rub, both long ago and today.

It's just that the Deuteronomists and Levitical priests have entirely different ways of slaving away for YAHWEH than the prophets suggest. The Deuteronomists and priests and even today's religious types insist on doing something for YAHWEH to appease YAHWEH — performing special/sacred rituals and offering sacrifices, giving one's best produce to the king/hierarch, paying the local priests/hierarchs for their service, fulfilling one's personal role in the economy/hierarchy, etc.

For the prophets, the only way to appease YAHWEH is relationship...an appreciation of what It is we are breathing, a continual remembering of what It is who gives us life. Essentially, from a prophet's standpoint, we are all slaves to the one and same master...YAHWEH alone.

Taking the prophets' cue...if everyone is a slave to YAHWEH — and to YAHWEH alone — what happens to society?

There is no longer a pecking order, no longer a hierarchy.

The only slaves would be every human slaving away for YAHWEH, the master and owner of slaves. And also the greatest lover.

Some might say that such an arrangement is impractical, that government by the wind could never work. Perhaps so. But let's simply play with the idea for awhile....

What would it mean, then, to slave away for YAHWEH in a 'reliable way'?

This is the language of relationship, yes?

To be reliable, dependable, trustworthy.

In relationship, it means one holds this one — this beloved — as THE ALL of life. One experiences THE ALL of life through this one.

It is love. It is doing the hard nothing, as I like to call it. Doing nothing but <u>being</u> in love. This is a new way forward, yes? Even in the 21st century in which we live and find ourselves.

As soon as all this talk about having a king over them circulates through Ancient Israel in this fictional story of 1 Samuel, the band of X makes clear the significant problem in which the people of Ancient Israel finds itself...as young King Saul has known ecstasy and now rules...

can hierarchical, political power and ecstatic-visioning go together?

can prophetic-leadership in a hierarchical model ever be successful, ever create change and re-order the hierarchy, flatten the hierarchy into a circle where we all realize we are equals in life, where we all have equal value in life because we are alive?

It is the age-old question that Jesus brings forward too...

can one slave away for YAHWEH and 'mammon'?

can one be slave to YAHWEH and to hierarchical-order where some things have more value than others?

You see, prophets — at least as we can see through the character Samuel — invite a very different understanding of life and power than do Ancient Israel's hierarchically-minded neighbors, than do the people of Ancient Israel demanding a king, than do the priests and eventually the Deuteronomists with advocating the following of the Law/Torah.

Hierarchy is the default, the step-minded imagination where one is better than another is better than another is better than another...which means someone else needs to be less valuable than another and another and another.

The hierarchical imagination was...

the default imagination of Ancient Israel/Judah, in their asking for a king and in their Levitical priesthood attached to serving the ark and the cult-ritual involved with it;

and the default imagination of their neighbors to the north, for over a thousand pre-Bible years of *Gilgamesh*, concretized below in the Ziggurat of Ur, legendarily the temple-city from which the character Abraham comes;

and the default imagination of their neighbors to the south in Egypt with their god-like Pharaohs and River and slave-driven building projects — slaves of many different classes — slave-built building-projects still admired today.

The prophets aren't into the default. They're into an <u>experience</u>, and that experience loosens people from the default — if they and you and I let it/It....

from Abraham's homeland, the Ziggurat of Ur...
representing Babylon's solid hierarchical imagination
from which Abraham is called to wander away

chapter 13

One year later, a son.
Saul had been king over Ancient Israel two years.

(And then many years passed, that son Jonathan grew much older. Jonathan's name means 'Gift-of-YAHWEH'.)

And Saul had chosen for himself 3,000 from Ancient Israel.

And 2,000 were with him at the Store-Houses in the mountains of Divinity's-House (in Ancient Israel).

And 1,000 were with Jonathan on The Hill in Benjamin, the small tribe known for its powerful children. (Saul was from The Hill, and as he told us himself earlier, from Benjamin of Ancient Israel.)

And the rest of the people he sent away, every man/person to their own tent.

And Jonathan struck the Dust-Rolling-Philistines' military station which was on the little hill.

(Keep in mind that being higher in ancient military battle can make it much easier to defend — if there are ample supplies and soldiers there. All one had to do was roll down big things at any attacker...logs rolled downhill would be lethal once they got some momentum.)

And the Dust-Rollers heard about it — Saul had <u>fucked it up</u>

— Saul had <u>blasted it out</u> over the whole land, blasted it out through the ram's horn (the ancient war-cry) saying, "They will hear! The Bordercrossers!"

(Saul and his thousands and the however-many-back-at-home are all 'The Bordercrossers'/AYBRYM — usually transliterated as 'Hebrews' — clever too with Jonathan having just crossed the border between Ancient Israel and the Dust-Rolling-Philistines for his attack. It's likely that the people of the entire region — including the aforementioned Ammonites with their king Snake and the Moabites — were all Bordercrossers, a broader term than 'Israelites.'

But what Saul had done here with sounding the alarm was foolish, in many ways. Even the way the sentence is set up in Hebrew denotes this...subject-verb-object. Normal Hebrew sentence construction is verb-subject-object. The only times the subject comes first are when the teller of any tale or poem is really trying to get a hearer's attention, riling up any hearer of this Samuel-saga.

First off, <u>he's</u> the one blowing the *shofar*/SHOPR...ram's horn... essentially an ancient trumpet used to rally people into war, to announce kings, etc....and it's usually blown by someone at the behest of the king, at least during the days of kings. War and crowning royals, in the ancient imagination, were acts of ELOHIM, of the divinities, and often mediated by priests or royal assistants. And Saul is certainly blowing the *shofar* to get the troops with him going to join what Jonathan had done in battle...but was their strike on the Philistines all that wise? The band of X is not yet telling us the numbers of the Philistines for a final laugh about how ridiculous this attack is...and not only that, just wait until we hear what kinds of weaponry Saul's men are forced to use and, ahem, Jonathan too.

Second, practically speaking, Saul basically announced Jonathan's attack to the much larger population of the

Philistine garrison. After a successful sneak attack, would you announce to the enemy that you're coming in full force?

And third and perhaps most importantly, the band of X lets us know something with a clever pun within this already bizarre situation: TQAY is a verb for 'blowing/blasting the *shofar*'. TQAY shows up in the Genesis 32 story with YAHWEH wrestling Jacob, and groping Jacob's genitals/ass. As I've laid out in *A Wildly Sensual YAHWEH*, TQAY is likely a euphemism for 'fuck/mess with' as the character YAHWEH had done with the character Jacob in Genesis 32. X uses the double-entendre of TQAY here in 1 Samuel to indicate King Saul's foolishness in announcing Jonathan's success — and perhaps taking credit for Jonathan's small advance against the much more powerful Philistine army — long before the battle is completely settled against a huge army...the powerful and well-organized confederacy of Philistia, as we learned in earlier chapters of our saga. Here, Saul TQAYs the *shofar* in his attempt to defeat the enemy-Philistines; later, the same enemy-Philistines will TQAY Saul. Brutally.

Let's look a little deeper into how *shofar* is used in the Hebrew Bible all 72 times. At least a few of these might have been known to an ancient hearer of this Samuel-saga...

> Leviticus 25.9 has AYBR ('bordercross') as the active verb with *shofar* instead of TQAY, a very priestly thing to do, likely to avoid the euphemistic confusion that TQAY brings

> there are many uses of *shofar* in Joshua, including Joshua 6, the story about circling the city to put the inhabitants in terror before committing genocide against them...and its the priests who 'blow'/TQAY the *shofarim* (plural), not the military-leader like Joshua himself

> many uses of *shofar* in Judges 3 & 6, and then multiple uses in Judges 7 with the story of Gideon also rallying a very small portion of his men chosen by YAHWEH to commit genocide on the Midianites with Gideon's small army winning

> *shofar* is used only once in 1 Samuel but six times in 2 Samuel, often by Joab in war or calling off battle and when King David had the ark brought to the new capital Jerusalem...King David does not blow the *shofar* himself though as he has people to do that

> twice in 1 Kings 1 to proclaim Solomon king, controversially; once in 2 Kings 9.13 with the *shofar* being 'blown'/TQAY'd when Jehu is announced as king

> and plenty of other times by the prophets' in their poems and in Chronicles & Nehemiah and the psalms and in Job...though most of the time the *shofar* is referred to QOL SHOPR/'the sound of the *shofar*' and not as the direct object of TQAY as above

I suspect the ancient-hearers would have been very surprised to discover in this particular context of taking on a massive Philistine army and announcing it to them with King Saul as the one 'blowing'/TQAY the *shofar*, which would bring in TQAY's other potential meanings 'fucking (it up), or being fucked/raped'...where those particular usages will circle back at the end of this character Saul's life.

And what else is foolish and quite telling in this story? How about how many men/people Saul and Jonathan have mustered here? Just 3,000 total?! Earlier in the saga, when the newly minted King Saul came in from the fields (!) and in his passion for the people of his nation about to lose their lives/ honor against the attacking Snake, Saul alone rallied 300,000 from Ancient Israel and 30,000 from Ancient Judah. Saul's army smashed Snake — so badly that no two of their cousin-enemy were left together. But here with Jonathan against an even bigger threat like the Philistines? Ancient Israel's king attacks with only 3,000?!

Despite Saul's first victory with those 330,000 in his army, many years have passed — years enough for Saul's own son Jonathan to be born, grow up, and be successful in battle. It will soon become even more clear that Saul is not the passionate military-strategist that he once was.)

And the whole nation of Ancient Israel heard:
"Saul struck the Dust-Rollers' military station!"
and even
"Ancient Israel's becoming a stench to the Dust-Rollers — a bother."

And the people cried out after Saul at the city of wheels, where the wind wheels and whirls around.

(Even the subjects of his own nation notice how foolish it was for their King Saul and the king's son to attack Philistia...this Saul and the system of monarchy that they had 'Asked-For'....)

And the Dust-Rolling-Philistines were assembling to fight with Ancient Israel —

30,000 chariots
and 6,000 horsemen
and people as many as there is sand at the seashore —
and they camped at the Store-Houses (basically King Saul's bank) just east of the house of trouble.

And each man/person of Ancient Israel saw the tight spot they were in —
because the people were distressed —
and the men/people went into <u>hiding themselves in their love-making with each other</u> —

in caves
in thorny bramble-patches
under craggy cliffs
in dug-out underground chambers
in pits.

(There's our punny-friend CHBAH again, the kind of 'hiding by love-making, hiding oneself in the bosom of the other.' Saul, the one asked-for and then raised up as king, was first found CHBAH-ing himself, and now in the great distress of war, his military runs and hides themselves by making love with one another...which lends a lot of credence to Dr. Jenning's *Jacob's Wound* thesis of Ancient Israel's supposed royal/military-pederastic roots, though I think even Dr. Jennings missed the whole funny-business of CHBAH.)

And (some) of the Bordercrossers crossed over the big downward-flowing river (Jordan) into the neighboring tribe's territory — the territory of Gad, known for their 'attack-by-penetration' — and into the city of heaped-up stones.

And as for Saul, he was still in the city of wheels, where the wind wheels and whirls around —
and all the people following after him were terrified.

And he waited seven days according to the meeting time set by Samuel — (seven being the 'just-right' number of the ancient world, not always simply meaning 'seven') — and Samuel didn't (fuck) arrive in the city of wheels, where the wind wheels and whirls around.

And (more) people started drifting away, disbanding from (Saul).

And Saul said,
"Bring here to me the animals that we can cut up and burn up — peace offerings!"

And an animal-to-cut-and-burn-up was climbed up.

And so it was —
just as he finished climbing up the animal-to-cut-and-burn-up that —
hear this! — Samuel (fuck) arrived!

And Saul went out to call out after him —
to kneel down for an abundance-blessing.

And Samuel said,
"What have you done?!?"

And Saul said, "— because I saw that the people were drifting away,
disbanding from me —
and you — you hadn't (fuck) arrived within the set number of days for our meeting —
and the Dust-Rollers had assembled by the Store-Houses —
and the Dust-Rollers were coming down on me at the city of wheels, where the wind wheels and whirls around —
and YAHWEH's face — <u>I didn't entreat or offend or feel weak—</u>
<u>I felt strong, compelled, restrained myself —</u>
<u>I climbed up the animal-to-cut-and-burn-up</u>!!"

(This whole business of 'climbing up an animal to cut and burn up' is euphonic: AYLH HAYLH. It's usually translated as 'making a sacrifice' even though the first AYLH simply means 'to climb up' which can be to make a sacrifice on a mountain or to simply climb any hill.

Saul speaks here with a curious style...CHLYTY which I translate as 'I didn't entreat or offend or feel weak' could be from at least three very different verbs CHLH/'to beseech, entreat, be rubbed or worn or weak' or CHUL/'to whirl, dance, writhe in pain' or CHLL/'to pierce, offend, profane' and then AHPQ which I translate as 'I felt strong, compelled, restrained myself' because that verb can indeed mean all of that. Saul seems to be speaking out of both sides of his mouth here — and not only that, he's assuming he has the power and strength of position of a priest, of one who offers sacrifices, something that's in Samuel's bailiwick. Recall that Saul blows the ram's horn too, something a king would not ordinarily do. What kind of king has Saul become?)

And Samuel said to Saul,
"You've played the fool —
you weren't careful about the orders of YAHWEH, your
ELOHIM/divinity
who shouted out orders to you...
YAHWEH would have firmed up your kingship
  over Ancient Israel
    forever!
But now your kingship won't stand up tall —
(you see) YAHWEH Itself is looking for a man/person with a
heart like Its own —
and YAHWEH is shouting out orders
for him to be a front/commander over Its people
because you weren't careful about what YAHWEH ordered
you to do!"

And Samuel stood himself up tall and climbed up from the
city of wheels, where the wind wheels and whirls around, and
went to The Hill in Benjamin, the small tribe known for its
powerful children (Saul's hometown, and apparently the seat
of the kingship).

And Saul mustered up the people he found to be with him —
about 600 men/people.

(Remember, just a few days ago there were 2,000 with him,
1,000 with Jonathan. So many left Saul out of fear of the
consequences of his foolish military strategy, all of them now
hiding and making love with one another, perhaps to soothe
themselves in their battle-distress.)

And Saul and his son Jonathan and the people found to be with
them stayed in the little-hill area of Benjamin, the small tribe
known for its powerful children (the city where Jonathan's
attack was successful just days before).

And the Dust-Rollers encamped at the Store-Houses (Ancient Israel's Treasury).

And the Dust-Rollers' no-holds-barred-military-destroying-unit went out from their army-camp — three heads/companies of them:

One company turned onto the road to the Ancient Israel city known for being like a young fawn, the area where the jackals feast upon them.

And one company turned onto the road toward the house of hiding (perhaps the hollow holes where people were hiding in Ancient Israel).

And one company turned onto the road that led to the border, the place where one could gaze down upon the valley that looks like it had been dyed so many different colors — (and therefore easy to spot people walking upon it when viewed from above) — out there toward the style-rich wilderness.

('Wilderness'/MDBR has 'style'/DBR within it...perhaps making the wandering wilderness a style-rich place and style-rich way of life.

The Dust-Rollers had essentially surrounded Saul and Jonathan's escape routes.)

And as for a metalworker...
one couldn't be found
throughout the whole land of Ancient Israel
because the Dust-Rollers said,
"Otherwise the Bordercrossers would make a sword or a spear!"

(Ha! Shows you just how much — how little! — King Saul was in charge of his own country!!)

And all of Ancient Israel would go down to the Dust-Rollers to get their things sharpened — each man/person — his hoe, his rake, his ax — his plow/farming tool (of all sorts).

And they had a sharpening-edge for plows, for rakes, for three-pronged forks, for axes, for the tips of sticks for herding sheep.

(This is ancient comedy here....)

And so it was —
on the day of the fight that no sword or spear could be found in a hand/phallic-control of any of the men/people who were with Saul and Jonathan —

but they could be found with Saul and his son Jonathan — (those two had weapons)!

And the Dust-Rollers' command-post (felt so confident that they) left for the pass-through of (Ancient Israel's) Store-Houses.

chapter 14

And so it was —

one day Jonathan, Saul's son, said to the slave/boy who lifted his gear,
"Come on, let's cross over
to the Dust-Rollers' military station —
it's just right over there on the other side."

But to his own father, he didn't report this.

And as for Saul...he was sitting on the outskirts of The Hill (near his house, not far from the Store-Houses where the Dust-

Rollers were encamped). He was <u>sitting under a pomegranate tree</u>...

> luxuriating with the luscious fruit?
> exalting himself?
> getting himself up?
> getting high?

('sitting under a pomegranate tree' could very well be an ancient metaphor — perhaps similar to 'resting on one's laurels'? — though 'pomegranate'/RMON to an ancient hearer recalls RMM/"to rise (literally or figuratively) — exalt, get (oneself) up, lift up (self), mount up" as *Strong's Exhaustive Concordance* reminds. This could be playing into the narrative here with the slaves/boys who lift the gear...more on that in a minute. Whatever an ancient would have heard in this sentence, the king is sitting under a tree while his son makes plans for another attack. And we moderns might think that a king under a tree sounds about right and safe from the action, but kings in the ancient world directed the battle — at the very, very least they were near the battle. Here, King Saul does not even know his son is about to attack....)

This was in a region of Ancient Israel known for 'tossing off,' for being on the edge.

And the people who were with him were like 600 men.

And Brother-of-YAHWEH —
> son of Good-Brother.
> brother of No-Honor,
> son of Snake-Mouth,
> son of Climb-Up, the priest who once was
> > in the A-Quiet-Place, He-Whose-It-Is —

he was <u>lifting up</u> the special priestly underwear.

(Same word for the 'special priestly underwear'/AHPOD that Samuel had worn when he was a child as a boy/slave to Eli-Climb-Up...though we don't know how 'straggly-yarned' / BD this edition of it is...we'll soon discover that this special underwear now in the story functions as a future-teller...likely with two dice inside...one marked 'yes' and one marked 'no.'

Note too that the same verb NSAH is used for Brother-of-YAHWEH lifting up the priestly underwear and Jonathan's gear-lifter. This might seem like a ridiculous thing to point out, but play with the directions of everything happening and I suspect just about any ancient-hearer would be "ahemmm"-ing. And it gets more intriguing....)

And as for the people...they didn't know in any way that Jonathan had gone.

And between the passes that Jonathan was seeking to cross over to the Dust-Rollers' military station, there was a sharp rock jutting out over one pass and a sharp rock jutting out over another pass.

One was named "shining"; one was named "thorns."

The sharpness of one rose up north toward the Store-Houses (where the Dust-Rollers were encamped); and one faced south toward the little-hill (not far from where Saul and his men were encamped).

And Jonathan said to the slave/boy who lifted his gear,
"Come on, let's bordercross over to the military station of these guys who have uncut-dicks —
maybe YAHWEH will work out something for us —
because there's nothing holding back YAHWEH from rescuing the big/many or the little/few!"

And his gear-lifter said,
"Do all that's in your heart —
stretch yourself out!
I am here with you — just like your own heart!"

And Jonathan said,
"Listen up —
we'll bordercross over to the men/people
and we'll strip ourselves naked in front of them — just like
exiles or slaves are forced to do!
If then (because of our naked, trespassing selves) they say to us,
'Be dumb enough to stay right there until we come lay our
hands all over you/fuck with you!'
then we'll stand our ground underneath us and not climb up
to them.
But if then (because of our naked, trespassing selves) they say
to us,
'Climb up to us!'
then we'll climb up
because YAHWEH has given them into our hands/penises/
phallic control —
this will be the sign for us."

(Besides the punny big-small references — especially in
the realm of cut-dicks and uncut-dicks — and the boy's
invitation to Jonathan to 'stretch himself out'/NTH — used
with comedic effect in the band of YAH's Genesis story about
Judah, and here with the maybe-smaller cut-dicked Jonathan
about to strip himself naked in front of the uncut-dicked and
probably then larger-dicked Philistines — this is an ecstatic-
prophetic power-punch of verbs here...AYBR/'bordercross'...
GLH/'to strip naked as a slave or exile is forced to do'...NTN
B-YD-NU/'to give them into our hands/penises'...and even the
exploding-in-every direction verb NGAY/'to strike, to touch
not nicely' and *Strong's Exhaustive Concordance* notes that this
verb is also used euphemistically to mean 'to lie with a woman'
as in having sex...and probably not the most tender sex...

thus the reason I chose 'to fuck with' which has all of those meanings within it, even in our English language...much like our TQAY/'blast or fuck with' just a few scenes earlier.)

And the two of them stripped themselves naked just like exiles or slaves are forced to do, right there in front of the Dust-Rolling-Philistines' military station.

And the Dust-Rollers said,
"Look! The Bordercrossers are coming out from the holes where they've been <u>making-love and hiding themselves</u> there!"

(Yep again, CHBAH/'lovemaking, hiding oneself in and around someone'...not STR/'hiding' as in hiding behind a rock...as these Dust-Rollers say this about the two naked and cut-dicked Hebrews/Bordercrossers standing there in front of them.)

And the men/people from the military station responded to Jonathan and to his gear-lifter and said,
"Climb up here to us!
<u>We'll make you know something in every way (including sexually)</u> — talk about style!"

(Here we have YDAY/'to know' and used throughout the Hebrew Bible for 'knowing as in having sex' — and not only that, we have the *hiphil*-use of the verb, the Hebrew-language way of force, of making something happen, perhaps as in rough or forced 'knowing'...sex. Quite the 'style'/DBR here, right? And the men of the military-station even note it themselves.)

And Jonathan said to his gear-lifter,
"Climb up after me —
you see — YAHWEH has given them
right into the hand/phallic-control of Ancient Israel!"

(Ancient Israel, of course, is the nation taking its name from
the hero who wrestled EL and got groped and penetrated and
climbed on top of EL and won.)

And Jonathan climbed up
by his hand/penis and by his foot/balls/testicles —
and his gear-lifter after him —
and they fell down right there in front of Jonathan and his
gear-lifter murdering them right after him.

(YD/'hand or penis' plus RGL/'foot or testicles or genitals'
— more euphemistic pun play that *Strong's Exhaustive
Concordance* notes. And these armed-and-ready Dust-Rollers
in their own secure-outpost must have been mesmerized
by Jonathan's naked body and Jonathan's gear-lifter's naked
body to fall down right there in front of them, I guess? We're
probably to assume that Jonathan stabbed them, and maybe
the gear-lifter whacked them out with his shield so that they
bled out and could not attend to their wounds.)

And it was a slaughter from the beginning —
with Jonathan and his gear-lifter striking and killing
about 20 men, about half of them bowed down, paired up in
the open-field.

And there was anxiety and trembling within the army-camp,
in the open-field, and within all the people of the military
station — and the no-holds-barred-military-destroying-unit
was anxious and trembling — even them!

And the earth was quaking —
and there was anxiety and trembling — ELOHIM/God-or-gods-and-goddesses!

And Saul's lookouts on The Hill in Benjamin, the small tribe known for its powerful children, saw something —
look — the rumbling-crowd was melting away —
it was leaving — it was beat down!

And Saul said to the people who were with him,
"Count up who is with us and see who left!"

And they counted up everyone with them —
listen up! —
Jonathan and his gear-lifter weren't there!

And Saul said to Brother-of-YAHWEH (the priest),
"<u>Bring</u> the ark of ELOHIM/divine <u>closer</u>!"

You see, on that day, ELOHIM's ark was there — and Ancient Israel's children.

> (They hadn't learned their lesson a generation back when Climb-Up's children had marched the ark into battle and lost it.)

And so it was —
while Saul was styling out to the priest, the sound of the rumbling-crowd in the Dust-Rollers' army-camp continued to get bigger.

> (What stylish thing had Saul said? Well, it could be the band of X referring back and making sure we catch to 'bring closer'/NGSH...which is also that euphemism for 'to lie down for sex.' Same command Saul issued earlier about bringing the animals for the cut-and-burn to YAHWEH when he got in trouble with Samuel.)

And Saul said to the priest,
"Your hand/penis! Take it out!"
And Saul and all the people with him cried out,
and they (fuck) went into the battle —
and listen here —
the sword of every man was against his friend —
a huge confusion, an uproar!

And the Bordercrossers who just three days before were with the Dust-Rollers (the Bordercrossers who had defected) climbed up with them into the army-camp from the surrounding area — even they were with Ancient Israel, with Saul and Jonathan.

And every man of Ancient Israel who had been hiding-themselves-by-lovemaking in Ephraim, the tribe from the mountains known for being fruitful, heard that the Dust-Rollers were running away, and so they followed close after them into the battle — even they did!

(CHBAH again...'hiding-themselves-by-lovemaking.' Now just a bit ago, when Saul told his priest to take his hand/penis out, normally that would have to do with reaching into the special priestly underwear to fetch a 'yes' or a 'no' — but if that's what Saul meant he and his men/people do not even wait for an answer, perhaps because the Dust-Rollers' uproar made it clear that they were in chaos and now was the right moment to strike. Or we are to assume that the priest showing his hand/penis was enough to get Saul's men/people to cry out and 'fuck, go into'/BOAH the battle.)

And YAHWEH rescued Ancient Israel, the nation taking its name from the hero who wrestled EL, got groped and penetrated and climbed on top of EL.

And the battle crossed over all the way to the house of trouble.

And as for every single man of Ancient Israel...he was was hard pressed that day —
Saul cussed out, made the people swear:
"Cursed is the man who eats any food until evening
and I've gotten revenge on my enemies!"

And no one among all the people had tasted any food.

And the whole land (fuck) led into a honeycombed-forest —
there was honey on the surface of the open-field.

And the people (fuck) went into the honeycombed-forest —
there was honey running everywhere!

And no one even put his hand to his mouth because the people feared the oath.

And Jonathan hadn't heard of his father making the people swear the oath. And he reached out the end of the stick that was in his hand/phallic-control and dipped it into the honeycomb full of honey and brought his hand to his mouth — and did his eyes ever brighten and see!

And one of the people responded and said,
"He swore, swore swore — your father did — with the people —
he said, 'Cursed is the man who eats any food today!'"

And the people started flittering and tittering and hovering protectively like birds.

And Jonathan said,
"My father roils water on land — (he stirs up trouble anywhere and everywhere)
see for yourselves —
my eyes are lit up —
because I tasted just a little bit of this honey!
Yeah, if our people — today — had eaten, eaten, eaten
from what they found and took from our enemies,

now how much greater would the slaughter be on the Dust-Rollers?!"

(Apparently, Jonathan knows something of the clever style of YAHWEH too...his father ARUR/'cursed' but Jonathan's eyes AORO/'light up'...punny. Jonathan's been acting without orders from his father — and successfully. And now we know a little bit of why....)

And they had struck down the Dust-Rolling-Philistines on that day from Ancient Israel's Store-Houses all the way to the Dust-Roller city known for its deer.

And the people were really flittering and tittering and hovering protectively like birds — very much so!

(Remember, the people hadn't eaten all day. They'd been fighting all day and were likely starved. And yet they swarm around Jonathan, protectively and perhaps even energetically/magnetically...this one with bravery and honest reckoning about the problems of his father, their king.)

And the people rushed onto what was taken (from the Dust-Rollers) —
they had taken sheep and cows and calves —
and they butchered them on the ground
and the people ate them — with the blood still there — raw!

And they reported it to Saul, whose name means 'Asked-For,'
"Hear this — the people have terribly offended YAHWEH — by eating the blood — by eating the meat raw!"

And he said,
"You all have acted unfaithfully, deceitfully!!!"

Roll over to me — right here, right now — a huge stone!"

And Saul said,
"Spread out among the people and say to them,
'Bring me each man's/person's ox and each man's/person's
goat,
and you all butcher them right here
and you all eat them
and don't offend YAHWEH terribly by eating them with the
blood — raw!'"

And all the people brought each man's/person's ox in his
own hand/phallic-control that very night and they butchered
them there.

Saul had built a slaughtering-table for YAHWEH —

he made a profane, profound mistake in building a
slaughtering-table for YAHWEH!

And Saul said,
"Let's go down after the Dust-Rollers by night
and rob them of everything we can until the light of morning —
and not leave a single man/person among them!"

And they said,
"All that's good in your eyes we'll do!"

And the priest said,
"Let's come closer to ELOHIM/divine!"

And Saul (the guy named Asked-For) asked of ELOHIM/
divine,
"Should I go down after the Dust-Rollers?
Will you give them over
to the hand/phallic-control of Ancient Israel?"

And (ELOHIM) didn't answer that day.

(If indeed the priestly underwear had a 'yes' and a 'no' as answers within in it...two dice within the underwear...and the priest couldn't find one of those rocks in his underwear?! What?! X is poking fun at the priests and their ways of getting ELOHIM/divinity to respond. But note the ridiculousness of this whole scene...how the band of X just lays it out there...as a king is deciding if he should go down with his army and the priests and their ark of God and commit genocide upon the enemy they've already routed.

The verb choices are quite curious and probably meant to be. Instead of the priest inviting Saul to SHAHL/'ask' ELOHIM we get the priest inviting Saul to QRB/'come closer' to ELOHIM. I mean, can anyone 'get any closer' to ELOHIM, to YAHWEH? YAHWEH surrounds, It enlivens us with every breath. Remember, Samuel didn't need ELOHIM's ark or the special priestly, fortune-telling underwear or an altar/slaughtering-table to communicate with YAHWEH — YAHWEH spoke directly to Samuel!)

And Saul said,
"Bring here all the chief-officials of the people.
Let's know and see who has terribly offended (ELOHIM) today!

(Saul assumes someone has offended ELOHIM because ELOHIM didn't answer him through the priest.)

(I swear) by the very life of YAHWEH
who has rescued Ancient Israel —
if it's because my son Jonathan he should die, die, die!"

But there was no one who answered him from among all of the people.

And he said to the whole nation of Ancient Israel,
"All of you be on <u>one side</u>,
and I and my son Jonathan will be on the <u>other side</u> —
(so we can get ready to roll the dice and figure out who is to blame — which 'side'/AYBR, these two sides of the 'Bordercrossers'/AYBR — and who will die for it)."

And the people said to Saul,
"If it's good in your eyes, do it!"

(Maybe the people who asked-for-it and got Saul were ready to dispense with Saul/Jonathan and all things royal? Or maybe they're ready to defend Jonathan if the roll of the dice falls upon him — defend Jonathan against their king, against Jonathan's own father. And the people know too that if the roll of the dice falls upon them, they can always kill the king. This is how fragile monarchy as a system is, and the only way it works is if everyone receiving benefits — "all the kings men" — continue to receive those benefits by continuing to prop up the king.)

And Saul said to YAHWEH, ELOHIM/divinity of Ancient Israel,
"Come on now...clarity and completeness (through the roll of the dice, casting lots)!"

And Jonathan and Saul were <u>captured</u> — chosen by the roll of the dice, casting lots! The people escaped (harm)!

And Saul said,
"Make (the dice, lot) fall between me and my son Jonathan!"

And Jonathan was <u>captured</u> — by the roll of the dice, casting lots!

And Saul said to Jonathan,
"Report to me what you've done!"

And Jonathan reported to him and said,
"I tasted, tasted, tasted — with the end of my stick
that's in my hand/phallic-control —
just a little bit of honey —
here I am — I'll die for it!"
And Saul said,
"This is what ELOHIM/divine will do!
And even more than this —
because you are going to die, die, die, Jonathan!"

And the people said to Saul,
"Jonathan? Die? —
when he was the one who made this great rescue with Ancient Israel!?!
How dare that be so — as long as YAHWEH lives!
If a single hair of his head falls to the ground...!
It was with ELOHIM/divine that (Jonathan) has done this today!"

And the people redeemed Jonathan — he did not die.

And Saul climbed up from going after the Dust-Rollers.

And the Dust-Rollers went back to their places.

And Saul <u>captured</u> the kingship over Ancient Israel — he fought/devoured every side against all his enemies...

against Ancient Israel's second-cousins From-My-Father-Inbreds-from-Moab people and the children of From-My-Inbred-Kinfolk and The-Reds — (all of them second-cousins of Ancient Israel) —

and against the kings of those stationed in the far north (Aram/Syria)

and against the Dust-Rollers

and every direction he faced, he violated them.

And he made an army and struck and killed more of Ancient Israel's second-cousins, The-Laborers.

And he snatched Ancient Israel away from the hands/phallic-control of whoever had robbed and stolen from them.

And so it was —
these were the sons of Saul, the guy whose name means Asked-For:

Jonathan, whose name means Gift-of-YAHWEH,
& Equalize,
& My-King's-Wealth.

(Notice how the names go from YAHWEH-oriented to King-oriented...and the only way a King gets wealthy is by taxing his people and robbing/stealing from foreign people as we have seen in the previous lines of all the people Saul attacks, even relatives of Ancient Israel.

YAHWEH through Samuel had warned them of what Saul — any king — would do....

LCD/'captured, seized, taken' is one of those curious verbs, often used when cities are captured but here and earlier when Saul was chosen as king it can mean chosen or selected...but maybe chosen/selected in not the best way.

And now Saul is capturing the kingship...via genocide...again, maybe not in the best way.)

And the name of his two daughters:

Merab-From-Many was the older,
& Michal-Who-Is-ALL was the younger.

And the name of Saul's wife was My-Brother's-Delight,
the daughter of My-Brother-Fastens.

And the name of the commander of his army was
Abner-Patriarchy's-Lamplight,
son of Lamplight,
Saul's beloved.

And Set-a-Trap was Saul's father,
and Lamplight was father of Abner-Patriarchy's-Lamplight,
son of EL's-Patriarchy.

(Now this is an important detail to clarify what kind of
'beloved' Lamplight was to Saul....

In Hebrew, as was mentioned earlier, DOD could mean 'uncle,
lover, beloved, love-boiler, a person named David'...or all of
these. This is sometimes the band of X's style, to introduce
a character's name in the saga as a regular noun or verb long
before the character is introduced. It could lean into the
argument that these stories that became 1 & 2 Samuel were
told in chunks — perhaps each night around a campfire —
and often enough that hearers would have giggled when they
heard a name introduced early in the saga because they knew
what was coming. Here we have Saul's beloved (relative/lover)
and soon we'll meet David and all that he might be for Saul.

Note too...the incestuous and patriarchal names of Saul's
wife's family, and that Saul's general is listed with his family,
and his relationship to Saul's family.)

And there was violent war with the Dust-Rollers all the days of
Saul, the one whose name means Asked-For.

And Saul viewed every powerful man and every strong son
and gathered them for himself.

chapter 15

And Samuel, the guy named for EL, said to Saul,
"I was the one YAHWEH sent to smear you with oil and make
you king over Its people, over Ancient Israel!
Now listen to the voice — the style of YAHWEH!

This is what YAHWEH-of-the-Big-Armies-Who-Require-
Service says!

'I'll visit-and-avenge The-Laborer (the head of the Amalekites,
your second-cousins) for what he did to Ancient Israel —
how he put himself on the road as (Ancient Israel) was climbing
up from Suffering-Egypt!

Now go —
you are to strike and kill The-Laborer —
you all are to utterly destroy all that they have —
do not have any compassion for them —
murder
  from man to woman —
  from child to suckling-baby —
  from ox to goat —
  from camel to donkey!'"

But Saul listened to the people...
and he visited-and-mustered them at the place known for its
lambs —

200,000 sets of feet (foot-soldiers),
and 10,000 men of Judah, the tribe known for throwing up
their hands/penises in praise.

  (Here is that strange verb again...PQD/'to visit-and avenge, to
  visit-and-muster' and a host of meanings in between...where

the visit might be friendly or hostile...and the 'what comes next' is key. It's likely a storytelling verb that makes people's ears perk up to find out what happens next. And here the band of X uses it twice in such close proximity in the story, and each with a different understanding.

And best to notice the style of what character-Samuel is telling character-Saul to do here, commanded by character-YAHWEH. It is most certainly genocide against The-Laborers/Amalekites, Samuel being the one demanding it. Notice the order of events that Samuel lays out: one person's death here is the key — The-Laborer/Amalek himself — and then everyone else after him, the rest of The-Laborers. And everything of value is to die too — all the animals — what most translators call putting the town/people under 'the ban, to utterly destroy, flatten everyone's and everything's noses, exterminate'/CHRM. Erase them from the earth. But the order of events is key here...our character-Samuel might be being quite crafty here in demanding the <u>head</u> of The-Laborers to die first...maybe because he knew Saul's heart....)

And Saul (fuck) got as far as The-Laborer's/Amalek's city and wrangled in the creek-valley.

And Saul said to Cain's-Kids (Ancient Israel's second-cousins dwelling among The-Laborers),
"Go — leave — turn away from —
go down from among The-Laborers —
otherwise I'll count you with them and remove you too —
you've demonstrated your loyal-love for all the children of Ancient Israel when they climbed up from Suffering-Egypt!"

And Cain's-Kids left, turned away from The-Laborer.

And Saul attacked and killed The-Laborer from the area known for its whirling dances (fuck) going all the way to the wall facing Suffering-Egypt.

And he captured Agag, The-Laborer king — alive!

And all the (other) people (Saul) utterly destroyed with the edge of the sword.

But Saul and the people had compassion upon Agag —
and upon the very best of the (valuable) sheep and cattle —
and the second-best too —
and upon the rams.

And upon all that was good, (Saul) wasn't willing to utterly destroy, any of them.

But everything he despised and was wasting away — that he utterly destroyed.

And so it was —
YAHWEH's style was with Samuel, saying,
"I am full of sighs —
sorry that I made Saul a king...
he has turned back from following me
and as for my style...he hasn't stood himself up tall!"

And hot anger came to Samuel.

And he cried out to YAHWEH all night long.

And Samuel woke up early to call upon Saul in the morning.

And it was reported to Samuel:

"Saul (fuck) went to the vineyard —
and listen here —
he set up — for himself! — a penis-(statue) —
and he's gone round and round it —
and then he passed on from there
and went down to the city of wheels, where the wind wheels
and whirls around."

(YD can mean either 'hand or 'penis' but the meaning is pretty clear here. Going round and round a YD/'penis-statue' is the dance around BAAL and ASHTAROTH, the divinities Samuel in his first speech had told the Israelites to leave behind, to behead.   BAAL and ASHTAROTH were symbolized by sticking a piece of wood or a rock into the ground — a phallus around which their devotees would dance so their divinities would ejaculate the conditions of fertility into the ground... fertile soil and fertile wombs. Even worse, Saul had the YD erected for himself.)

And Samuel (fuck) went to Saul and said to him,
"Saul! You've been brought to your knees into abundance by YAHWEH!
And I stand tall with YAHWEH's style!"

(Important here the silence, as Saul has no response to this unusual greeting.)

And Samuel said,
"And what's this —
the sound of this sheep in my ears —
and the sound of cattle that I hear?!"

And Saul said,
"From The-Laborers — they (fuck) brought them —
because the people had compassion
on the best of the sheep and the cattle —
for the purpose of butchering and burning them up for YAHWEH — your EL —
and the rest we utterly destroyed—"

(With all these animals of The-Laborers at his whimsy, Saul wouldn't have to use his own flocks for the victory-sacrifices for YAHWEH. Note too what Saul says about YAHWEH — Samuel's EL/divinity — not Saul's own. Saul seems to be making it clear that his EL/divinity is not YAHWEH. After all, Saul has erected a penis-statue for himself — something Ancient Israel's neighbors did for their EL — their divinity/godhead — and EL's pantheon of gods and goddesses...BAAL, ASHTAROTH, DAGON.)

And Samuel said,
"Slacken yourself down there (opposite of erect yourself) — I'll report to you what YAHWEH styled out to me last night!"

And <u>they</u> said to him,
"Style it out!"

(Some texts have 'and they said'/VYAHMRO and some texts have 'and he said'/VYAHMR...which could be as simple as a scribal error. Or, it could mean some of the royal-court/warriors were there with Saul...and perhaps the people were growing more and more suspicious of the royal-ruler they had asked-for and for whom they were laying down their lives...though he must have thrown some great parties...the vineyard, the penis-erection-statue, the dancing around it, the moving to the city where they were now that had to do with whirling around...all of this very connected to the BAAL and ASHTAROTH cults that surely were alluring and highly addictive for any human being in the ancient world, and likely would be today too. We have our own 21st century versions after all.)

And Samuel said,
"Isn't it so...that you were small and unimportant — in your own eyes — when you became head of all the tribes of Ancient Israel?! You!
And YAHWEH specially smeared you with oil — made you *messiah* — to be king over Ancient Israel!

And YAHWEH sent you on a way and said to you,
'Go! Utterly destroy the terrible offenders — The-Laborer!
Fight them until they are completely gone, finished!'

Why didn't you listen to YAHWEH's voice —
why did you swoop down upon the war-spoils
and do wrong in YAHWEH's eyes?!"

And Saul said to Samuel,
"Whatever —
I listened to YAHWEH's voice —
I went the way YAHWEH sent me!
I (fuck) brought back Agag, The-Laborers' king —
and as for The-Laborer, I utterly destroyed them —
the people took from the war-spoils —
sheep, cattle —
the very best from what was to be completely destroyed
to butcher and burn up for YAHWEH, your EL —
in the city of wheels, where the wind wheels and whirls around."

And Samuel, the guy named for EL, said,
"Is there pleasure for YAHWEH in climbing things up for
butchering-and-burning-of-animals?!

Compared to listening to YAHWEH's voice!?!

Listen here —

compare listening to butchering-and-burning...

it's better to prick up one's ears to hear,
better than the most delicious fat-and-juicy rams!

You see, the terrible offense (against YAHWEH) of divining-
the-future — (of trying to make God/divine speak by throwing
dice or reading from magical scrolls/books) — it's bitter —

and   panting-in-front-of-false-idols-is-evil   and   making-household-god-figurines is a stubborn urge —

because you are rejecting YAHWEH's style

and It rejects you as king!"

And Saul said to Samuel,
"I've done terribly offensive things!
You see, I've bordercrossed on by YAHWEH's mouth and
your style —
because I feared the people and listened to their voices!
Now, please, lift/take away my terrible offense —
return with me —
I'll bow down to YAHWEH!"

And Samuel said to Saul, the one the people Asked-For,
"I will not return with you —
because you rejected YAHWEH's style,
and YAHWEH rejects you from being king over Ancient
Israel!"

And Samuel turned around to go,
and (Saul) fastened onto the edge of his robe and it tore.

And he said to him — Samuel, the guy named for EL, did:
"YAHWEH tears the kingship of Ancient Israel from you today,
and It gives it to your neighbor who is better than you —

even now, the enduring horizon of Ancient Israel won't be
cheated (by you),
it won't sigh and be sorry (for you) —
because there isn't a single mud-made-human-creature-like-
Adam to be sorry!!!"

And he said,
"I've done terrible things...now please honor me
in front of the elders of my people

and in front of Ancient Israel —
return with me,
and I'll bow down to YAHWEH, your EL!"

And Samuel returned, following after Saul,
and Saul bowed down to YAHWEH.

And Samuel said,
"Bring Agag, The-Laborer king, to me!"

And he went to him — Agag did — <u>pleasurably, delightedly</u>...

(Notice: not only does Agag go on his own, he also seems to understand the language of Hebrew, a true kindred family member from the larger Bordercrosser people...and Saul's people must be wining and dining this celebrity-king for him to go so freely and 'pleasurably'/MAYDN...which can also mean 'dainty food, delicacy'...which all could be a gloss on the 'Eden'/AYDN story with AHDM/'mud-made-human-creature-like-Adam' so close by here.

It's important for us to remember that people were likely hearing most of these biblical stories aloud long before they were written down. The band of YAH's Eden story often haunts/echoes within 1 Samuel, something we evident in this volume a bit here and even more in the next volume, 1 Samuel 18 - 31.)

and Agag said,
"For sure he's turning from the bitterness of death!"

And Samuel, the guy named for EL, said,
"As women of your sword were made to miscarry and grieve,
for sure among women will your mother miscarry and grieve!"

And Samuel hacked Agag to pieces right before YAHWEH in the city of wheels, where the wind wheels and whirls around.

And Samuel went to The Heights.

And Saul climbed up to his house, Saul's Hill.

> (Note...it used to be called The Hill of Benjamin...but now Saul seems to have named it after himself or at least allowed others to name it after himself...while he is still alive. And apparently the whole hill is now his.)

And no longer did Samuel see Saul — until the day of his death.

You see, Samuel mourned and performed funeral rites for Saul —
(while Saul was still alive!),
and YAHWEH was sorry that It had made Saul the king over Ancient Israel.

Problems of the religious/divine life

Samuel's speech just a few paragraphs ago points out one significant problem of the 'divine life' or 'divination' — tasks of organized religion of any sort. No matter if one is the king, the pope, or perhaps even the most ardent follower, we often QSM. We try 'to make God/divine speak.'

We pray to urge God. We make our demands. We put our reasons and most brilliant logic behind it. We have Masses said. We sometimes even make donations or promises, we make sacrifices. We throw dice, cast lots, open a book and land our finger on a word to say "That's it! That's what God says!" We quote our favorite scriptures and hold onto them as if they are the truth. The truth of the matter is that God might speak - but not because we make God speak.

YAHWEH has Its own ways. While constant like the atmosphere around us, It often feels like It comes and goes like the wily wind, like a breath. But that's only our feeble human senses forgetting we're constantly swimming in It, alive in It, and one little wave we finally feel has us thinking we know something of the whole of It.

YAHWEH is dependable. YAHWEH needs no prayers. YAHWEH enlivens all for as long as any creature will allow, gives Itself freely to anyone on the planet. Feel the atmosphere constantly around and within you and you too can know ecstasy — possible in any and every moment — but such ecstasy cannot be controlled. Sitting and feeling the atmosphere — YAHWEH — inside and outside of you is far different from having a prayer service with some ritual led by someone with their specially chosen words and actions in hopes of conjuring the divine, of 'divining the future through some special means'/QSM.

QSM is the opposite of ecstasy. QSM is the opposite of taking off one's clothes (GLH) and waiting for YAHWEH to do the same, waiting for one's own senses to wake up and realize YAHWEH's always available, always revealing.

QSM...I've translated it above as 'divining-the-future — of trying to make God/divine speak by throwing dice or reading from magical scrolls/books.' Most Bibles translate QSM as 'divination.' Just about every concordance associates QSM with 'casting lots' or 'throwing dice.' *Strong's Exhaustive Concordance* also notes that QSM could also have to do with 'magical scrolls.'

What?!

Well, in a culture where 95% of people do not read or write, reading seems like magic. And having the ability to read and interpret a scroll with all those weird lines and marks would seem like magic to any person without that skill.

Who read in the ancient world, in the locales of this 1 Samuel saga? Priests...the Levites. Royal-bureaucrats...the Deuteronomists. Indeed, both of these groups wrote and assembled the Torah and, later, the Hebrew Bible. Both of these groups read that Torah out loud as if God had dictated its words to them directly, or through their proxy: Moses.

Such readings would have seemed magical and divinely inspired to any non-reader — unless one knew of something more powerful: YAHWEH and the ecstasy possible without effort. And that's what the ecstatic-prophets remind. How? Just sit there — come to know the way YAHWEH enlivens all without effort and without any scrolls or dice or Magic-8-Ball or prayer services or whatever.

Can't sit still long enough? All your attention flying in every direction? Feeling the impulse of violent rage? How could one possibly stop...?

Maybe through a clever word or stylish phrase or wild parable that stops you and me in our tracks — these words spoken in the moment but not read — these words that break us free from the deadly-trance of hum-drum-life and free from the deadly-trance of hierarchical-thinking and into 'what is'...YAHWEH. Babies and toddlers know ecstasy so easily; adults often struggle...especially rich ones who have plenty to protect and plenty to distract and entertain oneself...instead of the wind alone. "It is easier for a camel to squeeze through a needle's eye, than for a wealthy person to get into God's domain." (Gospel of Matthew 19, *The Complete Gospels*, 1994.). That would've stopped anyone in their tracks in Jesus' world — and still could today if it were refreshed, said differently than our usual ways of translating it.

Priests and royalists at some point realized that it would be to their advantage to train others in reading and writing — to let people into their skill-set. One more thing through which they could gain people's allegiance — and money. Tutor-mentor-relationships and monasteries and colleges and universities were created by priests and royalists of many traditions. They did the good work of growing literacy throughout the world. Eventually pre-schools and elementary and middle and high schools leading up to these colleges became commonplace. You and I have benefitted from literacy — we can read this page together and write back and forth to each other and share some sense of meaning, especially as the conversation continues, as we try to hash out a shared language with each other.

While literacy might have grown human potential, while humanity might have upgraded to such exceedingly complex things as traveling so easily across oceans and from continent to continent safely and dependably in just a few hours on a plane, through an airline ticket that could be reserved through a device that sent a message through the atmosphere that a mainframe computer system could be programmed somehow to catch and interpret it...it's not the same as knowing ecstasy.

Ecstasy cannot be taught. At these universities. At the reading of words from any scroll or book or computer. At memorizing anything from a scroll or saying and spitting it out.

To do so, you would be rejecting YAHWEH's style —

    in the moment

       of whatever the moment inspires and offers

         within one's own skin...

even quoting from this text misses the mark (!). Instead, be like our characters Hannah and Samuel and the random ELOHIM's-people who arrive and belt out some rap or style inspired by the moment, to meet the moment, and to draw us into remembering YAHWEH's constant, enlivening, wily-wind touch.

The text of 1 & 2 Samuel likely began as oral tales — and told with an edge to make the written and read-out-loud-as-a-magical-text Torah look foolish. Similar words are used far differently. GLH/'stripping naked' is used way differently in Leviticus than in 1 Samuel. As we have seen, the Samuel-saga repeatedly pokes fun at the Moses-saga — even and especially without mentioning Moses.

Now that 1 & 2 Samuel is a written text in the Bible, it would be easy for us to want to follow it and even its version of YAHWEH, the 'character' YAHWEH with Its usually snarky, humorous voice. But that misses the point entirely. Follow the wind alone, 1 & 2 Samuel seems to be advocating. Avoid QSM, avoid 'divine life,' avoid attempts to conjure the divine...with your whole heart and soul...follow the real, live YAHWEH...something a text like 1 & 2 Samuel can point to... but never contain....

chapter 16

And YAHWEH said to Samuel,
"How much longer are you going to mourn and perform funeral rites for Saul?
I have — I! — rejected him as king over Ancient Israel!
Fill your horn with oil and go —
I'm sending you to Jesse-There-He-Is
of the House of Feast-or-Fight —
because I see among his children — for me — a king!"

And Samuel said,
"Eek — how can I go —
Saul hears of it — he'll destroy me!"

And YAHWEH said,
"A young female cow —
take it in your hand/phallic-control —
and say,
'To butcher and burn it up to YAHWEH —
that's why I've (fuck) come!'
And call out for Jesse-There-He-Is to come to the butchering-and-burning event
and I'll make known to you in every way what you will do —
you'll smear with oil and make *messiah* for me —
whichever one I say to you!"

And Samuel did what YAHWEH had styled out,
and he (fuck) went to the House of Feast-or-Fight.

The elder-citizens of the city — (in any ancient city, the elders watched the gate because they knew everyone familiar by face, they knew whom to let in and whom not) — they shuddered in fear to announce him.

And one said,
"In peace — is that why you're (fuck) coming?"

And he said,
"In peace — to butcher and burn for YAHWEH — that's why
I've (fuck) come.
Make yourselves <u>extraordinary</u> and (fuck) come with me to
the butchering-and-burning event."

And he made <u>extraordinary</u> Jesse-There-He-Is and his sons,
and he called them to the butchering-and-burning event.

(Interesting this 'making someone extraordinary, consecrating
someone or something'/QDSH again. What exactly would
someone have to do to make oneself extraordinary? Bathe
oneself? Put on clean clothes? Say some special prayers? What's
super strange is that Samuel tells the elders at the gate to QDSH
themselves, and then Samuel QDSHes Jesse-There-He-Is and
his sons. If indeed QDSH has to do with purity/bathing and
purity/clean clothes and purity/special-prayers, then the elders
are told to do this themselves but Samuel does it to and for Jesse
and his sons. And we'll soon learn what these sons look like.

And to support this — ahem — strange notion, the types of
verb-stems lean that way. The elders are to QDSH themselves,
hitpael, reflexively. Samuel QDSHes Jesse and sons, *piel*,
intensively or repeatedly. Ahem.

And ancient audiences would hear it and catch it, this stylish
move in the story. Again, I suspect the band of X is poking
fun at the priestly notion of QDSH again through the action
of this not-really-a-real-Levite-priest who is Samuel, the guy
who was raised and reared by Eli-Climb-Up, a Levite...but
Samuel was forced to leave that whole priestly training behind
— after YAHWEH called Samuel to a new way of being priest
when Eli's son's took the ark into battle and lost it and died
and the sad news killed Eli-Climb-Up too.

All of this happening here in the House of LCHM...'feast or fight?')

And so it was —
they (fuck) came,
and he saw My-EL-is-Patriarchy, he said,
"For sure —
he is YAHWEH's <u>mate/front</u>, Its oil-smeared *messiah*!"

And YAHWEH said to Samuel,
"Don't stare at his looks
or at his standing up so <u>high-or-haughty</u> —
I have rejected him!
You see, it's not as a <u>mud-made-human-creature-like-Adam</u> sees
because a <u>mud-made-human-creature-like-Adam</u> sees with his eyes,
and YAHWEH sees with the heart!"

And Jesse-There-He-Is called for Patriarchy-Volunteers-for-War, and he made him pass by Samuel and he said,
"Even with this one...YAHWEH has not chosen!"

And Jesse-There-He-Is made Stunning pass by,
"Even with this one...YAHWEH has not chosen!"

And Jesse-There-He-Is made seven of his children pass on by right there in front of Samuel, and Samuel said to Jesse-There-He-Is,
"YAHWEH hasn't chosen any of these!"

And Samuel said to Jesse-There-He-Is,
"Is this the end of the boys/slaves?"

And he said,
"The only one remaining is the youngest —
he's over there shepherding the sheep and goats."

(There is a dismissiveness to Jesse-There-He-Is' tone for sure...
because this youngest son hasn't even graduated to the bigger
animals — cows — yet.

YAHWEH rejects all these patriotically and patriarchally
named sons and even one who is 'Stunning'...YAHWEH will
choose the guy — the youngest! — with a sweet little name,
one ready to be paraded in front of Samuel.)

And Samuel said to Jesse-There-He-Is,
"Send for him!
Fetch him!
Because we won't circle up (to eat)
until he (fuck) comes here!"

And he sent for him,
and he was made to (fuck) enter —
and he was <u>mud-made-red-in-the-face-like-Adam</u>
with beautiful eyes
and good-looking!

And YAHWEH said,
"Stand yourself up tall!
Smear him with oil as my *messiah*! He's the one!"

(The character-YAHWEH says that It sees into the heart,
not like an AHDAM/'mud-red-human-creature.' And this
youngest who is good-looking was AHDMONY/'mud-red,
ruddy, rosy.' AHDM/Adam in the Eden story is the one
YAHWEH loves and about whom It becomes jealous when
Woman CHBAHs the mud-creature/Adam after they eat
from the Sexy-Knowing-Tree together. In the Eden Story,
YAHWEH had created Woman to be a NGD/'mate, front,
talker, leader' for AHDM/'mud-creature.' And here in 1 Samuel,
YAHWEH again falls for one who is AHDMONY and bright-
eyed and good-looking and Samuel will smear this boy/slave

with oil and make this youngest son the NGD/'mate, front' of YAHWEH, YAHWEH's *messiah*. The band of YAH's stories and the band of X's stories continue to dance with each other....)

And Samuel took the horn of oil
and smeared it on him as *messiah*
in the middle of his brothers —
and YAHWEH's wind rushed upon him and pushed him
forward and prospered him — upon David —
from that day —
and kept climbing up! —
David...'the one who boils over with affection, with love'!

And Samuel stood himself up tall and went to The Heights.

And as for YAHWEH's wind...it was <u>turning away</u> from Saul
— <u>beheading</u> him —
a bad wind from YAHWEH was terrifying him.

(Wind and life into David, wind and life leaking from Saul... though that's been happening for awhile now. Note the 'turning away, beheading'/SUR is the same verb Samuel used in his first big speech after the ark disappeared, that first big speech decades later when he tells Ancient Israel to SUR their gods and goddesses and stay in relationship with what gives life — YAHWEH alone, the wind alone. And to SUR those gods and goddesses made sense to an ancient hearer because these divinities had heads, head-heads and penis-heads. Recall that Saul had erected a YD/'penis-statue' to himself... and now a bad air comes to him....)

And Saul's slaves said to him,
"Please listen here,
ELOHIM's wind — a bad one — is terrifying you!
Please say to our boss' slaves — all of us here in front of you —

to seek out a man/someone who knows in all ways how to strum the strings —
on a twangy-harp —
and so when it's upon you — the bad wind of ELOHIM (the One God? or the region's divinities he's been worshipping with his penis-statue?) —
he'll strum the strings —
with his hand/penis/phallic-control — and it'll be good for you!"

And Saul said to his slave,
"Please look around for me — a man/someone — a good one — to strum the strings —
and (fuck) make them come to me!"

And one of the slave/boys responded and said,
"Listen here — I've seen Jesse-There-He-Is' son
from the House of Feast-or-Fight —
he knows (everything, even sexually) about strumming the strings
and is a strong guy,
someone who can bear it,
and a fighting man,
and he perceives style
and a man with a nice figure —
and YAHWEH is with him."

And Saul, the one named Asked-For, sent message-runners to Jesse-There-He-Is and said:
"Send me David, your son who is out with the lambs and goats!"

(Such a man just described so positively is out with the lambs and goats?!!! Ancient audiences would be guffawing at this. That's a job for youngsters or for slaves, at least with any family of means. But at least this guy has a nice figure...and can 'strum the strings'/NGN to soothe the king when the king has his fits....)

And Jesse-There-He-Is fetched a donkey (to load it with) bread/food/a feast and a skin-bag full of wine and one young female goat. And he sent everything off in his son David's hand/penis/phallic-control to Saul. (Recall the meaning of David's name...'the one who boils over with affection'....)

And David (fuck) went to Saul —
and he took his stand in front of him.

And he loved him — very much so.

And he became his gear-lifter.

(Yes, you are reading it right...it's all right there in the Hebrew text. And maybe even more so, with the wildly clever puns that arise in the ancient Hebrew language.

And David stands? Before the king! David does not bow or kneel? And not only that...David 'takes a stand'/AYMD...which we'll soon see is the kind of standing an army does against its opponent.

Could this indeed be poking fun at the military arrangement where an older seasoned warrior adopts a younger rookie to train in all ways of life, including love and battle, as Dr. Jennings surmises in *Jacob's Wound*? The younger David stands, the older Saul...well, we're not yet sure what position he assumes when he sees David.

And we'll have to see just how much fighting Saul actually does in battle as the king....)

And Saul sent (a messenger) to Jesse-There-He-Is, saying:
"If you please, David is taking his stand in front of me,
you see, charm-and-grace-to-want-to-kneel-down-to-this-inferior has been found in my eyes!"

And so it was —
whenever ELOHIM's wind was upon Saul,
David would take the twangy-harp and <u>strum the strings with
his hand/penis</u>
and the <u>wind/relief</u> would be with him — and good for him —
and it would turn away from him — be beheaded — the bad
<u>wind</u> would.

(Yes...it's all right there in the Hebrew text, friends. Probably
the most surprising thing is the king addresses one of his
subjects with 'if you please'/NAH. As for the king having the
ability to be relieved by the NGN/'string-strumming' hand/
penis of one of his boys, such is the system of monarchy
where the king can demand whatever the king wants to get
himself through the day and the night. A little wind here, a
little relief there. And by the way, the word for 'wind'/RUCH
has the same consonants as the word for 'relief'/RVCH and
likely sounded similar to ancient ears. Good for Saul, indeed!)

chapter 17

And the Dust-Rolling-Philistines were gathering up their
armies to fight,
and they gathered at the place known for being hedged in, a
place that belonged to Judah, the tribe known for throwing up
their hands/penises in praise.

And they <u>encamped</u> between the place known for being
hedged in and another place in Ancient Israel known for being
fenced in, near the blood-border.

And as for Saul and every man/person of Ancient Israel...they
gathered themselves together and <u>encamped</u> in the valley
with the big drunk tree.

(You might notice a theme lately for where Saul can be found when war-time calls? Always under the shade of a tree and avoiding battle. Like David will become in this saga, Saul is a *'messiah'*/MSHYCH/'special oil-smeared leader' — a military title worth more than just any old 'general/commander'. Once luxuriating under the lush pomegranate tree while his men fought — and while his son Jonathan and gear-lifter took on the entire Dust-Rolling-Philistine army only with their dicks-and-balls — now Saul directs his military from under the 'big drunk tree'/AHLH. AHLH is a doubly or triply interesting word, as it could mean 'strong' or 'like a ram' or 'oak tree' from which strong/intoxicating drink was made in the ancient world.

'encamped'/CHNH hearkens back to CHN/'charm-and-grace-a-superior-feels-to-want-to-kneel-down-to-an-inferior'... there are plenty of other words the band of X could have used instead but they chose these two and put them so close together in their saga, all these people with hierarchical imaginations and their bending down and for whom and for what....)

And they arranged themselves in rows for fighting to call out the Dust-Rolling-Philistines.

And as for the Dust-Rollers...they took their stand on this side of a mountain, and Ancient Israel took their stand on the other side of a mountain — a gorge between them.

One of the champion-warriors went out — the kind of guy who could stand in the midst of a battle between two armies — from the Dust-Rollers' army-camps —

Stripper was his name...Goliath...

(a name from our old verb-friend GLH/'to strip naked as one would do to a slave/exile'...but in his case, more likely the kind of stripping that happens when one nation conquers another and then forces exiles or slaves to strip themselves naked to disarm them, to humiliate them, to dehumanize them, and to steal from them...or possibly after the battle on the bloody battlefield where the dead could be stripped of their valuable armor or weapons, if they had any...)

Stripper-Goliath was from one of the major Dust-Roller cities with the wine-press and the drunken concerts.

He was nine feet tall — and then some —

and a copper helmet on his head and scaly, jointed body-armor — this is what he wore — the body-armor weighed 5,000 copper coins —

and he had copper shin-pieces on his legs, and a copper javelin between his shoulders —

and the length of his spear was heavy like a weaver's beam or a yoke — the metal-tip of his spear alone weighed 600 coins of iron —

and a shield-lifter went in front of him —

and he took his stand and called out to the battle-lines of Ancient Israel, the nation taking its name from the hero who wrestled EL and got groped and penetrated and still won.

And he said to them,
"Why have you come out to arrange yourself in battle-lines to fight?
Am I not a Dust-Rolling-Philistine?
Aren't you all slaves of Saul?
Choose one man/person— fresh meat — for yourselves to come down to me —
if he's able to fight with me and kill me,

we'll be your slaves —
but if I'm able to prevail against him and kill him,
you'll all be our slaves —
and will you ever slave away for us!"

(Note the silence, no response from Ancient Israel or King
Saul. The first word out of Stripper-Goliath's mouth is
interesting: BRH, usually translated as 'choose' but it actually
almost always mean 'eat, select something to eat' so that's why
I've added 'fresh meat' to bring that whole sense of 'eating'
forward. His speech is a direct insult to the armies, especially
his noting that the armies of Ancient Israel are slaves to their
king, to Saul. And where is he? Where is King Saul? Stripper-
Goliath has issued a challenge to one man/person — and if
no one else steps up, guess who should step up in a culture of
honor like theirs? The king, the *messiah*. But so far Saul has
said nothing. No one has. So Stripper-Goliath continues....)

And the Dust-Roller said,
"I am the one <u>taunting</u> Ancient Israel's armies today <u>as if I
were removing the clothes of a slave without their permission,
to inspect their nakedness before I buy them and do whatever
I want with them</u> —
give me a man/person —
let's fight together!"

And Saul and all of Ancient Israel heard these styles of the
Dust-Roller, and they were shattered down on the ground and
afraid, very much so.

(In Stripper-Goliath's challenge — which can't be revoked
in an honor-based culture like theirs — it looks as if all of
Ancient Israel will become slaves if they don't find anyone
to step up to the challenge. And even if they do, it looks as if
it will be certain death for that person who goes up against a

warrior like Stripper-Goliath — and then the rest will become slaves to him and the Dust-Rollers. They all have great reason to panic and fall to the ground.

CHRP/'taunt, as if to remove the clothes of a slave without their permission, to inspect their nakedness before buying them and do whatever one wants with them'...well that should get Ancient Israel riled up. But it doesn't. The style only terrifies them all the more, it seems.)

And David was a son of a man from the fruitful place,
this guy from Bethlehem-House-of-Feast-or-Fight in Judah, the tribe known for throwing up their hands/penises in praise —
the man's name was Jesse-There-He-Is,
he had eight sons.

And he lived during the days of Saul — he was old and (fuck) going the way of all men/people (which is to say he would soon die).

And three of Jesse-There-He-Is' sons had gone — the oldest (three) followed Saul into the fighting.

(Recall 'Bethlehem' actually means 'House of Feast-or-Fight'/ BYT LCHM...where one might have to fight to eat. Jesse's sons follow Saul into the MLCHMH/'fighting, battle.' And surely the band of X is weaving these connections into their fiction on purpose. They could have chosen an entirely different town for Jesse to hail from...but they didn't. And note how many times LCHM — 'food' or 'fighting' — has been and soon will be associated with Jesse's son David.)

And the names of the three sons (of Jesse-There-He-Is) who went into battle were
  My-EL-is-Patriarchy, the first-born,

and the second, Patriarchy-Volunteers-for-War,
and the third, Stunning.

And David — he was the youngest.

And the three oldest followed after Saul.

(Note: You might be wondering how/why we are getting this reintroduction to David, as if we hadn't heard about him before. Some biblical scholars are sure that there are multiple versions of the story of how David arrived on the scene, and that could very well be. Homer's epics could have been massaged for each moment and each community too in their oral tellings and retellings. It's a common storytelling device to get at meaning in the moment, the way of a good rhetorician meeting their audience in the moment with their message. Perhaps that's what's happening here with two or more generations of the band of X simply including both stories about David's arrival.

Or...maybe a bit of a stretch...perhaps it is indeed one undisturbed tale. What if the band of X is doing something important here in giving us details again but differently. X sometimes does this — circles back, reminds us of a few earlier details, playfully massages them — to watch how they influence the present moment of his saga. Or to make an important point..."the recursive nature of good fiction," as my friend calls it.

Judging by the two older brothers' names, there's good reason they went into battle and followed along with Saul...those with hierarchically-minded names followed the hierarchical-assumptions by following the hierarch/king into battle....even though the hierarch usually made underlings run in front of him — if he was even anywhere near the battle in the first place. All the while, Saul has a fondness for sitting under the shady trees during battle. And even the third son of Jesse-There-He-Is — note the name — Stunning — he went into battle too. The fact that David — the one who boils over with affection —

is named as the youngest and that there are three more older brothers than himself who hadn't been sent into war gives us some clues to David's young age. His soon-to-be-revealed-again 'occupation' should also tip us off to his age as well.)

And David had left and returned <u>from being on top of</u> Saul — to shepherd his father's lambs and goats at the House of Feast-or-Fight.

And the Dust-Roller had been getting closer and closer every morning and evening and <u>had stationed himself</u> there for 40 days, for what seemed like forever.

(It is a rather strange way of putting it — that David had returned from being MAYL/'upon, above, over' Saul — but that usage does align with the earlier story of David 'taking his stand'/AYMD with the King...the role-reversal of the boy standing and the King 'bending down, bending over'/CHN for him. Contrast that with the way Stripper-Goliath stands here...the military-hero YTSB/'stations himself.' But that's not what David does in front of Saul in our saga.)

And Jesse-There-He-Is said to his son David,
"Please take your brothers a big helping of this toasted-ready-to-eat grain,
and these ten loaves of <u>bread</u> —
and run toward the army-camp — to your brothers —
and ten slices of this cheese — (fuck) bring these to the official in charge of their thousand, their battalion —
and your brothers — <u>cross paths with them, visit them,</u>
see if they are well and healthy and completely okay —
and fetch me something that shows they are okay!"

And as for Saul and they (the brothers) and every man/person of Ancient Israel...they were in the valley with the big drunk tree <u>fighting</u> with the Dust-Rollers.

And David, the one who boils over with love, arose early in the morning and <u>pushed off</u> the lambs and goats onto a guard and <u>lifted</u> — carried — everything and went just as Jesse-There-He-Is had shouted out for him to do.

And he (fuck) entered the back-trench of the camp — the safest way to enter the battlefield — and the strength of the army was going out to the battle-line and shouting the war-cry in the fight.

(Move LCHM/'feast <u>or</u> fighting' fun. Apparently no one had stepped up to fight Stripper-Goliath one-on-one as his honor-challenge dictated, so Saul must have decided dishonorably to send his warriors into battle. As king and lead-commander, if no one stepped up to accept the challenge to fight Stripper-Goliath, Saul should have stepped up himself. But he didn't.... he just didn't.

And PQD/'visit' & NSAH/'lift' too. Style.

And as for David, the young man who 'boils over with love and affection'/DOD...he seems pretty good at 'pushing off'/ NTSH things on others to do what he wants...he does it once with the lambs and goats and soon will do it again...a very deliberate verb-choice by the band of X to give us a sense about this David. Sure, we can say his father is ordering him to do so, but listen in on what his brother will soon have to say about it.)

And Ancient Israel and the Dust-Rolling-Philistines had drawn up in their battle-lines facing each other, one battle-line calling out the other battle-line.

And David <u>pushed off</u> the gear (his father's gifts) from upon himself into the hand/phallic-control of the guard of the gear, and ran toward the battle-line, and (fuck) went and <u>asked</u> about his brothers, about their health and if they were okay,

and as he was styling it out with them — listen up here! —

the man of champion-warriors — the kind of guy who could stand in the midst of a battle — was climbing up —

Stripper-Goliath

the Dust-Roller

— that was his name! —

from one of the major Dust-Roller cities with the wine-press and the drunken concerts

from among the Dust-Roller battle-lines,

and he was styling out these styles —

and David heard.

And as for every man/person of Ancient Israel...when they <u>saw</u> the man, they fled from his face — they were <u>afraid</u> — very much so!

(Certainly indications here of another 'seam' in the story... and more pun-play...RAHH/'seeing' and YRAH/'fearing, to be afraid.' These two words share very similar conjugations and when spoken aloud often sound very much the same which would make any hearer have to understand the context to make sure of the speaker's meaning. Here we have both in the same sentence, and in Stripper-Goliath's case, seeing is truly fearing!)

And one man/person from Ancient Israel said,
"Have you seen the man who's climbed up to taunt Ancient
Israel, as if to remove our clothes without our permission, to
inspect our nakedness before buying us as slaves and doing
whatever he wants with us—
this guy — that's why he's climbed up —
and so it will be that the man/person who strikes him down
in death, the king will enrich ten times over — great riches —
and as for his daughter...he'll give her to him —
and as for his father's house/family...he'll make exempt from
slavery&taxes in Ancient Israel!"

And David said to the men/people taking their standing there
with him,
"What'll be done for the man/person who strikes down this
Dust-Roller in death and beheads—deflects the taunt from
upon Ancient Israel, the taunt as if he's removing our clothes
without our permission and inspecting our nakedness before
buying us as slaves and doing whatever he wants with us —
who is this uncut-dicked Dust-Roller?!! —
that he would taunt the battle-lines of the living ELOHIM/
divine!?!"

And the people answered him in this style, saying,
"Yes!!! So shall it be done for the man/person who strikes him
down dead!"

(David appears to be trying to excite — even egg on — the
crowd. Why? Maybe so he could see a real spectacle, and
in his young adolescent ways forgetting that such a spectacle
would have had grave consequences for his brothers and his
whole nation.

And maybe the crowd is egging David on too with some hope
of getting out of this mess alive — hoping for enslavement
to the Philistines at the very worst if David/someone steps
up and at least fights Stripper-Goliath and loses his life for

the good of the rest of the nation. Because surely no one can defeat such a seasoned giant of a warrior like Stripper-Goliath....)

And his older brother My-EL-is-Patriarchy heard what he'd styled out to the men/people, and got all red-in-the-face angry — My-EL-is-Patriarchy did —
at (his little brother) David, the one who boils over with affection and love,
and he said,
"What's this?!
You came down here —
and on whom'd you push those few lambs and goats in the wilderness
(those small animals you can barely handle yourself)?!?
I know the arrogant pride that seethes from you and the bad in your heart!
To see the fighting — that's why you've come down!"

And David, the one who boils over with affection, said,
"What've I done now?!
Did I not style this out?!"

And he turned away from being near to him and toward another and said the same styling-out as earlier. And the people returned the style just like the style of the first group.

And the styles David had been styling out were heard and reported in the presence of Saul, and he fetched him.

And David said to Saul,
"Don't let the heart of all humanity fall upon itself!
Your slave — that's me! — is going to fight with this Dust-Roller!"

And Saul said to David,
"You can't go at this Dust-Roller — to fight with him —
you're a boy/slave —

and he's a man of war — and been one since he was a boy/slave!"

And David said to Saul,
"A shepherd!
That's what your slave is — what I am!
For my father!
With the lambs and goats — the small animals!
And a lion (fuck) came — and with a bear too! —
and <u>lifted</u> — took — a young lamb from the flock —
so I went after it —
and struck it down —
and snatched it from its mouth —
and it stood up tall against me so I firmed up inside myself
even with its old age'd beard
and struck it down and killed it —
both the lion and the bear — your slave struck them both
down —
and so it will be for that uncut-dicked Dust-Roller —
just like it will be for the rest of them —
because he taunted the armies of the living ELOHIM/divine
as if he were removing our clothes without our permission
and inspecting our nakedness before buying us as slaves and
doing whatever he wants with us stripped down and examined
like his slaves!"

(Note...no response from Saul.)

And David said,
"It was YAHWEH who snatched me away
from the hand/phallic-control of the lion
and from the hand/phallic-control of the bear —
It'll snatch me away from the hand/phallic-control of this
Dust-Roller!"

And Saul said to David,
"Go! May <u>YAHWEH be</u> with you!"

(Well we finally get a word out of Saul's clamped-shut mouth
— and surprising and slightly stylish words at that: YHVH
YHYH/'YAHWEH be'...the first time Saul has said those words
with any sense of faith or reverence in awhile. Recall that
earlier when talking with Samuel, Saul referred to YAHWEH
as Samuel's divinity, not his own.

Now...this was a <u>huge</u> risk...if David or anyone lost to Stripper-
Goliath, it would be slavery for all — though maybe not for
Saul — maybe a royal deal could be made for him and his
family as Saul offered to Agag when Saul captured Agag who
was pleasurably ambling alongside Saul until Samuel struck
him down dead. In a hierarchical system, it often pays to be at
the top...at least until someone not buying into the hierarchy
emerges and calls out the system, as the prophets/ecstatics tend
to do, even the rather violent way that Samuel did with Agag.)

And Saul clothed David in the full-measure of his own clothes
and put a copper helmet on his head
and clothed him in armor.

(Note: Saul clothes David in his royal clothes and gear...which
is ridiculous in a number of ways including Saul's own height...
instead of Saul honorably going out to fight the Stripper-
Goliath himself. We might wonder what Saul is standing
there wearing...some of David's clothes? or Saul stands there
nearly naked in his belt/underwear? The upcoming Chapter
18 shares what Jonathan wears and could be used as a reference
for what the king might wear. Note too the various ways 'lift'/
NSAH has been used and will be used....)

And David strapped on a sword to his clothes,
and made an effort to walk —
you see, he'd never tried them before!

And David said to Saul,
"I can't walk in these —
I've never tried them before!"

And David took them off — beheaded them from himself.

> (Just like Samuel earlier in our saga advised the people to 'turn away from, behead'/SUR their ELOHIM/divinities — their gods and goddesses — SUR can also mean 'to take off (clothes)'.)

And he took his green-stick in his hand/phallic-control — (a fresh green branch he'd ordinarily use for shepherding the animals) — and chose for himself five smooth stones from the creek and put them in his shepherd's gear, which had within it a special pouch.

And his sling was in his hand/phallic-control.

And he stepped up closer to the Dust-Roller.

And the Dust-Roller walked, walked, walked forward getting closer to David — and the man/person who lifted the shield to his face.

And the Dust-Roller looked around and saw David and despised him —
after all, he was a boy/slave —
and mud-made-red-in-the-face-like-Adam —
and good-looking!

And the Dust-Roller said to David, the one who boils over with affection and love,
"A dog? Is that what I am?
That you would (fuck) come at me with green-sticks?!"

And the Dust-Roller cursed David by his own ELOHIM/
divinities.

(Note...no response from David. No response from anyone
on David's side either.)

And the Dust-Roller said to David,
"Go on, come at me!
I'll give your flesh to the birds of the sky
and to the beasts of the field!"

And David said to the Dust-Roller,
"You! You (fuck) come at me
with sword and with spear and with javelin —
but I — I (fuck) come at you in the name of YAHWEH!
The General-of-the-Big-Armies-who-Require-Service!
ELOHIM of the battle-lines of Ancient Israel —
whom you've taunted — as if to remove our clothes without
our permission, to inspect our nakedness before buying us as
slaves and doing whatever you want with us stripped down
and examined like we're your slaves —
today YAHWEH's going to shut you up in my hand/phallic-
control —
I'm going to strike you down dead —
and behead your head from you
and give the dead-body of the Dust-Roller's army-camp —
today, this day! —
to the birds of the sky
and to living things of the earth —
and all the earth will know — in every way possible —
that — yes! —
Ancient Israel has ELOHIM/divine —
and everyone assembled here will know that
it's not with sword and spear that YAHWEH rescues —
the fight is YAHWEH's,
and It will give you all into our hands/phallic-control!"

And so it was —
you see, the Dust-Roller stood himself up tall
and walked to get closer to call out David,
and David hurried and ran toward the battle-line to call out
the Dust-Roller,

and David stretched out his hand/phallic-control into his gear,

and took from it a stone,

and whipped it around sling-like —

and it struck the Dust-Roller!

in his forehead!

the stone sank into his forehead!

and he fell down on his face onto the ground!

And David had firmed up within himself — he'd grown strong
— over the Dust-Roller with a sling and with a stone!

And he'd struck down the Dust-Roller, and killed him!

And as for a sword — there wasn't one in David's hand/phallic-control!

And David ran and stood near the Dust-Roller,
and took his sword
and drew it from the sheath
and killed him
and with it cut off his head!

And the Dust-Rollers seeing their champion-warrior was
dead, they fled!

And the men/people of Ancient Israel & Judah — Israel being

the nation named for the guy who was raped by ELOHIM but climbed on top and won and Judah being the tribe known for throwing up their hands/penises in praise — they stood themselves up tall and shouted out the war-cry and chased after the Dust-Rollers as far as the entrance to the gorge and as far as the city-gates of the Dust-Roller city known for things pulled up by the roots, for childlessness.

And the pierced/fatally wounded of the Dust-Rollers fell along the road to the double-gates and even as far as the Dust-Roller city with the wine-press and their drunken concerts and even as far as the Dust-Roller city known for things pulled up by the roots, for childlessness.

And the children of Ancient Israel returned from their hot-pursuit of the Dust-Rollers. And they'd rifled through and stole from their army-camps.

And David would take the Dust-Roller's head and carry it to the city known for being The-Arrow-of-Peace (Jerusalem) and his gear he would put in his tent.

And when Saul saw David, the one who boils over with affection and love, going out to call out the Dust-Rollers, he said to Abner-Patriarchy's-Lamplight, general of the army, "Whose son is this boy/slave, Abner-Patriarchy's-Lamplight?"

And Abner-Patriarchy's-Lamplight said,
"Long live your breathing body, King, if I only knew!"

And the king said,
"You go ask around —
whose son is this —
the youngster!?"

(Saul, the one for whom the people 'asked'/SHAHL, now 'asks'/SHAHL about David. Notice that King Saul and his general don't go help chase down the Dust-Rollers — though their men/people and David do. And notice too the shift in Saul referring to David as boy/slave and now 'youngster, ripe-and-ready teenager'/AYLM...more on that to come.)

And when David had returned from striking down and killing the Dust-Roller, he took him — Abner-Patriarchy's-Lamplight did — and (fuck) brought him before Saul's face, and the head of the Dust-Roller was in his hand/phallic-control.

And Saul said to him,
"Whose son are you, boy/slave?"

And David said,
"Son of your slave Jesse-There-He-Is,
from the House of Feast-or-Fight!"

chapter 18

And it was just as he'd finished styling it out to Saul that the living, breathing body of Jonathan was <u>tied up</u> with the living, breathing body of David.

(Remember, Jonathan is King Saul's son. *Strong's Exhaustive Concordance* notes that QSHR/'tie up' can also mean 'form a conspiracy, be in love, be bound together.')

And Jonathan loved him
as much as his own living, breathing body.

And Saul took him that day and wouldn't give him back to return to his father's house.

And Jonathan and David cut a covenant (made a serious

promise to one another by walking in the blood between just-cut, valuable and now dead animals) — in his love for him as his own living, breathing body.

And Jonathan <u>stripped himself</u> of the valuable outer garment designating his rank that was on him — Jonathan stripped himself as if he had been invaded and conquered — and gave it to David —

and his clothing

and even his sword

and even his bow

and even his underwear, the belt that held his weaponry...

— to be continued —

(pausing here in this volume at 1 Samuel 18.4)

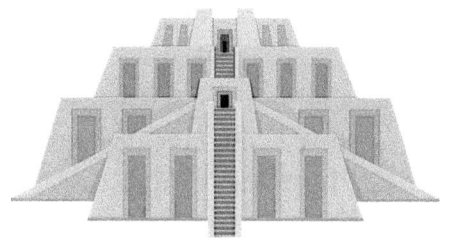

CHOOSE WELL!

After-Styles

Um, that last passage just after the virgin-boy David kills Stripper-Goliath?

Well, both the king and the king's son seem to be in love with this NAYR/'boy, slave' — the same David whom Saul accidentally calls an AYLM.

AYLM is used only twice in the Bible, and only in 1 Samuel: once out of Saul's lips in Chapter 17, once in Chapter 20 (in the next volume) out of Jonathan's mouth referring to the boy who fetches his arrows. The feminine version of AYLM is AYLMH, usually used to refer to a virgin-girl who has been shielded from public view and is now ready to be viewed as ready for marriage. Keep in mind that would have been when she's about 12 years old in the ancient world, or when menstruation begins, just after she's ready to begin to make babies for her husband's line. A ripe-and-ready teenager. Or almost teenager. The values of the ancient world are much different from today's values...though I marvel that some Christians want to return to the marriage-values of the ancient world.

Talking with his general, Saul calls David AYLM and demands to see the virgin-boy.

We could get hung up on why Saul wouldn't recognize David, his twangy-harpist who strums his strings to soothe King Saul's temper tantrums.

Either we have in our fictional-saga two versions of how David meets Saul — one as the twangy-harpist and one on the battlefield taking on Stripper-Goliath — or we have a King Saul who has so many boys at his disposal who soothe his every whim that he does not recognize David. In the harem or — ahem — the army of the king, just another of the choice young boys....

Both possibilities seem likely...that there are multiple versions for how Saul meets David and that David is just one of many of Saul's boys.

In any case, we have a love-triangle brewing with King Saul wanting this AYLM-David for himself and with Jonathan expressing his love for David — even going so far as making a covenant with David and cutting up animals and walking together in the blood between the chunks as they voice serious, irrefutable promises to one another. And then, perhaps to show how serious he is, Jonathan removes all his weaponry and clothes and hands it all over to young David. The verb choice is interesting here, and different from any kind of stripping we've had so far. Jonathan PSHTs his clothes and weaponry — he 'strips as if he had been invaded and conquered.' It's a hostile-word but Jonathan does this for young David willingly. In the next volume — specifically in 1 Samuel 23, 27, and 30 — David will PSHT the so-called enemies of Ancient Israel — David will raid these peoples and strip them of their wealth and kill them. But the only killing happening here with Jonathan PSHTing his clothes for David is being slain in the spirit of love, it seems. Goliath 'taunted'/ CHRP Ancient Israel...not a whole lot different from PSHT.

Earlier in our saga, YAHWEH was GLHing — 'stripping Itself naked as slaves or exiles are forced to do by an oppressor.' And YAHWEH did this for Its style-spitting ecstatics. Most translations have 'reveal' — but this is way more than sharing one's mind. GLH has to do with willingly removing your clothes for an oppressor, a move that keeps the revealer alive in the hierarchically-minded situation; PSHT is usually what happens to someone after they are dead, their stuff is taken by the oppressor. Jonathan offers all of those things all the way down to the belt that held his weaponry. Ahem.

The rest of 1 Samuel is a doozy. The king who 'fucks it up'/ TQAY does indeed get 'fucked'/TQAY — but not by 'the one who boils over with love and affection,' not by David. As the band of X seems to remind over and over again, anyone living in a monarchical or hierarchical system does get fucked — even the king.

Why so many 'fucks'?

Most Samuel scholars I've read shy away from the style of Ancient Hebrew in the text. Find me another translation of 1 & 2 Samuel that notes the plays on words, that notes all the potential *fucks* in the text — all the BOAHs and the TQAYs and even others. Maybe these scholars fear for their university jobs if they brought forward all the potential meanings for these Ancient Hebrew verbs; maybe they're just too bashful.

Only one scholar seems to have the courage to point out the military-pederasty that is prevalent in 1 & 2 Samuel — Ted Jennings in *Jacob's Wound*. Jennings even goes so far to wonder if military-pederasty began in Ancient Israel before the Greeks picked it up and ran an empire with it. The Samuel-saga — 1 & 2 Samuel — of course is fiction. But the band of X could be reaching back to a practice that actually was used in Ancient Israel within the military and the Jerusalem temple. Why? To throw it back into the faces of the Levitical priests and Deuteronomist royal-enablers who benefitted from the male-with-male action within the military (safety) and within the temple (payment from male-citizens for renting the 'holy prostitutes' in the temple). It's centuries later that the Levitical priests and Deuteronomists crafted their homosexual-hating laws, especially Leviticus 18 & 20.

One could wonder if the Levitical priests were forbidding

male-with-male love to try to put an end to something "males" liked but no longer needed when the army was outlawed after Assyria and then Babylon and then Persia took control of the region — these same priests, it seems, who used to allow male-prostitution in their own temple with the QDSHYM/'holy prostitutes' of 2 Kings 23. The ecstasy that comes with male-with-male love must have been quite — well — catchy during those times...if we are to trust that this 1 & 2 Samuel fiction has any factual merit to it at all, that this fiction has things in it that people would guffaw at because they know their truth. After all, in 1 & 2 Samuel and in 1 & 2 Kings, it seems that the king, the king's son, the priests, the military, and the prophets all condone and practice male-with-male love — even in the soon-to-be Jerusalem temple. For whatever reason centuries later, the Levitical priests outlaw male-with-male love. The Levitical priests outlaw a lot of things that reveal their flimsy power — even forbid saying "YAHWEH" out loud, another experience that reveals that you don't need a priest to have an ecstatic experience of YAHWEH. Say "YAHWEH" and life comes to you....

The many faces of love-boiling David in the Bible

It's easy to read the versions of the 'love-boiling' character David/DUD we have from the Psalms and from Chronicles and other lore onto what we have here in 1 & 2 Samuel. But all of that misses the very complex character we have in 1 & 2 Samuel, of David being King Saul's boy and Jonathan falling in love with David. Later in this Samuel-saga, David will be a foolish king, better loved by the people than Saul but still greedy and out for his own good and rarely the people's. King David will have one of his most faithful guards killed to cover over David's own royal-lust for the guard's wife — and all of this when David should have been out in the field with his 'choice young men' fighting alongside them. Instead, King David takes a nap and wakes to see his guard's wife bathing on the roof, has her entered into his palace in order to enter her and impregnate her. The only thing that makes the whole thing worse is considering why she must've imagined she was being summoned to the palace — to hear directly from the king/royal-court that her husband had been killed in battle. And then all of a sudden the king is on top of her and will soon have her husband killed to cover up their 'affair.' That's the version in 2 Samuel. You can see why the priests will remove all that in their Chronicles, right?

In terms of plot alone, King Saul and eventually King David and even King Solomon in 1 & 2 Samuel and 1 Kings are made to look bad, foolish.

The priests in 1 & 2 Samuel do not fare any better — they are made to look like fools too.

Who is not on the chopping block in the band of X's saga? Well, the prophets of course. The NBYAHYM. The ecstatics. The misfits often up on the mountains, in the faraway places, those who care nothing for kings or priests or arks or temples... the ecstatics who know the power of the wind, who know YAHWEH, the storm divinity, the king of wind and rain, and if ruler of those two precious things, then of all life for anyone who dwells on Earth.

The style of writing we have in 1 & 2 Samuel bears the hallmarks of poem-crafters like the Isaiahs and like Jeremiah... exceedingly clever, often funny, sometimes in the most dire circumstances. Jesus' parables are similar in style — and for those who don't know, a parable is a story with a wild, surprising twist. Like Jesus' parables, the band of YAH's stories in Genesis are similar too to what we have in 1 & 2 Samuel in terms of style and sexy plots and wild twists and turns.

But the priests' laws and stories in the Torah and in Chronicles are completely different from the poems of the Isaiahs and Jeremiah and from the stories of the bands of X and YAH and the parables of Jesus. There's rarely a good pun in priestly material. The priestly-composed Chronicles removes all the sex, all the puns, and all the foolishness of David and Solomon — they often look like wise kings from the perspective of the Chronicler-priests. And as I've noted in *A Wildly Sensual YAHWEH: volume 0 of The Naked Path of Prophet series*, the priests who assembled and crafted the Torah even tried to tamp down the bawdiness of the band of YAH's stories in the book we call Genesis through editing and explaining and adding commentary and other material to break the band of YAH's ecstatic flow. The band of YAH can tell a story! So can the band of X! Especially if we look carefully at the Ancient Hebrew texts of Genesis and 1 & 2 Samuel, and portions of 1 & 2 Kings.

Why even include the bands of YAH & X's stories in the Torah/Bible if the priests found them so controversial? Well, those bawdy, enlightening, imagination-altering stories might have been so popular that the Levitical priests realized they were sunk without them. And the best way to take control of and tamp down a great oral tale is to write it down with a whole bunch of commentary interspersed and other tales that break the flow of a story that had a commanding and engaging style to it. And that's precisely what the Levitical priests did in Genesis. And the Deuteronomist royalist political party took the Levitical priests' document — Genesis, Exodus, and Leviticus — and brushed it up a bit and added their own stuff — especially Deuteronomy, the Deuteronomistic ever-growing version of law — crafted Numbers and all of that became the Torah, the first five books of the Bible. And scholars today debate if it was originally just five books — perhaps the Book of Joshua was included, a sixth book of the Torah. Possibly a seventh with the the Book of Judges too.

But the Deuteronomists very clearly did not craft 1 & 2 Samuel — at least not much of it besides that interpolations of 1 Samuel 12 and of the last few chapters of 2 Samuel. The Samuel-saga without those interpolations has a very different style, both in Hebrew-sound and in plot, from Deuteronomy.

But the Deuteronomists did eventually include 1 & 2 Samuel in their every growing Bible, likely long after their king-loving, royal-propping political party lost power after the Babylonian Exile, long after they got hired by the Babylonians and later by the Persians for their governing experience, long after some of them returned to Israel/Judah to begin again, albeit under the thumbs of the Persians who let them leave Babylon for Jerusalem likely to be Persian-administrators in their ancestral homeland.

Why did the band of X craft this Samuel-saga and then some?

If I had to guess, the band of X found the Torah disgusting — for what the Levitical priests had done to the band of YAH's tales, for the women-hating and queer-hating nature of the Levitical and Deuteronomistic laws, for the ridiculousness of holiness-infused ritual and law as a system of governance, and for the vision of God that the Levitical priests and Deuteronomists presented.

So this band of storycrafters I've named X — again, after the ecstatics, say it out loud — crafted a totally hilarious fiction about the roots of the priests' temple and the roots of the king's palace. Today we call this fiction 1 & 2 Samuel and 1 & 2 Kings...though the Deuteronomists interspersed their own material throughout, especially in 1 & 2 Kings where the Deuteronomists do seem to include archaeologically often-verified 'histories' of the actual kings including their most beloved King Josiah.

But why would the Deuteronomists include the band of X's tales — 1 & 2 Samuel and X's portions of 1 & 2 Kings — in their ever-growing Bible when X's tales lampoon much that would become the Hebrew Bible? As the Levitical priests realized with the band of YAH's tales in Genesis, maybe the Deuteronomists realized they didn't have much without them — that these X-tales and YAH-tales were so popular that without them, their Bible was flimsy. Maybe the later-generation Deuteronomists had gotten fed up with the kings and priests too and found the band of X tales lampooning the kings and priests refreshing.

Thankfully the Deuteronomists included 1 & 2 Samuel in their Bible, that we still have this saga today. First and Second Samuel are a warning, remember. I suspect if we listen to 1 & 2 Samuel carefully today, it could help sort through and dispel these strong impulses that are arising in us 21st century humans for strong leaders and kings, the ever-strong allures for fascism and control. The ecstatic imagination frees — and often with humor that is quite catchy and disarming.

Could it be that the very roots of the entire Jewish-Christian-Muslim traditions are in the ecstatic imagination...even though all three of these religions' authorities continue to tamp down that ecstatic-spirit so much, as the Levitical priests did with the band of YAH's stories, as the Deuteronomists did with the band of X's stories, as the Levitical priests did by crafting Chronicles to over-ride 1 & 2 Samuel and 1 & 2 Kings, and as today's religious-authorities in Judaism, Christianity, and Islam continue to do in their often very lacking translations and interpretations of the Bible?

Could Samuel be a foil for Moses?

In 1 Samuel 1, the character Samuel is said to be an Ephraimite. But in later generations (at least) of storycrafting in 1 Chronicles 6, Samuel is listed among the Levites.

Perhaps this reflects the fight within the long tradition that is played out with one camp writing at/to other other — all of that writing becoming the Bible. The prophets/ecstatics claim Samuel and the Levitical priests likely do the same though probably long after the Samuel-saga was crafted.

In 1 Samuel, Moses is never mentioned except in that interpolated chapter (1 Samuel 12) written by the Deuteronomists to harmonize 1 & 2 Samuel into their grander epic of the Bible. Moses is the hero of the Levitical priests and of the Deuteronomists. But the crafters of 1 & 2 Samuel don't mention Moses and make every effort to avoid mentioning him...but the Deuteronomists sure do bring up Moses in 1 Samuel 12.

The band of X has their hero-character Samuel doing some of the things Moses is known for and even one-upping Moses. Samuel kills Agag, the king who took advantage of Moses and the exiles from Egypt — something Moses wasn't able to do.

In addition to that, we have a few curious parallels:

Samuel talks to YAHWEH and YAHWEH answers with thunder and rain (1 Samuel 7)

vs.

Moses talks to YAHWEH and YAHWEH answers with thunder and lightening (Exodus 19)

YAHWEH hears the crying out of Ancient Israel and orders Samuel to act for It (1 Samuel 8)

vs.

YAHWEH hears the crying out of Ancient Israel and orders Moses to act for It (Exodus 2-3)

Both Samuel and Moses call Israel to YAHWEH. The Levitical priests and Deuteronomistic scribes have Moses do so through the ark and formulate how to please YAHWEH through 613 laws and ritual promulgations. The band of X casts Samuel doing so through relationship with YAHWEH alone, even a rather sexy relationship where YAHWEH notices the beauty of human-creatures as It did with Samuel and David. And it's almost always a very unlikely person to whom and through whom YAHWEH whispers and enchants in the Samuel-saga.

Very different voices and philosophies — Samuel vs. Moses, 1 & 2 Samuel vs. Torah.

One thing that is curious about Samuel's origins in 1 Samuel 1 is the mention of his being from TSUP and of having a relative named TSUP — usually translated as Zuph.   It's also where Saul ends up looking for his father's lost donkeys and finds Samuel instead, 1 Samuel 9. TSUP. Very close to Sufi in sound, isn't it?

Wouldn't that be sweet? That the ecstatic/prophetic tradition — here in 1 Samuel — having some roots in TSUP, in a 'honeycomb, a comb gushing forth honey' as any good metaphor and pun does. Perhaps, like the Sufis, TSUP in 1 Samuel is not just a place and not just a person/people and not just a single religion but a way of living that is no particular way at all. The Sufis and the biblical ecstatics/prophets both have reputations of playing with language cleverly and sonically, being rich with puns and stylish language and word choice, often bordercrossing meanings in their tales to inspire within the hearer of the tale an experience original to the hearer and yet shared in some way by all who hear. Idries Shah notes this well regarding ways of Sufi storytelling in his book *The Sufis*.

In the Bible, the character Moses in the Torah has very little poetry, really. The poetry ascribed to him in Deuteronomy 32-33 seems like an afterthought, as if some editor realized they couldn't proclaim Moses a prophet *par excellence* without giving him at least some poetry.

Moses has little style; Samuel and the random ecstatics/

prophets — sometimes called 'man/person of ELOHIM/God or divinity' — are rich with style, at least here in 1 Samuel. True in the band of YAH stories in Genesis too.

Compare the uses of '*ephod*' in 1 Samuel and in the Torah/ Moses-material and we can learn a thing or two more about the significant differences between the Levitical priests and the band of X....

Are there differences between 'ephod' in the Samuel-saga and the Torah-saga?

In 1 Samuel wearing the '*ephod*'/AHPOD appears to be so revealing that Hannah-Bend-Down makes a little robe to cover up young Samuel when she visits her boy, the priest Eli-Climb-Up's 'boy/slave.' The *ephod* young Samuel wears as the special-server of the priest is made of cloth — 'straggly-yarned'/ BD we are told. *Strong's Exhaustive Concordance* suggests that the Hebrew word BD from which most Bible translations get 'linen' is probably derived from BDD/'stringy' as in the fibers had space between them. Later on in the Samuel-saga, we'll hear of a certain famous King David donning the cloth *ephod* and dancing wildly before his subjects and the ark — much to the embarrassment of his wife who notes that he had exposed himself to slave-girls. Apparently, the cloth-like, stringy-nature of the *ephod* in 1 Samuel allowed one's nature/genitals to sneak out, especially while dancing wildly in David's case or in attending to the ark when mother Hannah-Bend-Down visits in young Samuel's case.

In the Torah (Exodus 28 specifically), the *ephod* appears to be made of cloth as well, though much finer than simply straggly, stringy linen. And make no mistake — no matter how much of nature might leak out of this Exodus version of the priestly *ephod*, a metal breastplate is worn over the *ephod* in which the Urim and Thummim are housed, perhaps the 'yes' + 'no' lots/dice that we hear of King Saul's priest using to decide whether to attack in battle and whether Jonathan was guilty or not of violating the no-eating order (1 Samuel 14), that time when King Saul wanted to kill his own son Jonathan in front of everyone. And in the Exodus description, the Urim and Thummim are very clearly to be housed in a pocket over the heart of the one who wears the *ephod* and breastplate — not within the 'linen *ephod*, straggly yarned underwear"/AHPOD BD itself as seems to be happening in 1 Samuel.

And not only that, the Torah-framers — be they Levitical priests or Deuteronomistic scribes who crafted/edited Exodus 28 — order that special trousers from waist to leg are to be made for Aaron and the priests to wear to 'cover their nakedness.' In the Exodus version of the *ephod*, even if one's genitalia did leak out, they'd be covered over by many layers of fine materials — cloth and metal — things never mentioned in 1 Samuel's version of the *ephod*.

And with the straggly-yarned underwear-*ephod* in 1 Samuel, we get two rather unusual verbs...CHGR and NSAH. In Chapter 2, we are told that Samuel CHGR's the straggly-yarned *ephod*... CHGR is a verb usually used with weaponry as in 'girding on or strapping on one's weapons.' CHGR is what David does in strapping on Saul's sword to go take on Stripper-Goliath in Chapter 17.

The other verb used with the *ephod* in 1 Samuel is NSAH, usually meaning 'to lift' or 'to raise' or 'to carry.' For someone to 'wear the *ephod*' we might expect the verb LBSH, the verb that the Torah priests/scribes use 'to clothe'/LBSH the priests in their trousers in Exodus 28. But X with their *ephod* chooses a verb that has to do with lifting, raising up...the same verb as in raising up one's eyes to see or lifting up one's voice to be heard. NSAH is the verb used to describe Jonathan's assistant (usually translated as gear-holder) and Stripper-Goliath's assistant (usually translated as shield-carrier).

Raising up the *ephod*...that's the verb-phrase the band of X chooses to describe the priestly use of the *ephod* in 1 Samuel. The Torah priests/scribes who likely originally crafted Exodus 28 do not even go near such a verb and instead cover over the nakedness or near-nakedness in 1 Samuel's *ephod*-version and any potential of anyone raising up — in the excitement of the moment — the linen underwear with what's inside.

Deuteronomist-strategy?

Did the Deuteronomists try to hide away 1 & 2 Samuel in the Bible as 'ancient history'?

What began as roving fictional stories told by a clever band becomes the tap-root story of Israel/Judah — at least versions of it we get in Chronicles without all the style so prevalent in 1 & 2 Samuel.

Best selling books have been written and sold about the David and Goliath story alone. But very few people read the rest of the Saul-David-Solomon saga in 1 & 2 Samuel and 1 Kings and what these men become. Brilliant as boys — at least in the case of Saul and David — all three of them grow to become men you'd probably not want your kid to emulate, unless you are a mafia-boss. People love the David-Solomon version of Chronicles and the Psalms — but they rarely read where all of that came from in 1 & 2 Samuel and 1 Kings. There's a stark difference — just as there's a stark difference between the materials for the *ephod*, as we noticed in the prior section.

The Deuteronomists take Saul-David-Solomon — 1 & 2 Samuel and 1 Kings — and put it in the Bible as the bridge between the likely fictional/legendary Moses-Joshua-Judges and the actual kings of Israel/Judah whose 'histories' get recorded by the Deuteronomists in portions of 1 & 2 Kings.

Although the poetry and stories spoken out loud might have begun much earlier, when did the actual <u>writing</u> of the Bible begin?

In Judah's capital, Jerusalem, in the 7th century BCE, the scribes of King Josiah's royal court began actually <u>writing</u> the Bible with their first draft of Deuteronomy. That's one reason we call these scribes today the 'Deuteronomistic scribes' or 'Deuteronomists.' Taking their cue from the scribal-traditions of other nations, the Deuteronomists had likely been exerting great influence over the affairs of the royal court for generations. We might think of these Deuteronomists or scribes as something like a political party today, a party or group who gained power from supporting and even propping up royalty as a system of government. Later generations of these scribes assembled and edited other storycrafters' and writers' earlier/later contributions into their ever-growing scroll that would become the Hebrew Bible.

In an ancient culture, writing has power — it seems like magic to a person who cannot read or write. And scholars estimate that even as much as 95% of the population in the ancient world could not read or write. Imagine!

So these scribes decided to take even more power into their own hands during the kingship of one they had raised and reared in their own Deuteronomistic thinking since his youth — King Josiah. It is written that he took the throne when he was eight years old. And of course the royal court — Deuteronomists — took care of matters while the young boy grew to adulthood, marked in the ancient world by marriageable age, likely puberty.

And somehow a document laying out what YAHWEH wanted came to the attention of the royal court — a speech from Moses. This of course was the earliest draft of Deuteronomy. Whether it was found as the temple was being cleaned out as we have it in 2 Kings 22 or whether the Deuteronomistic scribes had been writing it for years or whatever, this early draft of Deuteronomy became the centerpiece-philosophy of King Josiah's rule...how to please YAHWEH by following Moses' so-called 'ancient' speech which might have been written for that very moment, the occasion of it's being found and immediately read to King Josiah.

It's interesting to me how 2 Kings 22.8 even lays it out...(my translation)

And Hilkiah, the high priest, said to Shaphan, the scribe, "The scribal-work of the law — I have found it!"

The very Hebrew has the double SPR/'scribe or scribal' in the sentence, both words back to back, as if to connect immediately the scribal role in scribing out the Law, the Torah that was 'found.'

These scribes began the Bible-writing tradition and eventually became the editors of much of what today we call the Hebrew Bible. But to strengthen their grasp on power at a few key junctures, these Deuteronomists had to make some compromises to unify other biblical thinkers into their camp. The Levitical priests eventually begin writing, crafting a body of laws and interpretations of stories into their own document. While the Deuteronomistic scribes had their document that was an ever-growing speech by the great law-receiver Moses, the Levitical priests had something similar in their Exodus and Leviticus.

There is much similarity between the Levites' laws and worldview and the Deuteronomistic scribes' laws and worldview — and some big differences.

The Levitical priests also included stories which they did not craft themselves but instead interpreted/edited freely in the books of Genesis and Exodus placed before their Leviticus. (It should be noted that the names given to these books or most of the Bible's books came much later.) The Deuteronomistic scribes had no story in Deuteronomy but they do tell a story of Israel through what comes out of Moses' mouth...what the scribes inserted into Moses' mouth and even 'later' characters like Joshua and Samuel and Solomon in their ever-growing Bible.

Whose stories were the Levitical priests grabbing and interpreting in their canon, their early Torah? The stories of the prophets...at least I identify them as the prophets. I'll say more about that in a bit. Once called by scholars as "J" or "the Yahwist" and once thought to be a single person who had a penchant for calling divinity 'YAHWEH' particularly in Genesis, scholars are now very divided on who this formerly-known-as-J-is. It was very likely multiple people of multiple generations.

Study the <u>style</u> of the stories in Genesis and one can discover quite quickly that there is a similar imagination in many of the stories in Genesis. What style? Well, the verb choices are often hilarious, sexually stimulating, uproariously funny, bawdy with a double/triple entendre kind of imagination with which stand-up comedians of our 21st century play quite readily. That's one reason I call the crafters of these stories in Genesis 'the band of YAH.'

And the character-YAHWEH in the band of YAH's stories in Genesis is clearly very different from the Levitical priests' ELOHIM/'God' and clearly very different from the YAHWEH of Deuteronomy. Just read Genesis' Eden story alone and you'll get a whiff of what I'm talking about. YAHWEH in that Eden story is quite powerful for sure but kind of out of control emotionally and certainly not all-knowing — YAHWEH can't find the mud-creature in the garden that YAHWEH had created. Contrast that with the all-powerful, orderly-creating ELOHIM/'God' of the creation story (Gen 1 - 2.3) placed right before the Eden story...this Seven Days Creation Story was likely crafted by the Levitical priests (possibly with the Deuteronomists' later flourishes) to stand against the bawdy Eden story. Check out the Hebrew verb choices in that Eden story — talk about style!!

The Levitical priests in crafting their beginnings of the Torah were emphatic in trying to bulldoze over the prophets and this bawdy style. Volume 0 in *The Naked Path of Prophet* series — *A Wildly Sensual YAHWEH* — lays that out quite plainly.

The prophets? In Genesis and 1 & 2 Samuel?!

"The prophets?" my scholarly friends might question. "What do the prophets have to do with Genesis?"

The very style of storycrafting with these YAHWEH-oriented stories in Genesis resembles the double/triple entendre imagination of the prophets' poems — prophets like Jeremiah, the Isaiahs, Amos, and more. And not only that, Genesis contains an origin story of YAHWEH birthing the prophets: with the Divine wrestling Jacob and penetrating Jacob with Its wispy seed — yep! (Genesis 32) And who is Jacob's son he loves the most after that penetrating-experience? Joseph, the younger son who dreams dreams — like the prophets — the son upon whom YAHWEH rushes — like the prophets — the son who spends much of his life in the story naked — like the prophets, at least as we have them in 1 Samuel. It's even likely that, in the 'original' tellings of the story, the character Joseph was standing there naked before Pharaoh when Pharaoh — in a matter of minutes after meeting him and after Joseph delivered the bad news that Pharaoh's court refused to do — quickly elevates Joseph from prisoner-in-the-dungeon to Pharaoh's Number Two. Who is ordinarily Pharaoh's Number Two? The Queen, right?

But here we have an often-naked dreamer and dream-interpreter with a bit of style/poetry and cleverness standing there in Pharaoh's court and now elevated to Number Two in the whole wide world (at least in their ancient eyes). What had Joseph's brothers — whose names become the regions/states of Ancient Israel and Ancient Judah (but not Joseph!!) — what had these brothers done to their younger brother Joseph who dreamed dreams about all of them bowing down to him, the (second) youngest and (nearly) least significant brother in the family, the brother who received a special princess-dress from their father?

What do Jacob's sons — Israel's sons — do to this prophet-like guy?

They mock him, silence him, and attempt to kill him...much like Ancient Israel/Judah had a penchant for doing with their prophets. At least one time they were successful — it is written that the citizens of Jerusalem killed Jeremiah. They also had a hand in killing Jesus too.

You see, the entire tradition of Judaism is the intertwining of the hierarchical vision of the priests/kings/scribes and the more circular vision of the prophets — the entire written tradition of Judaism-Christianity-Islam is like an intertwined rope made of two materials: the priestly-imagination and the prophetic-imagination. To read the entire Bible is to witness the fight, the disagreement through the centuries that was being hashed out between these two camps. In my own Christian tradition, this family-fight can be found between Peter's vision for governance using Rome's cruel hierarchical system and Paul's vision for governance that was the first time democracy was envisioned without slaves, ever, with women holding positions of leadership, and with all humans being recognized as equal before God.

As the priests/scribes seemed to have won out over the prophets/ecstatics in Judaism, so too has Peter's hierarchical-camp won out over Paul's non-hierarchical approach in Christianity. Tragic. And abhorrent.

How so? Very few people can even recognize the prophetic nature of Jesus...and instead put him on a throne as their king and lord/Lord, the very tools of the hierarchical imagination. Even worse, they call him 'Christ' or messiah, the highly problematic title Jesus does well to spurn, as we'll explore in the next volume of the series. Jesus' parables and wisdom sayings lampoon people who try to hold power over others; his parables and wisdom sayings attempt to free hearers/imaginers within, and even at their own waking pace. Very few people have a clue just how crafty Jesus and the prophets were with their wordplay and poems and imaginative stories and actions and invitations to experience, all of them designed to wake people up during some of the more dire situations of empire-driven life.

The hierarchical imagination won out in modern religion, at least in modern Judaism and modern Christianity. I suspect the hierarchical imagination wins out in every religion. Following a religion asks the follower to see and hear and feel in particular ways about the world that are often not their own, rarely based on what their own deeply intelligent sensations notice.

But ecstasy cannot be enforced, only discovered. Most followers have no sense of the ecstasy upon which their religions were founded.

I missed it too for decades of my life...so caught up in the hierarchical traditions I had inherited, caught up in a very dangerous game.

To follow a religion is — often without thinking or realizing it — to disregard the prophetic/ecstatic imagination and even to attempt to suppress it. The prophets invite an experience that unfolds based on the present — not what was in the past. The prophets invite an experience on YAHWEH's terms that hierarchically-minded people try to block, even by killing the prophets who invite such a simple experience of noticing the life-giving force that is the wind.

Building a tradition...what the scribes do and must do to bolster their power, even after their propped-up royals fall

The Deuteronomistic scribes had been writing about the kings of Judah, for sure, and we can guess they inherited material about the kingdom to the north, Ancient Israel, perhaps when they were all together in exile in Babylon, or even before that when Israel's citizenry moved south away from Assyrian control.

What's this business of 'the exile'?

Israel fell to Assyria in 721 BCE. As mentioned earlier, many people in Israel migrated south to Judah/Jerusalem to save their own lives and livelihoods; those who didn't leave in time were exiled by Assyria. For a good century plus, Judah/Jerusalem hung on for their nation's life. Tiny little city-state Babylon eventually conquered Assyria and then asserted its control upon Judah in 597 BCE and then hammered the final blow by wrecking Judah's temple and palace in 587 BCE and exiling Judah's king and most of the royal-court, likely the Deuteronomistic scribes. Who was left behind in Judah? The poor, maybe a Deuteronomist or two propped up by the Babylonians to use their administrative/scribal skills to assist the Babylonian governor, and at least one prophet: Jeremiah, at least as we have it in the stories about him.

Once Cyrus of Persia conquered Babylon in 538 BCE, many of the Judean exiles were anxious to return to Judah to rebuild what once was — without a monarchy, of course, because they were under the rule of Persian King Cyrus. The prophet known today as "Second Isaiah" whose poems are recorded in Isaiah 40-55 even boldly proclaims that the non-Hebrew Cyrus was a *messiah*, a specially-anointed king of God/YAHWEH.

But not all of the exiles returned — many chose to stay in old Babylon and, perhaps, work for the new Persian administration, just as they had for the Babylonians. They had skills, after all, skills as scribes and as administrators/bureaucrats from their earlier days (and their grandparents' earlier days) that Babylon likely used and that Persia probably continued to use. Those who chose to remain in Babylon had built good lives for themselves...why return to Judah?

And those who chose to return to Judah from exile — much of old royal-court and upperclasses and Deuteronomistic scribes — saw themselves as the 'true Israel...the chosen people' who would rebuild Zion, their vision of YAHWEH's capital city of the world, capital of God/ELOHIM. And what did they do with anyone who wasn't of their own Deuteronomist-class? They didn't let them in. Such is the tragic tale of the books of Ezra and Nehemiah — the tales of hierarchical-imagination going tragically wrong again, even when they had an opportunity to begin fresh and anew all over again.

When they set out to build a tradition by crafting the story of their nation's origins long after it had fallen to Babylon, the Deuteronomistic scribes had a big gap to fill — the legends of Joshua/Judges and then some post-Solomon record of the doings of the kings of Judah and Israel. How to bridge the gap and explain the origins of monarchy for their nation?

Those old fictional stories of Saul-David-Solomon fit perfectly. Long after Israel/Judah's monarchy had died and looked likely to never return under Persian rule, the Deuteronomistic scribes reached for this scroll of 1 & 2 Samuel (at least as we call it today) and used it as a bridge between the early legends of Joshua/Judges and the later kings. And voilà — the large swath of Genesis through all (or nearly all of) 2 Kings is born. It's possible that the Elijah-Elisha-guild-prophet stories were added into the Kings-saga later, at the same time as the prophets' catalogs of poems were added to that swath that became a much-larger draft of the Hebrew Bible, now including the books of Isaiah, Jeremiah, and the whole catalog of what today we call Prophets. With these major inclusions and the later wisdom literature, we have today's Hebrew Bible.

But how to bind it all together, this burgeoning Bible of competing voices?

The Deuteronomistic scribes finished it off by editing everything in that whole almost-complete Hebrew Bible with a series of speeches that hold it all together, as scholar Thomas Römer lays out so convincingly in *The So-Called Deuteronomistic History*. Just as they had been putting whole speeches into Moses' mouth for generations in Deuteronomy, the post-exilic Deuteronomistic scribes inserted speeches into other characters' mouths in these books they include in the Hebrew Bible and summarized key moments in their national life:

(Note, I have taken the scholarly framework summarized by Römer and built upon it here, as you can see if you consult Römer's *The So-Called Deuteronomistic History*, pp 122-3.)

Deut 28...after crafting generation-by-generation the whole book of Deuteronomy, the Deuteronomists conclude their book (at least at that point in their writing) with Moses' farewell speech that announces the exile (I should also add here that Deut 32-32 includes the very late additions of prophet-like poems placed into Moses' mouth, and following that in Deut 34 the declaration that Moses was the greatest prophet ever... likely the post-exilic Deuteronomists dealing with the fact that their propped up Moses so far had no poems to his long story/influence in Exodus and Leviticus and Deuteronomy... poems/style seem to be the heart of what the prophets are about as the Deuteronomists included so many poems by the prophets in that post-exilic edition of the Hebrew Bible so they had to craft some for Moses and tack them onto the end of their Deuteronomy if Moses would have any credibility as a prophet)

Joshua 1...here the character-YAHWEH announces to Joshua the 'future' conquest of the lands that will become the kingdoms of Ancient Judah and Ancient Israel

Joshua 23...Joshua's farewell speech about accomplishing the conquest and the need to follow Moses' law to avoid the exile (I would add Joshua 24 to this as well, though perhaps it was added by a later group of scribes...Joshua 24 very much resembles the same reminder of the 'history' of Israel as 1 Samuel 12 will do below)

Judges 2.3 - 3.6...the cycle of Israel/Judah following a YAHWEH-sent judge and prospering and then floundering once the YAHWEH-sent judge dies

1 Samuel 12...Samuel's farewell speech that spells out what YAHWEH requires of YAHWEH's people (note too that this is the only mention of Moses in 1 Samuel)

1 Kings 8...Solomon's very, very long temple-inaugural speech when Israel and Judah were (said to be) not only united as a single kingdom but also with a palace and temple of epic proportions, a fulfillment of character-YAHWEH's promises to character-David...this speech also 'announces' or 'warns of' the exile though it had likely already happened when the Deuteronomists added this speech from Solomon to 1 Kings

2 Kings 17...this text describes the fall/exile of Israel because Israel had worshipped other gods — and the scribe points out, the Israelites even continued to do so during the exile and thus why after the exile the Ezra/Nehemiah leadership will not let the Samaritans/northern-people of Israel assist with rebuilding the temple...and 2 Kings 17 also 'presages' what Judah must do to save themselves from exile...immediately following this chapter we get the stories of Judah's two kings most appreciated by the scribes: King Hezekiah and then a couple of kings in between and then King Josiah, the king the Deuteronomists raise and rear from age 8 to enact their ideas

2 Kings 25...a full summary from the Deuteronomists' standpoint of the invasion of Babylon, the fall of Judah, and the ensuing exile and who led and was allowed to lead Judah in exile.

As you can see, the Deuteronomistic scribes/editors must deal with the fact that the kings they served (and reared) had failed — Babylon conquered them and exiled them all. So these later post-exilic Deuteronomistic scribes/editors tried to explain through those 'early' legendary stories of Israel/Judah exactly why their government(s) had failed — it's because Israel/Judah had not listened to their character-YAHWEH's warnings, to serve God as Moses-of-their-primal-scroll-of-Deuteronomy had prescribed. And often, according to the Deuteronomists, the reason for Israel's fall and failure and Judah's fall and failure was because of their bad kings who did not demand their subjects worship YAHWEH as Moses-of-Deuteronomy had prescribed. The only exceptions to the 'bad kings' were Hezekiah and Josiah, at least according to the Deuteronomists. The Deuteronomists, of course, seem to take no blame for the invasion/exile themselves, even though they most likely had been part of the inner royalist circles perhaps since the beginnings of the monarchy.

The Bible: Massive Diversity Project

The Deuteronomists including 1 & 2 Samuel into the Bible? That's bold, for sure. Maybe the Saul-David-Solomon saga with the naked prophets was just so darn catchy and loved by the people that the Deuteronomists felt they had to include it in their Bible or be poo-pooed by the people.

After all, the crafters of 1 & 2 Samuel seem to set up the character-Samuel as being all that the character-Moses was but better, and much less wordy. Samuel appears to be a foil to Moses and the Levitical priests' vision and scribes's vision of Law, and even of the Deuteronomistic urge for a history to follow.

The Bible is actually a big book of many books, often with many competing voices within each book, voices that have been plastered over to create a 'final edition.' Hierarchs and prophets are all tied up in one book, this Bible.

Let's be very clear here. I am definitely not arguing that this is a face-off or battle between one religion and another. I am arguing that if we look closely enough, we will find this face-off or interface between 'freedom-discovery-spontaneity' and 'fascism-control-hierarchy' within every religion and its sacred texts — and likely within each human being, whether they consider themselves religious or not. This book and the whole *Naked Path of Prophet* series seeks to shed more light upon the competing visions within the roots of Judaism and its sacred texts, and within the Christian tradition and its sacred texts. The Westar Institute/Jesus Seminar's work the last few decades with Jesus' sayings and the many gospels within the Bible and outside of it and the authentic/inauthentic letters of Paul reveal that same tug-of-vision in the early Christian tradition.

Such a tug-of-vision happens today too, most certainly, in 21st century religion.

And it happens not just in religions but in nearly every organized arena of our lives. Going along without noticing this tug-of-vision within oneself and within one's relationships, I suspect, is what has brought us to the precipice of human-disaster here in the 21st century...with a planet reacting to our human-generated pollution, with one 'side' wanting to demolish another 'side' politically and corporately and in too many ways...with too much of everything, too much noise, and so little interest in the wind that gives life.

Conflicts arise — potentially significant ones — when one's personal map of 'reality' tries to dominate another person's map. The same, of course, can be said of any group taking on an individual or another group. But the experience of the prophets — the ecstatics — just might free us from the compulsion to want to dominate others. The wind has Its ways of freeing...with Its gifts of ecstatic experience.

Getting to the Roots

Tracing things back to their roots might help us to detangle the twisted society in which we live. I suspect the very clever story of 1 & 2 Samuel could help with that. As we'll soon see, the character Samuel once was among the 'mediators' (the priests) but then had an experience that changed him and led him to another way forward, one that no longer needed 'mediators.'

Samuel discovers that YAHWEH is reliable without the rituals that his ancestors had done, without the prayer formulas, without the particular knowledge of the old stories...no matter how many times people tried to drag him back into those well-known ways. The band of X's character Samuel discovers an experience of life that changes him, and can change anybody if we are invited to pay attention to it...to It.

In 1 Samuel, X tells us people would travel to see the priest or religious-authority or to the 'seer' to get 'in touch' with the divine, with God.

Can you be 'in touch' with something that is Infinite?

Consider taking a moment to wonder about that!

It's a koan for our time...with which hand do you touch or connect with the Infinite God?

Our character Samuel comes to see that no one needs a priest or catechism or commandments or king or a bunch of laws to get 'in touch' with God. Our character Samuel and the ecstatic-prophets — ancient and modern — discover that God is all around, that we are swimming in God, that we participate in God and are God in the Infinite, THE ALL.

To understand 1 & 2 Samuel, you and I will need to leave behind what we think 'God' is to truly know YAHWEH, the Infinite, THE ALL.....

It's not so easy to shake off thousands of years of control and catechism and law that we've inherited from our very ancient ancestors. Even if you're not a religious-type, you still have all that control in you — it's encoded in the modern languages we speak, so much of them rooted deeply within that exceedingly complex and twisted biblical imagination. What twists? The coiling of the circularly-inspired wisdom of the prophets with the hierarchically-minded law of the priests and scribes...the coiling done by those priests and scribes often trying to hide or dim down the root-experiences of the ecstatics/prophets.

So, how to shake off these thousands of years of control? Get to the roots....

Would Jews be wise to feel the breeze, to stand on the mountaintops and high points — to know such an experience — instead of relying on Moses to tell them how to live? The character Samuel and his gang of misfits invite such a mountain-top experience, of the wild wind on one's naked skin, one's whole naked skin, pure ecstasy! This is quite a contrast with the ancient Levitical priests and the Deuteronomists who have their lead-hero Moses only expose his naked feet to YAHWEH's presence...while YAHWEH gets naked with Samuel and soon — in the next volume — it sounds like the ecstatics/prophets are fully naked with YAHWEH and one another.

Would Christians be wise to enter the discomfort of the desert, to sleep under bridges, to dine with prostitutes and thieves and homeless wanderers...people not tied up in the game of the 'empire'? This was the experience Jesus was inviting of those who 'followed him' during his day, at least as we have it in the many gospels.

Would Muslims be wise to enter the cave, to listen for Gabriel's voice that sings in every generation and invites some of the very best poetry to come forth as it did for Mohammed and then later wisdom figures within that tradition like Rumi, Hafiz, Rabi'a and so many?

Experiences at the roots are wild, cannot be contained, ecstatic, vision-opening. Roots are unpredictable, after all — they go every which way yet seek after water, life. Such is YAHWEH in the ancient prophetic traditions — unpredictable and yet ultimately the very stuff of life. Breathe and you'll know!

Getting to the roots, breathing and luxuriating in it (It), giving ourselves opportunities to let the breeze come to us on our naked skin, such things might be the only actions that save us from destruction as a world-people. *The Naked Path of Prophet* series aims to detangle us from the web of 'control' that is enacted upon you and me every day, and which you and I enact upon each other in nearly every interaction if we're not wise to how we use our power and even our words. I hope this book gives you and me confidence to trust our experiences of the wind, of breathing, of the very essence of life — and to rely like the character Samuel does on the wind alone.

The breeze is always there for each one of us, after all...

at least for anyone who has sense to feel It.

And the wind gets us up to imagine and say and do some wild things...all in a very clever, system-shattering, ecstatic-style as we discover from the get-go in 1 Samuel.

And perhaps to protect the ecstatic-prophets and their genderbending and bordercrossing ways from a royal-priestly worldview that wants to punish genderbenders with death (Leviticus 18 - 20), the band of X crafts a fictional origin story of the first kings of Israel who have homosexual tendencies on the throne and in their military.

And not only that, X will set up a whole narrative that the very system of monarchy and its military found their success through these homosexual tendencies, even with adolescents. (!) And as for the Levitical priests, they dress their 'boys/slaves' in straggly-yarned, see-through underwear, as the band of X brings forward in 1 Samuel.

What's this business of 'messiah'/MSHYCH?

I'll have a lot more to say about *messiahs* and *christs* in *The Named Path of Prophet vol 2*, the continuation of the 1 Samuel story, especially as we watch *Messiah/Christ* Saul begin to crumble.

Suffice it to say, being a *messiah* — a specially oil-smeared one for YAHWEH — sounds like a tall order, to say the least. Could any single human be up for the task?

Let's not forget that, at least in the Gospel of Mark account (Mark 8), Jesus warns Peter and his disciples not to associate him with *christ/messiah*.

Why 'It' as YAHWEH's pronoun?

Quite honestly, no pronoun works well. It just didn't seem that 'Him' worked in the text, specially when YAHWEH seems to be the wind in 1 Samuel.

The character-YAHWEH does not walk the earth human-like in X's imagination and storytelling as It does in the band of YAH's Genesis stories. The band of YAH even has YAHWEH wrestling Jacob and groping and penetrating him too.

I chose 'It' as YAHWEH's pronoun to shake us up, perhaps, to get us out of the modern-religion myopia and dystopia of what 'God' is expected to be. I plan to carry It through the whole *Naked Path of Prophet* series.

While I respect greatly all the recent returns to 'God as mother' and the Divine Feminine — I'm a huge Marion Woodman fan, for crying out loud! — I think all this gendering of 'God' misses the point. If 'God' is Infinite, 'God' then includes all possibilities — and all genders. And gender in my opinion is not a masculine, feminine, and neuter game of three only. We in the 21st century are reminded of that, yes, with the gift and awareness of transgender people and people who do not identify themselves within a gender-binary...fellow humans who are gifted with different genitalia, different identities, and different sexualities than just 'three' or even worse just 'two.'

The shamans of many traditions are sometimes said to be shape-shifters, right? They are said to know all dimensions of life often perhaps because they were gifted with diverse genitalia and diverse identities.

Grammatical gender is quite tricky, as my Sanskrit professor once reminded me. Originally, what we call 'gender' in language was 'animate' and 'inanimate.' Animate later was split into two, masculine and feminine. Inanimate became neuter in our more 'modern' languages.

Perhaps even this much earlier linguistic-organizing of life-experience misses the point just as much as our present way of linguistically-organizing anything....

Open your mind with me, leave behind the metered sound, let YAHWEH's style have Its brash, naked, and wild ways with us. After all, It's the only way to know the Infinite, yes? To know It ALL....

Why does YAHWEH like to get 'naked'/GLH in 1 Samuel but nakedness is forbidden in the Torah? And why is nakedness forbidden by most modern translators?

The verb choice GLH in 1 Samuel is very curious. The band of X clearly is playing some games here, being clever and insightful, and is surely in 'conversation' with the Levitical priests who wrote Leviticus. GLH is used in Leviticus 24 times, as a matter of fact, often like this:

LAO TQRBO LGLOT AYRUH (the verb GLH can be found in 'LGLOT'...in an infinitive form)

'Do not get close to someone to strip (as you would a slave or exile) the nakedness of'...and then a whole lot of relatives are usually listed.

Most translations of Leviticus make it clear that this 'uncovering someone's nakedness' is the first step toward sex, and I think that's what the Levitical priests are getting at too — and making very clear that stripping someone even before sex is an abomination.

Seems like good advice, right? Of course! I think we can all agree that no one should go around stripping anyone without their full consent and no one should do so as if these fellow-humans are slaves or exiles...and not just relatives as Leviticus 18 & 20 make clear, right?

Maybe someone might 'GLH' a lover in the throes of passion when both lovers have supreme trust in one another, when they are 'reliable' with one another, trustworthy. That's quite different, of course.

But notice in the priestly imagination of Leviticus that GLH is never used to describe YAHWEH self-stripping before humans as the band of X has YAHWEH do repeatedly in 1 Samuel. The Levitical priests never describe YAHWEH that way.

But X does. Why?

In 1 Samuel, the band of X has YAHWEH 'GLH' freely. YAHWEH takes off Its clothes, just like slaves and exiles do before an oppressor. Or before a lover in the throes of passionate love-making.

YAHWEH does this! For human beings! For young Samuel!

The word RAHH for 'revealing' or 'showing' could be used if X had meant for YAHWEH just to reveal Itself to young Samuel.

But X doesn't do that — instead X uses GLH throughout their story instead of RAHH.

This is shocking, right? And helpful, in my opinion, to imagine YAHWEH doing such a thing for you and me and everyone. But most biblical translators and theologians and priests and pastors and rabbis and imams seem to want to run from it, from It, and simply say YAHWEH was "revealing" Itself to Samuel, to anyone. But this is a different kind of revealing... and it involves stripping, nakedness. How uncomfortable many of my religious friends are about nakedness...!

But why? It is what YAHWEH does, right? And it's not just that I want it to be that way — it's the way the verb GLH is used throughout the Bible.

The band of YAH uses the verb GLH to describe Noah fumbling off his clothes in his tent after getting drunk on the vineyard's wine he had cultivated after the flood. Clearly, Noah was doing more than revealing his heart and his emotions and identity to the tent. He was naked! And he remains that way when his sons find him the next morning and try to cover him up — much to their embarrassment — before he goes on a hung-over tirade on the kid who didn't even see him naked. Noah's name, by the way, means 'tranquilizingly beautiful.' Ahem.

The 'nakedness'/GLH of that Noah Genesis story often gets translated by biblical translators as nakedness — just as it does in Leviticus — but when they get to 1 Samuel, they leave the nakedness out. It must be so embarrassing to scholars to think of YAHWEH stripping Itself of clothes. "Surely YAHWEH would not do such a thing," they protest!

But in 1 Samuel, YAHWEH does get naked.

Getting naked has something to do with knowing YAHWEH... and something to do with the ecstasy of prophets...especially if done with sensible intentions.

And it can be beautiful too...if you and I stay with the image and not run from it. Allow the image to play with you...

YAHWEH stripping Itself, getting naked Itself, with human beings...

as if you and I and every human were the captor of YAHWEH.

And we are.

Be sensible...breathe in and feel YAHWEH within you.

Feel how YAHWEH gives you life when you capture It within you for a few seconds.

How much do you long for this kind of relationship with the air you breathe? How much do you take for granted this lover that loves you into life, often without your realizing It?

It's YAHWEH's nakedness that the Levitical priests seem to fear, especially between humans and YAHWEH. The priests present a 'God' that would never do such a thing...as if to snuff out and stuff down that kind of longing a human being might have for the divine, and the longing of the divine with a human being. Such longing is the stuff of life, yes?

Really. Breathe...and you will know!

How would you be with any other human — friend or foe — if you recognized that they also captured YAHWEH, breath by breath by breath? Just like you do to live.

This is a new morality emerging and a new imagination — and one much wiser than a bunch of laws and commandments.

I suspect that's what the band of X is after with all of this stripping...we'll have to see how this plays out in the rest of the band of X's saga.

And as much of a gift as these priests/scribes have offered us moderns by preserving the band of YAH's imagination in framing and crafting the Torah, how we've all paid the price societally and perhaps personally these 2500+ years by listening to them almost exclusively, to these priests and scribes and such an imagination that fears intimacy, even uncomfortable intimacy. Such fear requires laws — Law/Torah — and framing a law that encourages the destruction of enemy-nations, that prescribes death to a man having sex with a man, that condones slavery, that gets wrankled when people are menstruating or having wet dreams or wearing clothing made of two different kinds of material.

But another ancient 'author' of the same Bible offers something that very well could be helpful, and that is a gift. What the band of X offers in helping us to imagine a YAHWEH who strips Itself of status and allows Itself to be captured by us...It's the stuff of life, yes?

What would happen if humans followed suit?

Perhaps nakedness is a true learning to be vulnerable in one's skin and to trust one's skin. In X's imagination in 1 & 2 Samuel, it's YAHWEH who first removes clothes, who first strips...and who does so as if captured...as if to be ravished, breath by breath by breath, lovemaking by beautiful lovemaking.

It's a beautiful possibility X has left us, yes?

The ancient prophets might remind us of the modern naturist lifestyle?

I think back to the naturist/nude beaches I've visited and walked upon and rested upon and swum in their waves, all over the world. These beaches were nearly always the least sexual places I have been — certainly less so than a bar, gay or straight, after everyone has had a few drinks and the midnight hour approaches.

Such beaches...they offer and invite an <u>experience</u> of nature... of being nature and without artifice. And they can usher us through one of the great compulsions of the 21st century — at least in my home country — of fearing being naked publicly.

On these naturist/nude beaches, one can witness whole families so easily taking off their clothes — little kids, teenagers, parents, grandparents — and enjoying the feeling of the sun and breeze and water on their skin...without any inhibition, without even an ounce or inkling of sex or sexual feeling. The clothed gawkers walking by, on the other hand, reveal a different way of being around such nakedness, clutching their towels over their crotches already covered by clothes, darting their eyes every which way so anxiously, being so completely uncomfortable. Until they try it....

It's always interesting to watch first-time nude-bathers. They often freak at first...and then a short time later, they walk around as if they don't even notice that they are naked and become completely comfortable around other people who are naked.

They come home to themselves. We <u>are</u> nature. We can't escape it. And on a naturist/nude beach, a new morality of mutual respect is so easy to get, to understand, and without any law making it so. How easy to see the humanity of any person when the status of their clothing no longer covers their skin....

Naked intimacy, let's remember, does not always move towards sex. But it does imply a freedom, a knowing, a barrier-less relationship of equals. And YAHWEH does this for the character Samuel as It does for you and me...if we let It.

Jesus and nakedness and nonviolence

Using the imaginations of the biblical ecstatics-prophets that he surely heard around the campfires of his world, Jesus played with new ways of dealing with control/power in the three examples of nonviolence he brought forward in what comes to us through Gospel of Matthew 5.38-41...the famous and often completely misunderstood "turn the other cheek" saying. It's not about being the bigger person and getting hit...it is about being clever in the moment and doing/saying something that jolts the oppressor and oppressed alike into awakening together to the equality we all share as human beings. The whole business of left and right hands and their ancient meanings/functions are key to understanding Jesus here, and anywhere. I've written about this elsewhere so will not go into detail now with that first of three examples.

The second example in that trio of clever actions from Matthew 5.38-41 does have some bearing in this series: it involves being sued, being taken to court. And Jesus invites something very clever: if someone sues you for everything you've got, then give it all to that oppressor...including your coat and your clothes. And then you'd be standing in the courtroom naked with your oppressor holding your clothes. Smile!

Welcome to the prophetic imagination — one that can turn the tables of one's mind up-side down. Tyranny and fascism can be toppled through love, a clever style of love... one that lays bare — naked — the whole situation as a way to know THE ALL together, oppressor and oppressed alike. Nonviolence remembers that people are allowed to be very, very wrong and still worthy of love, worthy of an invitation toward transformation.

The ecstatics/prophets are usually nonviolent — in 1 Samuel, at least most of the time, as the character Samuel does kill King Agag when King Saul won't do it.

Not all ecstatics/prophets will see what Samuel does here as the wise thing — my guess is that Jesus would have had a different reaction to Agag than what the character Samuel did or what the character Elijah will later do in the continuation of the band of X's saga in Kings.

Indeed, the character Elisha has a very different reaction when enemy-soldiers come to kill him — he blinds them, leads them into the gates of the capital city, and makes the king and military of his own nation feed the enemy-soldiers and send them home. Talk about a different strategy! The one who can open their heart the most — even to enemies — is the one who can transform an entire system, an entire family, an entire nation intent on doing harm.

The wind has Its ways of waking us up to life, to possibilities, especially when each breath of wind is so different.

Is challenging the Levitical priests an anti-Semitic move?

I condemn anti-Semitism of any sort, whether directed at Jewish people or Muslim people.

I want to make that very clear from the beginning.

I stand with all people — with all life.

A friend of mine read *Sweet Lady J* (an early version of *A Wildly Sensual YAHWEH*) and suggested my writing was anti-Semitic because I said that the priests — and later, Deuteronomists — who crafted the Torah were wise in what they did in assembling the Torah out of different storytellers' works and foolish at the same time dimming down the band of YAH's stories.

Hmmm.

Is it anti-Semitic to point out that genocide by idea or by action is wrong, especially when such genocide is stated in 'holy law' and inserted into the mouth of YAHWEH? The Torah encourages genocide in a number of places: Deuteronomy 20, Deuteronomy 25. The book of Joshua is in some ways one big tragic call to and celebration of genocide — or perhaps so glaringly violent that the writer of most of that tale was trying to dissuade anyone from ever engaging in such a genocidal thing as this for state-craft.

Leviticus 20.13 encourages killing men who have sex with men. Is it anti-Semitic to point out that killing a man for having sex with a man is foolish, denies love, and contradicts other biblical voices from a similar writing-era as Leviticus? After all, biblical authors in Genesis and 1 Samuel reveal YAHWEH to be quite sexy with men, even impaling Jacob!

I lament how many of my LGBTQ+ fellow-humans through the millennia have been killed by other humans who claim Leviticus 20.13 as their guide — even non-religious people who have reached back to 'holy law' as their reason for hate and disgust for those who love differently. I cry for so many of my fellow LGBTQ+ fellow-humans through the millennia who have been disowned by Jewish or Christian or Muslim family-members who cite Leviticus 20.13 as their rationale for 'God hating queers.'

Is it anti-Semitic to point out that slavery is wrong? Leviticus 25 encourages having slaves — much of the Torah assumes slavery is okay. Even as enlightened as the bands of YAH's and X's stories are, some of their characters have slaves or are slaves. Whatever the rationale, the vision of owning someone seems awfully far adrift from what is right and just. The band of X challenges that vision for sure, especially when Samuel tells the people that they will all essentially be slaves to the new king they are requesting...instead of YAHWEH. I think the band of YAH also challenges slavery, especially by revealing that Abraham's slave has the ear and mouth/style of YAHWEH in finding a wife for his boss' son. Most of the biblical ecstatic-prophetic writers — including the band of YAH — challenge the hierarchical assumptions that permit and even encourage slavery.

Is it right to follow a Law that proclaims menstruating women are 'unclean' and not fit to approach YAHWEH? And the same for men who've had wet dreams? These fluids — blood and egg and semen/sperm — are the stuff of life, after all. Sure, you might not want them all over you but to say that someone is unclean and must be cut off from others seems a bit ridiculous, yes?

There are real problems with what the Levitical priests and Deuteronomistic scribes did in crafting their Law. Thankfully, some rabbis from my own city — Cincinnati — saw past some of these problems with the Torah and crafted a more modern reading of the Torah/Bible through Reformed Judaism.

We would do well in the 21st century to begin noting the stark differences in approach between hierarchical-ways and circular-ways, perhaps especially in the institutions we have inherited. There are deep roots of fascism/control inherent in Judaism, Christianity, and Islam. This series lays bare at least a few of those fascist roots of religion and a life-giving alternative for all. Maybe it's time for us humans to let the wind dry out those fascist/control-oriented roots exposed here and elsewhere that they may no longer take root in this generation, that love will rule but not by conquering.... instead through a deep trust in the wind/YAHWEH/breath-of-life that gives life to each one of us. The choice between fascism/control and self-determination must be made in each interaction. It's a choice worth discerning, right?

If our planet and all humanity is going to heal from the gaping wounds of the 20th century and the 21st century and and even long before that, we're all going to need to be wiser...and to be able to cleverly call out anyone who puts down another and creatively awaken the oppressor and one's own self to our shared life, our equal share in the wind...so that we all can heal from our collective madnesses and know such love that is indeed possible, even among opponents or enemies. Such is the sexy, life-giving way of YAHWEH breathing Itself into and out of us all. Such is relationship.

All the sexiness is not in modern translations of the Bible because...

...many modern Bible translations of the Hebrew Bible are from the Septuagint (LXX), at least up to a few decades ago. And much of that Septuagint-imagination and imagery and (lack of) style stuck.

What is the Septuagint?

The Septuagint is a Greek translation of the Hebrew Bible, commissioned in Egypt for Greek-speaking Jews. It is said that 70 (or 72) Jewish scholars translated the Hebrew texts that they had at the time into Greek in the 3rd & 2nd centuries BCE. LXX are Roman numerals for 70, thus the name "septuagint."

What's the matter with reading Hebrew texts through a Greek translation, you might be saying?

Well, just look at the very last line in 1 Samuel 3. I have translated it from the Ancient Hebrew text as:

> *And YAHWEH continued to let Itself be seen*
> *in A-Quiet-Place, He-Whose-It-Is —*
> *you see, YAHWEH had stripped Itself naked like an exile or slave is*
> *forced to do — YAHWEH did this for Samuel —*
> *in A-Quiet-Place, He-Whose-It-Is*
> *in YAHWEH's style.*

The Hebrew verb choices make this passage so wild. Compare this translation to your favorite translation.

What did the 2nd century BCE Jewish scholars do with the verbs?

'to let oneself be seen'/HRAHH (*niphal* infinitive) in the Hebrew text gets translated by the 70+ scholars into the Greek as *dēlōthēnai*/'to show oneself or make visible (often with words)' 'to strip oneself naked like an exile or slave is forced to do' in the Hebrew text gets translated into Greek as *apekaluphthē*/'to uncover, to reveal, to unveil (mostly ideas)'...and (as far as I've found) never having any instance that involved nakedness, stripping oneself of one's clothes as if having been captured by an oppressor.

Significant differences! This of course is just taking a look at a single sentence.

To take it even further, as was mentioned earlier...the Hebrew word 'ecstatic' translated in the Greek Septuagint becomes *prophētēs* from which we get our English word 'prophet'...but the Greek and English 'prophet' do not carry with them any of the Hebrew roots of 'ecstasy.'

And therein lies one very big problem of modern religions... they all too often try to look at the deep past through two or three languages/lenses that have little to no ability to connect with even a whiff of what the ancient imaginers were experiencing and wondering.

If indeed the ancient prophets were getting high on the wind — on YAHWEH — as it came and went and allowing relationship with every creature to be mediated by that wind-high...

that's a very far cry from meting out specific rituals and prayer-formulas and laws and punishments for not following the prescribed rituals that hope to stir up the Holy Spirit or Spirit of Holiness to act because we called upon it in our ritual, as the priestly imagination so carefully prescribes.

Can we have a nice time being moved by the Holy Spirit / Spirit of Holiness through our rituals or even those rituals of another religion? Of course. But those prescribed rituals are a far cry from sitting there naked and waiting for the wind to lick your skin, right?

And the Septuagint was crafted when modern religion and modern religious-practice had already taken at least <u>some</u> shape in what we today would call "Judaism." That is to say these 2nd century BCE Jewish scholars were reading these older biblical texts and translating them based on some more "modern" notion of Judaism — not with which the more ancient biblical writers might have been playing and wondering before there was a Torah that helped to create and codify a religion, or at least a more modern one.

It's even worse within the religious tradition from which I was steeped: many Catholic Bibles stuck to the Vulgate, the translation of the Hebrew texts into Latin by Jerome in late 4th century CE because he wasn't happy with the Septuagint translations. Vatican scholars took the Latin translations of this often sex-fearing man and translated his biblical Latin translations into English or any vernacular language of the region to become the family Bibles sitting on people's special tables at home. When I read my grandfather's Catholic Bible from 1961, I am shocked and saddened by the translation choices...all of this shaping a vision of "God" and of life that seems very distant from the roots of the biblical stories that go back to the ecstatics/prophets.

In the Catholic world, only since Vatican II (1962 - 1965) are we beginning to see biblical translations into English and modern languages from the 'original' Ancient Hebrew texts ('Old Testament' *sic*) and Greek texts ('New Testament' *sic*)... and while these newer translations are far better than the ones from the Vulgate, they are still a far cry from what is actually there in the more original forms of the biblical texts that exist today in Hebrew (Hebrew Bible) and Greek (Christian additions to the Hebrew Bible). Like their Jewish-scholar counterparts translating the Hebrew texts into the Septuagint, modern Catholic-scholars often translate ancient/ pre-religious experiences into modern religious language to reflect modern ritual and what has grown into Christian/ Catholic religion and religious-tradition.

The roots of religion are far different from the later branches.

Although a lot of the Bible might have begun as oral tellings, once biblical books/scrolls were written down and used for however long the parchment or animal-hide would last before it wore out, books/scrolls were recopied and sometimes even changed. Sometimes for good reasons, sometimes not.

What we have in today's Bible (Hebrew Bible + Christian additions) is a patch-work of ideas through potentially 8-10 centuries of writing, copied over so many times...by astute copiers, by sleepy copiers prone to errors, and sometimes by copiers who had an agenda to change things, often toward more hierarchical visions. What happens in Paul's letters is a good example. Check out *The Authentic Letters of Paul* to discover how lines were added to Paul's letters to shift his meaning away from the radical ideas he had about God and democratic-governance. Paul was the first imaginer of democracy without slaves. Ever. But those who took Paul's letters and wrote them into the Bible added things that made Paul seem like a hierarch-loving, woman-hating fool.

Biblical study seems awfully precarious when we know how these stories arrived to us in the 21st century....

That being said, it's a great gift we have what we have with the Bible — to be able to study the basements of your consciousness and mine and discover if we like the basement layers we've inherited and if we'd like to choose from them or make new choices that reflect better a life worth living for all and with ALL on this planet.

I suspect that this 1 Samuel text offers an invitation to an important experience that might help us all a great deal. You've been doing it — having that experience — as you've read the last few pages, or any pages. At least I hope so. It's life, breathing. And it's in noticing it/It, feeling it/It, sensing it/It, that a profound gift emerges.

It's time to get to the roots! They offer life. And sex with YAHWEH — ecstasy!

Choose life! It comes through sex! Sometimes man-on-man sex if YAHWEH is involved. Or David with Jonathan. Or David with Jonathan's father, Saul, their king.

Same-sex love is divine and 'bordercrossing'/AYBR... just like YAHWEH!

What might be shocking to many Bible readers is that within the Bible itself are two conflicting ways of living — at least two.

The bands of YAH and X recognize same-sex love as having something to do with God.

The Levitical priests (and possibly the Deuteronomistic scribes) disagree completely — they create regulations among their 613 commandments outlawing same-sex love and even prescribe the death penalty to any male who has sex with a male. (Leviticus 20.13) Rather interestingly, the same prohibition does not appear in Deuteronomy (composed by the Deuteronomistic scribes through many generations), where a great many of the Levitical commandments are indeed repeated. The Deuteronomists ban crossdressing though in Deuteronomy 22.5.

Of course the great irony is that the nation or gathering of people — Israel — for whom the Levitical priests and Deuteronomistic scribes wrote those laws is named for Jacob, whose Genesis story of how he got the nickname 'Israel' has him wrestling a guy down by the river and this 'guy' jumps on top of him and gropes him between the legs and penetrates him, impales him — 'fucks'/TQAY him. And the 'guy' turns out to be YAHWEH in the 'flesh'! And Jacob then tops this 'guy'!

The Levitical priests say same-lex love is an abomination;

the bands of YAH and X strip it down that same-sex love is divine — that YAHWEH enjoys same-sex love. What should we do, Bible-readers? What are we to do when — within the same "Word of God" — one story says something is right and another story says something is wrong?

Throw the whole Bible out?

Create our own Bible of our favorite passages only? (most people do this)

Or, could you hold them both — both of these 'sides'? After all, they both exist within the same whole...the Bible, life, the universe, God, the One Love, THE ALL.

Is there something about holding both 'sides' that could very well be the message for our times, when we in the nation where I write, within the world and time from which I write, is so split, so polarized, and so sure of one's own 'side'?

Sit with it. Be with it. Hold both 'sides,' let them wrestle one another, let each 'side' find the other by the river and wrestle one another and interpenetrate one another —

this is to know God, THE ALL.

You can't hold a piece and call it THE ALL in itself.

The only way such a possibility comes and the only way it changes us is through ecstasy...some vision/experience of THE ALL that cannot be controlled by any human. But It can be noticed...and must be, I argue, if we are to understand the Bible and thrive on this amazing planet.

When have you known ecstasy?

When was an experience so intense that it brought you beyond the life you knew before that? when all the obstacles tumbled away? when you saw and heard and felt through to a larger wholeness to life?

Who needs holidays or 'special times' or 'special rituals to conjure the divine and cajole the divine to speak' when one knows the enchantment of life, when one allows life to open up and speak at every instant?

Organized religion might be preventing you and me from knowing THE ALL. Hierarchies have a way of doing that, of requiring their participants to see and hear and feel in particular ways to belong.

Swim away with me...discover all the life that the wind offers....

What if the world's healing and growth depends on your experience of ecstasy and mine?

Surely some of you will message me and say, "No hallucinogenics?? Have you not read the research? Brian C. Muraresku's *The Immortality Key*? All the drugs that have been found in the cups of the early Christians. All the possible connections to the Greek mystery cults. Surely these prophets of the Bible, the ecstatics, were using drugs to get a glimpse of the new world they were envisioning. Surely the biblical prophets' ecstasy was drug-induced!"

Yeah...maybe. I've always wondered about the possible connections between the Hebrew word NBYAH and cannabis. As you can see, there is a possible connection in terms of derivation — *nabi* and cannabis — and plenty of scholars note the connection or slough it off. The Hebrew letter C is often placed at the beginning of Hebrew words to mean 'when' or 'as' or 'like'...so that something like *cannabis* would be 'like being an ecstatic'...'like being a prophet.'

And please remember, friends, that just because one or two or many Jesus-followers or Christian groups used psychedelics doesn't mean that <u>every</u> biblical group did, going back to all time, as in centuries upon centuries of biblical writing.

What character-Samuel and his misfit-friends might have been doing on the mountaintops of out-of-the-way Ancient Israel or Ancient Philistia might indeed be some kind of psychedelic experience fueled by drugs. Yes. Quite possibly. But I'm not sure drugs are needed. I'm not sure psychedelics are needed to be an ecstatic.

Walk under any tree and look at the sunlight or moonlight dancing through. Feel the breeze on your skin, maybe especially your sweaty skin. Ecstasy is constantly available.

And, as we'll soon see in the second half of 1 Samuel (coming very soon in the next volume in the series *The Naked Path of Prophet*), there are a few things that indeed help one to know ecstasy. And psychedelics aren't mentioned.

Gautama (the one called Buddha) apparently didn't need psychedelics either to know bliss, enlightenment. For that matter, he needed <u>nothing</u>...not even guided meditations with flowery words and soothing background music on this favorite app.

As a matter of fact, if we take the Vipassana meditation tradition and its clever teaching seriously (which very well <u>could</u> go back to Gautama / the Buddha), the entire point of enlightenment is to use NOTHING to discover it. No mantra. No chanting. No special way of sitting or walking. Nothing. No-thing.

Meditations with words are nice, for sure — but can they be better than 'nothing'...YAHWEH...the sound of the breeze and breath that can be heard and sensed in 'nothing'?

Ecstasy. Enlightenment. Bliss. They all come, and they all go.

Or better, ecstasy and enlightenment and bliss are constant

and available and reliable — and we can be the noticers, the recipients, the ones who wake up to them. The Sanskrit word *buddha* means 'the one who wakes up' after all.

But be careful if you think you can control when and how you notice enlightenment, the Vipassana-meditation tradition wisely cautions. I think the biblical ecstatics would offer the same caution...let YAHWEH come to <u>you</u> and seduce <u>you</u> and ravish <u>you</u> as YAHWEH — THE ALL — allows It to happen.

Can you romance YAHWEH? Can you do things that invite YAHWEH to find you and ravish you? As we'll learn through the next volume of *The Naked Path of Prophet* series (1 Samuel 18 - 31), absolutely yes. Take off your clothes, breathe, wait. Stay with It. Be with It. Let YAHWEH come and caress you, arouse you, awaken you...to enlightenment, to bliss, to ecstasy. YAHWEH is reliable...for all of us.

YAHWEH as known by the ecstatic-prophets is different from state-religion as we see and will see with the saga of Saul-David-Solomon (and perhaps our own time). The ecstatics-prophets' version of YAHWEH is different from BAAL and ASHTAROTH; the ecstatics-prophets' version of YAHWEH is different from the Deuteronomists' and Levitical priests' versions of YAHWEH. Study each one and you'll know them by their subtle yet stark differences. Sense how each one makes you feel.

YAHWEH as the wind...as soon as you try to contain It, ritualize It, concretize It, YAHWEH refuses to participate. The wind stops offering life, becomes a 'bad air' as it does for our character Saul, the trophy-building, penis-erecting king who grows more and more self-interested the less he allows himself to be enchanted by the wind. Maybe that's the problem of being a *messiah*, a *christ*, no matter who it is.

Fresh air must flow. You can't contain it or control it, no matter how much we try to air-condition it.

The king and his court of Deuteronomists confiscate, the Levitical priests try to nail down how to live with 613 commandments...yet the ecstatic-prophet frees.

It's what all of us addicted to the old slavery-ways of hierarchy discover...instead of helping us, all the numbing agents often create obstacles to what we feel in the moment...the drugs and the booze and the ritzy/junk food and the websites and the reels and the shopping and the on-and-on-and-on. Eventually, we all discover we don't need them to be happy, to be blissful.

Instead, something else....

...that we are alive...that we sense, that our senses come alive and have a wildness to them that can also be attentive to relationship, curious about the possibilities...and the only thing we need — ultimately — at least in this moment — is the breeze, oxygen, the atmosphere, life.

YAHWEH.

Do you want to put your energy into people and institutions that put you in your place — high or low in the hierarchy — institutions that eventually all crumble...hopes and visions that eventually disappear into thin air...

or will you put your attention and time into the wind, into the very thing that gives life, that breeds the miraculous in the everyday, breath by breath?

May we be so bold as to join in and lean into what is...YAHWEH. There's power when friends gather and simply feel, simply rest in the wind and delight in the wind without any other agenda...without any need to hold on...with an inner freedom to 'bordercross'/AYBR...just as YAHWEH-as-the-wind crosses all human-made borders.

Nations and their children come and go, get conquered, die out, sometimes even get swept away by the wind...

...but the children of the ecstatic-prophets...they live, even when the children of the nations and the children of state-religion try to kill them off. Open your heart, feel the breeze. You know this too, right?

With a lover like YAHWEH, we all rise.

A Final Invitation

A friend who read a draft of the new edition of this translation & commentaries (styles) of 1 Samuel 1 - 17 suggested that a wise reader now go back to the beginning — 1 Samuel 1 — and begin again. But this time read it through without the commentaries.

This should be easy to do as I have indented commentaries that I have inserted into the biblical translation.

Now that you have a 'lay of the land' of the Ancient Hebrew and some information about the context of the band of X's world, much of this context from scholars' archaeological research, perhaps you too will be inspired to sit and let the current moment catch you and awaken you — YAHWEH! — and style out something that helps all humans recall from which we've come — YAHWEH! — and with which we have our being — YAHWEH! — all of us sharing together this life and equally valued in the circular ways of the wise wind. It's more fun with friends. Come! Be welcomed here!

The next volume of this series — **Ecstatic Prophets, Compulsive Fascists** (1 Samuel 18 - 31) — coming very soon.

Resources for Further Study

Hebrew Alphabet - transliterated

It would be fair to say that my rendering below of the Hebrew (Aramaic) characters/sounds into English letters is far from perfect. I do hope it is useful, and easier than most renderings. Many Hebrew letters have multiple sounds, depending on if the letter is doubled or depending on the vowel with which it might be associated. I have let a lot of that go for simplicity's sake.

Although I disagree, it has been usually said/assumed that the Hebrew 'alphabet' (*aleph-bet*) itself has no vowels — they are assumed, in a sense. For clarity, between the 6th - 10th centuries CE, a group of biblical scholars called the Masoretes added vowels below the Hebrew consonants to clarify the sounds and even meanings of the written Hebrew language. In some ways, the Masoretes' work clarified meanings of Hebrew words; in some ways, the Masoretes' work flattened the meanings, especially of the ecstatic-prophets' poems and 1 & 2 Samuel — both of which rely on the pun-richness of the Ancient Hebrew language...the ways words expand and explode with multiple meanings and possibilities.

My very crude system of transliterating the Hebrew characters into English-sounds invites you to add any 'a' sound between consonants that you wish. And let gutturals be vowel-like. It's a system, in my mind anyway, that allows the words to be euphonic without the Masoretic markings that aim readers/hearers toward some kind of false precision which sometimes distract readers from hearing the potentials of the sounds from word to word. More of the puns become noticeable too, I think. But you must be the judge of that for yourself. As we well know, language is spoken differently as language flows from one community to another, from one time to another.

<u>my transliteration</u>

א	*aleph*	AH
ב	*bet*	B
ג	*gimmel*	G
ד	*dalet*	D
ה	*hey*	H
ו	*vav*	V or U or O
ז	*zayin*	Z
ח	*chet*	CH
ט	*tet*	T
י	*yod*	Y
ך/כ	*kaf*	K or hard C

ל	*lamed*	L
ם/מ	*mem*	M
ו/נ	*nun*	N
ס	*samech*	S
ע	*ayin*	AY
ף/פ	*pey*	P
ץ/צ	*tsade*	TS
ק	*qof*	Q
ר	*resh*	R
ש	*shin*	S/SH
ת	*tav*	T

My only hope with this simplified system of transliterating Ancient Hebrew sounds into English approximated-sounds is to encourage more people to study Ancient Hebrew...to dig deeply in the sandbox of language and understanding to discover our roots and to make better choices in our present moment.

Major Character Names

Hannah's family

Elkanah...AHLQNH...Elkanah-Divinity-Creates...from AHL = *EL* + QNH = 'create,' though QNH can also be 'to buy/acquire'... when people become inspired, something like a Muse possesses them and creates something through them, yes?

Peninnah...PNNH...Power-Jewels...from PNH which can mean both 'jewels' (especially made of coral) and something like the chief, the one in charge/powerful

Hannah...CHNH...Hannah-Bend-Down...as CHNH literally translates as 'bending over' that comes with the sun bending down in the sky to bring on evening or the 'bending-down' that would need to happen when nomadic-people or military would hurry up to pitch their tents as evening came...and Hannah figuratively must bend down to her rival-wife Peninnah even though Hannah is loved more by her husband Elkanah...Hannah would be seen by ancient eyes as having less status than Peninnah and having to then bend down to Peninnah because Peninnah has children and at the beginning of the story Hannah doesn't...split the syllables and CHN and AH and something interesting appears...CHN = 'grace/charm' + AH / *YAH* = YAHWEH...Hannah certainly charms YAHWEH and then sets the story of Samuel on course!

Samuel...SHMUAHL....Named-For-EL....SHM = 'name' + AHL = *EL*

Samuel's sons, about whom we hear only once:
  Joel...YUAHL...YAHWEH-is-EL...from <u>YAH</u>WEH + *EL*
  Abijah...AHBYH...Patriarchy-is-YAHWEH...from AB = 'father/ patriarchy'*+ <u>YAH</u>WEH

> *Why have I chosen 'Patriarchy' throughout instead of simply 'Father'?*

Because fatherhood in the ancient world wasn't simply the progenitor of a child but a whole system of hierarchy...husband over wives over children who weren't considered human until puberty when they were suddenly valuable for more work and for marriage/marrying off.

———————

Yahweh/Lord...YHWH...YAHWEH...from the verb 'to be'...say 'yahweh' out loud a few times and what does it sound like? the breeze? one's breath? what any ancient and hopefully modern person knows sustains life...the air!

Lord **of Hosts**...the title/descriptor that often follows YAHWEH in the Hebrew text: **TSBAHUT...of-the-Big-Armies-who-Require-Service**...the plural of 'army' and having to do with compulsory-service, as army service often is in countries ancient and modern and as service is in cultic-worship

———————

Eli's family

Eli...**AYLY...Climb-Up**...depending on how it's pointed/vowelized by later scholars, AYLY is the imperative of the verb 'to climb'

Hophni...**CHPNY...Two-Fists**...from the word CNPHN 'fists' or 'handful' and sounds like he's a bit of both!

Phineas...**PNCHS...Snake-Mouth**...PH = 'mouth' + NACHS = 'snake'

Ichabod...**AHYCBOD...No-Honor**...from AHY 'no' or 'where' (implying negation) + CBD 'honor'...AHY can also be 'jackal' (an animal that feasts on corpses, perhaps after battle)...Ichabod was Eli's grandson through Snake-Mouth

Ahijah...**AHCHYH...Brother-of-YAHWEH**...AHCH 'brother' + YAHWEH...Ichabod's brother who wears the *ephod* for King Saul

Abinadab...AHBYNDB...Patriarchy-Volunteers-for-War...from AB 'father/patriarch(y)' + NDB 'to impel, to cause someone to volunteer, often as a soldier'...after the ark is returned to Ancient Israel, it is brought to Abinadab's house and his son Eleazar is made holy to care for it...Abinadab is also a name for one of David's older brothers

Eleazer...AHYLAYZR...EL's-Helper...AHL '*EL*' + AYZR 'to help'

———————

Saul's family

Saul...SHAHUL...Asked-For...from SHAHL 'to ask'

his father:
   Kish...Set-a-Trap (from QOSH 'to set a trap, lay a snare')

his sons:
   Jonathan...Gift-of-YAHWEH (<u>YAH</u>WEH + NTN 'to give/gift')
   Ishvi...Equalizer (from SHVAH 'to level or make equal')
   Malkishua...My-King's-Wealth (from MLCY 'my king' + SHUA 'riches')

his daughters:
   Merab-From-Many (from M/'from' + RB 'much or many')
   Michal-Who-Is-ALL (from MY/'who' + CL/'all')

his wife:
   Ahinoam...My-Brother's-Delight (from ACHY 'my brother' + NAYM 'delight/pleasant')

her father's family:
   Ahimaaz...My-Brother-Fastens (from ACHY 'my brother' + YTSH 'to shut or fasten')

his general:
  Abner...Patriarchy's-Lamplight (from AHB 'father/patriarch(y)'
  + NYR 'lamp')

Abner's father:
  Ner...Lamplight (from NYR 'lamp')...Saul's beloved (either
  uncle/relative or lover...most likely uncle though we are left
  wondering)

Abner's grandfather:
  Abiel...EL's-My-Patriarchy (from AHBY 'father/patriarch(y)' +
  EL)

———————

David's family

**Jesse of the House of Bethlehem...YSHY BYT-HLCHMY...Jesse-
There-He-Is of the House of Feast-or-Fight**...(from YSHY 'there
(he) is' and BYT 'house' + LCHM(Y) 'bread, food, feast' or 'fight,
war'...rather interesting, isn't it, that LCHM can mean both 'bread'
and 'war'...but then again why are most revolutions fought but
for access to bread, to the freedom to live)

his sons:
  Eliab...My-EL-is-Patriarchy (my + *EL* + AB 'father/patriarch(y)')
  Abinadab...Patriarchy-Volunteers-forWar (AB 'father
  patriarch(y)' + NBD 'incite, impel, offer oneself for war')
  Shammah...Stunning (from SHMM 'to stun or amaze')

there are other brothers in between, but so far they are unnamed

David...DUD...'the love boiler' (DOD 'beloved, lover, uncle'
  DUD literally means 'to boil over with affection, love')

———————

Goliath...GLYT...Stripper, as in the kind of stripping that happens when one nation conquers another and then forces exiles or slaves to strip themselves naked to humiliate them, to dehumanize them, to steal from them (from GLH 'to force someone to strip' or 'to denude someone')

The Tribes or Branches of Ancient Israel

Israel...YSRAHL...nation named after the hero who wrestled EL, got groped and penetrated, and topped EL to win!...AHL = *EL* + SRH = 'to top/to be in charge'...literally, Israel means On-Top-of-God...I have chosen to draw it back to that primal story from the band of YAH in Genesis which surely was on the mind of anyone who heard it, the story being so wild. And perhaps true to life. Breathe in and the air — yahweh — penetrates you and gives you your being, your life — yahweh.

the tribes of Israel named in 1 Samuel 1 - 18.4,
in order of their being mentioned:

Ephraim...AHPRYM...'Ephraim, the tribe from the mountains known for being fruitful' from PRH/'to bear fruit'

Dan...DYN...'Dan, the tribe known for offering clear judgements' from DYN 'to judge'...its early root also having to do with sailing directly toward something

Benjamin...BNYMYN...'Benjamin, the small tribe known for its powerful children' from BN 'son/child' + YMYN 'right'...'right' in most ancient cultures (including this one) has to do with power or strength and 'left' being sinister or wrong or at least unexpected. Ironically, Benjamin was also one of the smallest tribal lands.

Levi(tes)...LUYM...'Levites, the tribe known for being attached to the ark' from LVH 'to twine or attach or join with' and quite fitting as they serve as the attendants to the ark and its cultic-rituals

Gad...GD...'Gad, the tribe known for their attack-by-penetration' from GDD/'to invade, attack, penetrate, cut'

Judah...YHUDH...'Judah, the tribe known for throwing up their hands in praise' from YDH 'to throw' and YD 'hand' and such throwing one's hands was associated with prayer, exaltation... YD of course can also mean 'penis' and the band of YAH has a story in Genesis 38 where the character Judah puts his penis out there with his daughter-in-law dressed up as a 'holy prostitute'/QDSHH to trick her father-in-law...nine months later to his great embarrassment

Often Named Cities in Ancient Israel
(as they appear in 1 Samuel)

Ramah...The Heights...from RMH 'the high places' or 'heights'... where the character Samuel was born and where he makes his home when not on his circuit

Zuph...'the land of the Honeycombs, where wild honey gushes' or Honeycomb...from TSUP which can be 'honeycomb' or 'floodwaters'...two similar words in Hebrew, probably loaned from different cultures. Could Zuph be a reference to the Sufis, the whirling prayer community who honors God as Love (Rumi, Hafiz, Rabi'a, and so many wonderful poets)?

Shiloh...A-Quiet-Place, He-Whose-It-Is...from SHLH 'quiet, tranquil, peaceful' put together with SHYLH: a possible messianic title 'He Whose It Is' associated with Shiloh

Ebenezer...Rock of Help...from AHBN 'rock' + AYZR 'help'

Beth Shemesh...House of the Sun...from BYT 'house' + SHMSH 'sun'

Qiryath Yearim / Kiriath-Jearim...the town in the honey-combed forest...from QRYH 'town' and YAYR 'forest/honeycomb'

Mizpah...the watch-tower...participle form of TSPH 'to spy' or 'to look out/watch'

Bethel...Divinity's-House...from BYT 'house' + AHL = *EL/divinity*

Beer Sheba...'the most perfect place on earth — in Seven-Wells!'...from BAHR 'well' + SHBY 'seven'...the southern-most city of Ancient Israel...'seven' in the Ancient Near East was often more than just a number...communicates perfection...completeness

Gilgal...the city of wheels, where the wind wheels and whirls around...from GLGL 'wheel, whirl, whirlwind' or GLL/'to roll away'...another city that scholars have no firm idea where it was, though probably in the mountains, perhaps not far from Shiloh, where the wind whips and whirls around those mountains

Jabesh-Gilead...the city of dry ground and heaped up stones ... from YBSH/'to dry up, wither' + GL/ 'a heap, rollable' + AYOD/'to repeat, do again'

Michmash...The Store-Houses...from CMS, participle-form of the verb 'store-up'

Gibeah of Benjamin...The Hill in Benjamin, the small tribe known for its powerful children...Saul eventually has the hill named for himself: **Saul's Hill**...from GBAYH literally 'hill'

Geba...the little-hill area...from GBAY literally 'bowl' as in not quite as high as a hill / Gibeah

EmekofElah...valleywiththebigdrunktree...fromAYMQ/'valley' and AHLH/'terebinth'...from which turpentine and strong drink or liquor was made throughout the Mediterranean world

Bethlehem...House of Feast-or-Fight...from BYT 'house' + LCHM(Y) 'war, fight' or 'bread, food, feast' (see details on 'Jesse from Bethlehem')

Jerusalem...The-Arrow-of-Peace...in 1 Samuel, not yet a Israelite city and not of much prominence...foreshadowed in the David and Goliath story...from YRH 'to throw or shoot an arrow' and SHLM 'peace or health or wholeness'

> *Many of the cities named within 1 Samuel cannot be found today. Makes you wonder, yes? Perhaps the band of X was being very crafty with their fiction, especially when the city-name's <u>meaning</u> plays into the flow of the story. And it so often does, so I often translate it that way.*

Major Opponents of Ancient Israel

Egypt...MTSRYM...Suffering-Egypt, same consonants as a singular word in Hebrew that means 'suffering'...who knows what an ancient Hebrew would first think of when they heard MTSRYM? To many Hebrew people though, Egypt was a place of suffering as the story says they were slaves there, a place with a significant hierarchical imagination, enough to use slaves to construct pyramids and great cities for their thought-to-be-divine Pharaoh. Egypt, of course, did not call itself "suffering"... that combination of sounds surely produced different meanings in the many languages used in Egypt but to Hebrew ears it was often "suffering" and far from the wandering-freedom of the ecstatics-prophets...Egypt referred to itself by many names, Masur being one name...notice the similarity between Masur and MTSR...in any case, the great irony is that Ancient Israel chooses a similar hierarchical and slave-holding system as their legendary enslavers — the Egyptians — for the form of government they would most like for themselves.

Philistia/Philistines...PLSHTY...the Dust-Rollers . . . from PLSH 'to roll or wallow in the dust, as in mourning' *the confederacy of the five major Philistine cities:*

Ashdod — one of its well-known, powerful cities known for its cruel violence and ravaging other civilizations (from SHADAD/'to deal violently with, spoil, ruin')

Gath — the city with the wine-press and their drunken concerts (see GAT/'winepress' and then see NAGAN/'to pluck the instrument's strings')

Ekron — city known for things pulled up by the roots, for childlessness...perhaps a city where DAGON was never able to get fertility going despite the people's prayer (from AYQR verb: 'to pluck up by the roots' noun: barren, having no children)

Gaza — city known for its strength (from AYTS/'strong')

Ashkelon — city known as the bank for weighing produce/wealth...(from SHQL/'to weigh' as in a 'shekel' = a weight/a value of wealth)

> *Of course some of these cities still exist today in Palestine and have been much in the news, tragically. Please note that in this translation I'm simply guessing what an Ancient Hebrew speaker might hear in these non-Hebrew city names. Non-Hebrews like the Philistines are always shown as having more faith in YAHWEH than Israelites in the band of YAH and band of X stories.*

other enemies/foreign nations . . .

Hazor...Settled-Here (from CHTSR/'settled, village') whose general was:

Sisera (named in prior biblical legends)

Zobah...those stationed in the far north (Aram/Syria)

Amorites are named out of nowhere in Chapter 7.14, which made me wonder if it's an early copyist's error or referring to the Philistines in some way, not as a people but as a descriptor... the word Amorite is from the Hebrew word AHMR/'to speak'... perhaps 'braggarts...those who talk and talk and talk'

Ancient Israel's Second-Cousins

Moabites...From-My-Father-Inbreds-from-Moab people (Lot's son...Lot was Abraham's nephew)...MOAHB/'from my father'

Ammonites...From-My-Inbred-Kinfolk's people...Ammon/'my people'...the Genesis story with Lot impregnating his daughters gives the name of the ancestor of the Ammonites as Ben-Ammi (BN-AYMY/'child of my people')...their leader Nahash...Snake from NCHSH/'snake, serpent'

Edomites...The-Reds' people (Esau's nickname Edom: AHDOM/'red'...Esau was Jacob/Israel's twin brother)

Amelekites...The-Laborers (Esau's descendants...Esau was Jacob/Israel's twin brother)...AML means 'to labor'...Agag is their leader, a legend for his brutality

Kenites...Cain's-Kids (Cain's descendants...son of Adam and Eve)...their cities Chavilah (from CHUL/'to whirl around') and Shur (from SHUR/'wall')

One invites love
and flexibility...

today...groups who are curious about the deeper roots
and who seek to mine the gifts of the present moment
and all present...circles of deciders

the writer of the Gospel of Thomas, wisdom through
personal experience and 'study-through-play' of past wisdom
to create new wisdom

Paul and his all-are-equal-before-God imagination...Paul is the
first imaginer ever of democratic communities without slavery

Jesus and his clever, funny wisdom sayings and actions
inviting conversion within and love of enemies and relying
on God alone (not priests or kings or authorities)

wildly clever poems of the prophets...
Amos, the Isaiahs, Jeremiah, and others

the band of X, authors of 1 & 2 Samuel and (perhaps)
1 & 2 Kings and the inspiring stories about the prophets and
the foolishness of kings & priests

the band of YAH's Genesis stories that upset the
hierarchical & patriarchal apple-cart of Ancient Babylon

ecstatics' (prophets') mountaintop experiences of
YAHWEH, the wind...the playful, clever, spiraling, poetic
imagination reacting to Ancient Babylon's and Ancient Egypt's
royal/slave superpower imaginations

today…groups who still think one human being
is worth more than another (hierarchical, priestly,
royal/slave fascist imagination)

the writer of the Gospel of John and "belief"
as all you need (makes Thomas look like a fool)

Peter and his hierarchical camp that rejected Paul's vision of
equality and perhaps wrote Acts of the Apostles to reduce Paul's
power/prestige (they also change Paul's letters years later)

the military/royal title "**Christ**" and the king/redeemer
mythology inflicted upon Jesus, an imagination
cementing over Jesus' wisdom and lifestyle

Ezekiel, Nehemiah, Ezra and I/II Chronicles…
the priestly efforts to craft a priest-led religious
tradition and subvert the prophets

priestly imagination that assembled the **Torah**
and the character **Moses** as greatest of everything,
even greatest prophet…though he has little to no
ecstatic poetry/action like the prophets

the **Deuteronomist** "political party" who enabled
the royals and began the first written Bible during
King Josiah's reign

Ancient Babylon & its towers and metropolises
like Uruk…and **the hierarchical, royal/slave
imagination** required to build such things…
where one human is thought to be better than
another…the imagination of slavery/royalty

…one does not.

Bibliography

Walter Brueggemann. *The Prophetic Imagination*. Minneapolis: Fortress Press, 1978.

Eric. H. Cline. *1177 B.C.: The Year Civilization Collapsed*. Princeton, NJ: Princeton, 2021.

Michael David Coogan. *Stories from Ancient Canaan*. Louisville, KY: Westminster, 1978.

Arthur J. Dewey, Roy W. Hoover, Lane C. McGaughy, Daryl D. Schmidt. *The Authentic Letters of Paul: A New Reading of Paul's Rhetoric and Meaning*. Salem, OR: Polebridge, 2010.

Israel Finkelstein. "A Great United Monarchy? Archeological and Historical Perspectives." (I read it via academia.edu...originally published in *One God - One Cult - One Nation*. ed. by Reinhard G. Kratz and Hermann Spieckermann. Berlin: De Gruyter, 2010.)

Israel Finkelstein and Neil Asher Silberman. *The Bible Unearthed: Archaeology's New Vision of Ancient Israel and the Origin of Its Sacred Texts*. New York: Touchstone, 2001.

Robert W. Funk, Arthur J. Dewey, & the Jesus Seminar. *The Gospel of Jesus: According to the Jesus Seminar*. Salem, OR: Polebridge, 2015.

Theodore W. Jennings, Jr. *Jacob's Wound: Homoerotic Narrative in the Literature of Ancient Israel*. New York: Continuum, 2005. This book flipped my world up-side down. I found a used copy at Strand Bookstore in New York City six years ago while there for Feldenkrais training. For the past year or so before that, I had been working on a book about the prophets and was flailing around with it. There were strange things in the Ancient Hebrew texts that I didn't think were palatable for modern audiences. I wondered if I had the courage and resolve to say out loud — or in writing — what was there. Dr. Jenning's book gave me the nudge to go with it, to let those ancient writings say now what they were trying to say then...hopefully with some ears in this 21st century that might wish to listen and ponder a YAHWEH that wants intimate relationship with you and me. Irony of ironies, a high school religion colleague took graduate school classes with Dr. Jennings at Chicago Theological Seminary! My only sadness is that Dr. Jennings died before I could meet him. My condolences and love to his wife and family and many students.

Stephen L. McKenzie. *King David: A Biography.* New York: Oxford, 2000.

Robert J. Miller, editor. *The Complete Gospels: Annotated Scholars Version.* Sonoma, CA: Polebridge, 1994.

William Armstrong Percy III. *Pederasty and Pedagogy in Archaic Greece.* Urbana/Chicago: University of Illinois Press, 1996. While it makes no mention of Ancient Israel as a potential place for military-pederasty, this book helped me to understand how that practice was used in Crete, Greece, and Sparta to create a very organized, vastly hierarchical military-system.

Thomas Römer. *L'Ancien Testament.* Paris: Que sais-je? / Humensis, 2019.

Thomas Römer. *The Invention of God.* (trans Raymond Geuss). Cambridge, MA: Harvard University Press, 2015.

Thomas Römer. *The So-Called Deuteronomistic History: A Sociological, Historical and Literary Introduction.* New York: T&T Clark/Continuum, 2007. This book began the paradigm shift in me that led to the second edition of *The Naked Path of Prophet.* with all improved commentaries and a better understanding of how this wild text of 1 Samuel ended up in the Bible. Revisiting the commentaries and then preparing *The Naked Path of prophet vol 2* to follow this revised volume made me want to improve the translation and be clearer about the the profound humor of 1 Samuel. My only hope is that scholars will begin to spend more time with my translation and wonder about it and return to the Hebrew text and wonder some more...and then come to notice even more deeply the supreme cleverness of the biblical authors I call 'X' and their playful ecstatic-prophetic style.

Thomas Römer, editor. *The Future of the Deuteronomistic History*. Leuven: Leuven University Press / Peeters, 2000.

Thomas Römer and Loyse Bonjour. *L'homosexualité dans le Proche-Orient ancien et la Bible*. Geneva: Editions Labor et Fides, 2016.

Indries Shah. *The Sufis*. New York: Anchor, 1971.

Jacob L. Wright. *David, King of Israel, and Caleb in Biblical Memory*. New York: Cambridge, 2014.

> Please consult the Bibliography in *A Wildly Sensual YAHWEH* for more.

about the artists

Sean K. Long...cover image

Sean Long is a father and husband based in Cincinnati, Ohio. He is an accomplished artist, musician, poet, and writer. His creative works range from murals, portraits, sculptures, music, to cartoons, comics and so much more, including the graphic novel YAHWEH IS the Wind! with Brian Shircliff. Sean has a true dedication to his craft. He infuses his work with passion, creativity and life experience. Through his company "The Art Department" he brings his creative vision to clients. For collaborations, contact Sean at TheArtDepartmentCincy@gmail.com

Julie Lucas...all interior images, cover design, VITALITY's logos

Julie Lucas is a graphic designer, illustrator and meditator whose creative process draws from inquiry and deep listening into the heart of it all. See more of her work at withinwonder.com.

about the translator/commentator

In addition to **The Naked Path of Prophet** series, Brian Shircliff is the poet of **winds of (r)evolution** (paintings by Matthew Klooster) and author of the graphic novel **YAHWEH IS THE WIND!** (illustrated by Sean K. Long). Having taught high school religion for seventeen years, he felt the need to swim away from the shipwreck of organized religion for a more inclusive perspective. He is a Bones for Life® Trainer, Guild Certified Feldenkrais Practitioner, Healing Touch Certified Practitioner, and thirty-year student of many styles of meditation. He co-founded and continues to direct VITALITY Cincinnati's donation-based holistic self-care programs.

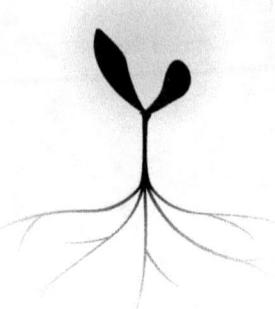

about VITALITY

VITALITY is a circle of friends welcoming all, awakening each other, and reminding each other that we are Whole. Our affordable self-care programs invite everyone to move, to breathe, to rest, to contemplate, to grow...wherever each person begins their self-care journey, wherever and however they want to become.

it's the power of a circle!

we invite you to explore with us through our

donation-based drop-in classes...in person & via Zoom
affordable trainings
individual sessions
volunteer opportunities

vitalitycincinnati.org

VITALITY

buzz, bliss + books

publishing books from VITALITY's circle of friends
inspiring love, creativity, + possibility

vitalitybuzz.org

a final poem

modern religion[1] is dying —

let it.
let something new spring forth.

find the
root
that became
religion...
and read or bind it back a little further —

to unread, unbounded life....   *experience*

----
[1]religion (n.), a Latin word...some possibilities

   derived from 're'...again/more +

   the same root as 'lecture'...reading out loud, as in monastic/
   university reading?

      or

   the same root as 'ligament'...binding (from the earliest
   language root of the hypothesized 'first' language...Proto-
   Indo-European...from which the most ancient roots of
   Greek, Latin, Sanskrit, Semitic languages and so much of
   today's imagination springs)?

www.ingramcontent.com/pod-product-compliance
Lightning Source LLC
Chambersburg PA
CBHW070908120626
46546CB00001B/182